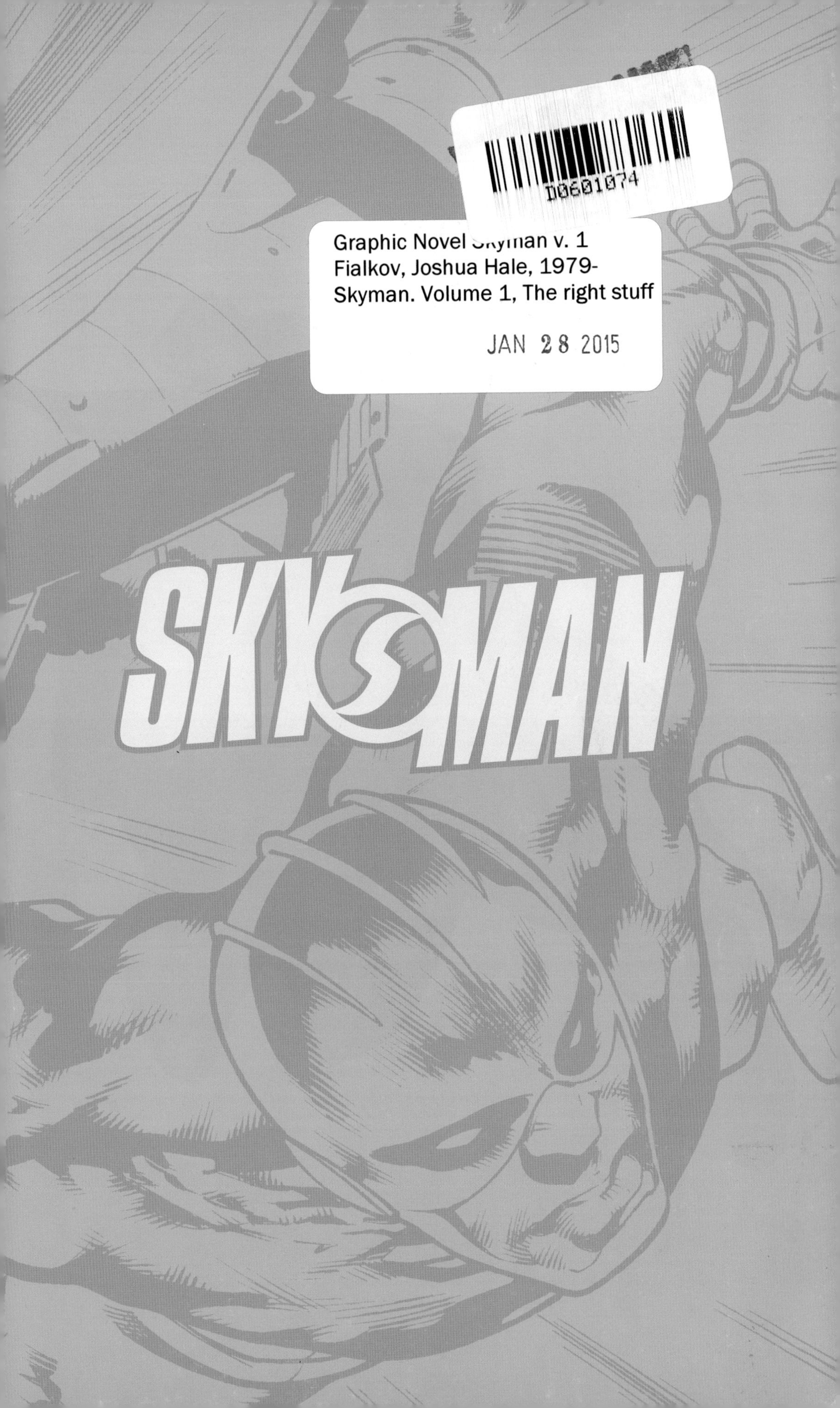
SKYMAN

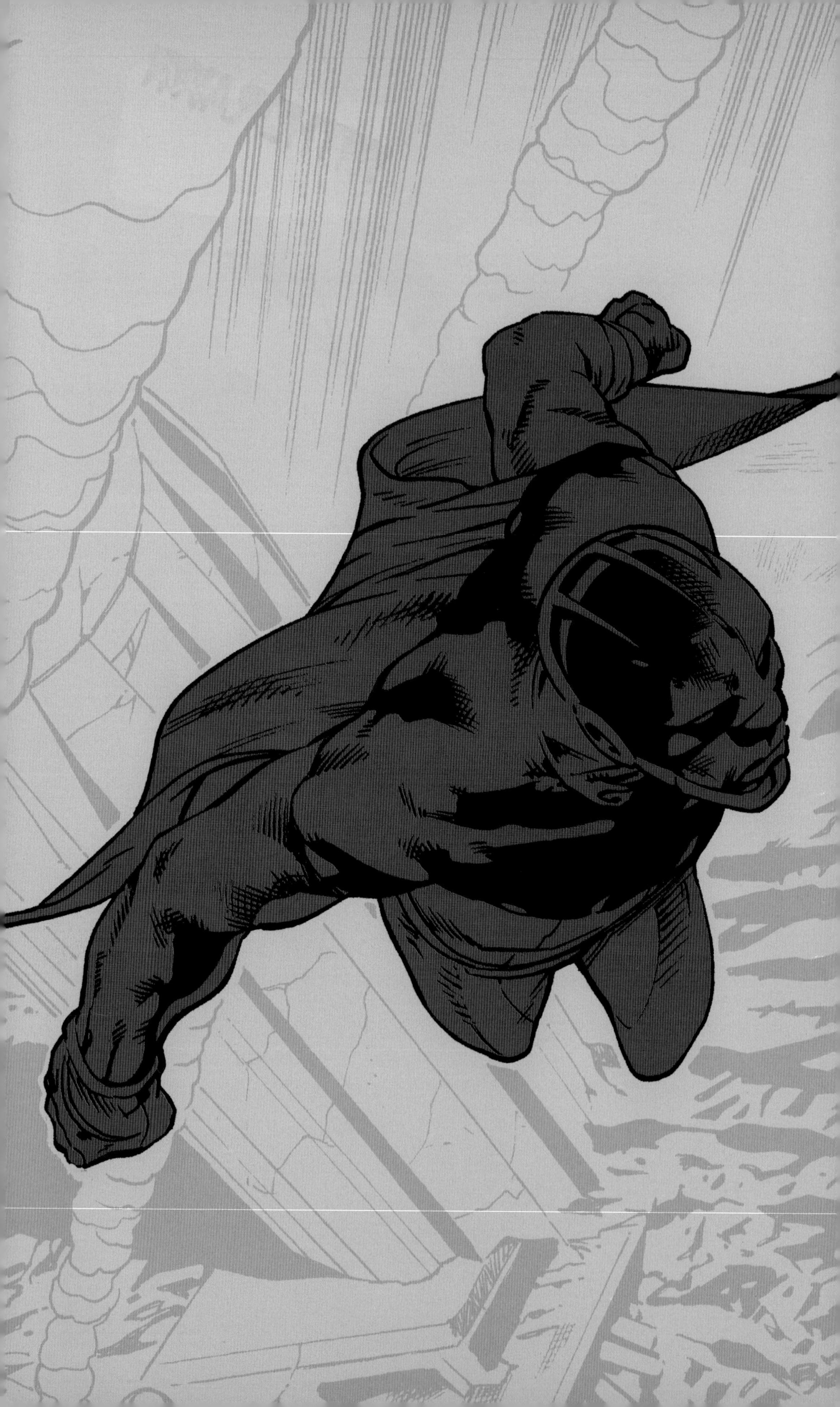

# SKYMAN

## VOLUME 1 THE RIGHT STUFF

STORY BY
**JOSHUA HALE FIALKOV**

PENCILS BY
**MANUEL GARCIA**

INKS BY
**BIT**

COLORS BY
**MARTA MARTÍNEZ**

LETTERS BY
**NATE PIEKOS** OF **BLAMBOT®**

COVER AND PINUP BY
**FREDDIE WILLIAMS II**
AND **DAN SCOTT**

CHAPTER BREAK ART BY
**FREDDIE WILLIAMS II**
WITH **DAN SCOTT**
(CHAPTERS 1–2)

**FREDDIE WILLIAMS II**
WITH **JEREMY ROBERTS**
(CHAPTERS 3–4)

DARK HORSE BOOKS

PUBLISHER..................MIKE RICHARDSON
EDITOR.....................JIM GIBBONS
ASSISTANT EDITOR..........SPENCER CUSHING
DIGITAL PRODUCTION........ALLYSON HALLER
COLLECTION DESIGNER.......NICK JAMES

Special thanks to Mike Richardson, Randy Stradley,
Scott Allie, and David Macho Gómez and Spanish Inq.

Mike Richardson, President and Publisher | Neil Hankerson, Executive Vice President | Tom
Weddle, Chief Financial Officer | Randy Stradley, Vice President of Publishing | Michael
Martens, Vice President of Book Trade Sales | Anita Nelson, Vice President of Business
Affairs | Scott Allie, Editor in Chief | Matt Parkinson, Vice President of Marketing | David
Scroggy, Vice President of Product Development | Dale LaFountain, Vice President of
Information Technology | Darlene Vogel, Senior Director of Print, Design, and Production |
Ken Lizzi, General Counsel | Davey Estrada, Editorial Director | Chris Warner, Senior Books
Editor | Diana Schutz, Executive Editor | Cary Grazzini, Director of Print and Development
| Lia Ribacchi, Art Director | Cara Niece, Director of Scheduling | Tim Wiesch, Director of
International Licensing | Mark Bernardi, Director of Digital Publishing

Published by Dark Horse Books
A division of Dark Horse Comics, Inc.
10956 SE Main Street
Milwaukie, OR 97222

First edition: August 2014
ISBN 978-1-61655-439-2

1 3 5 7 9 10 8 6 4 2
Printed in China

International Licensing: (503) 905-2377
Comic Shop Locator Service: (888) 266-4226

**SKYMAN VOLUME 1: THE RIGHT STUFF**

This volume collects Skyman #1–#4 from Dark Horse Comics.

# CHAPTER 1

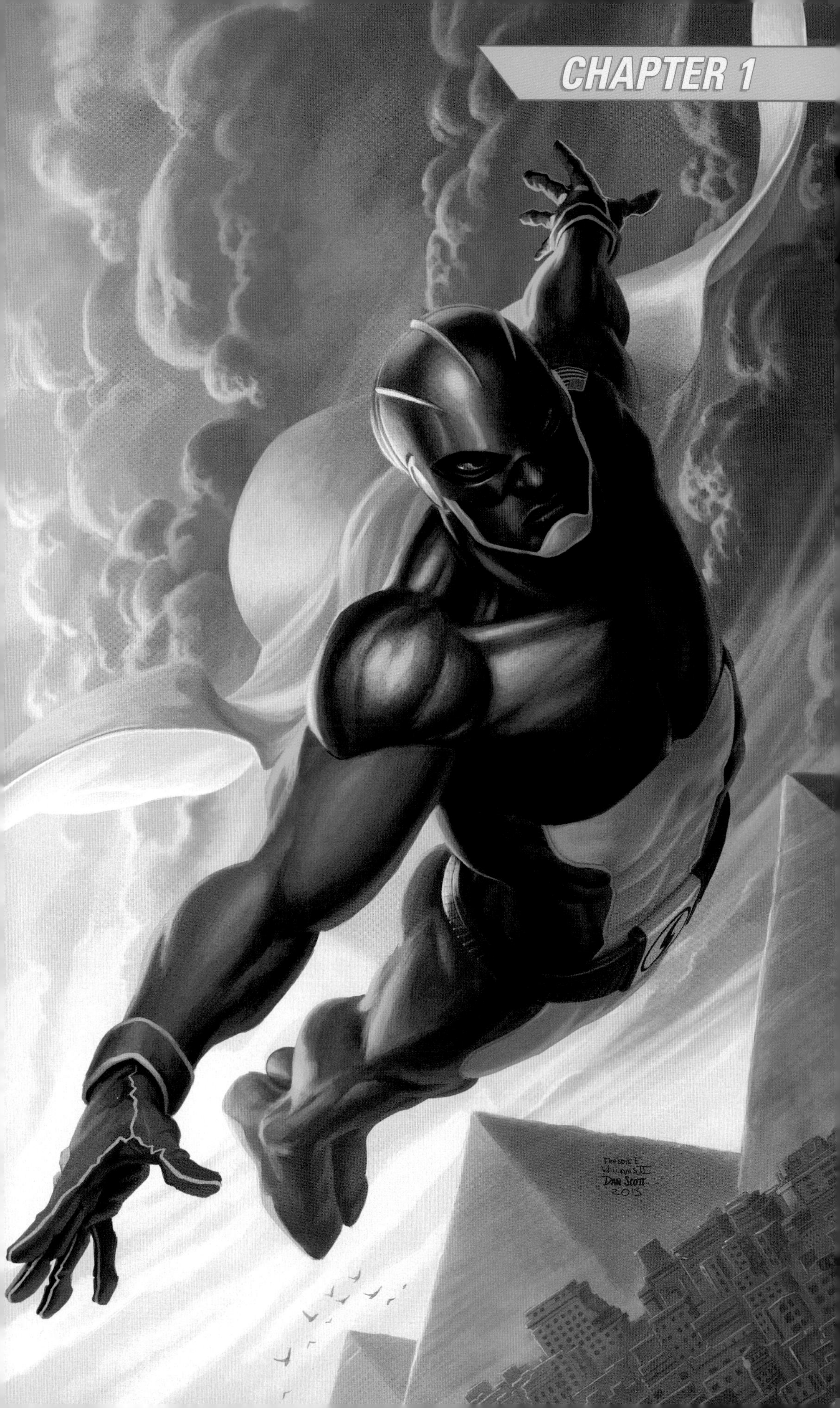
FREDDIE E. WILLIAMS II
DAN SCOTT
2013

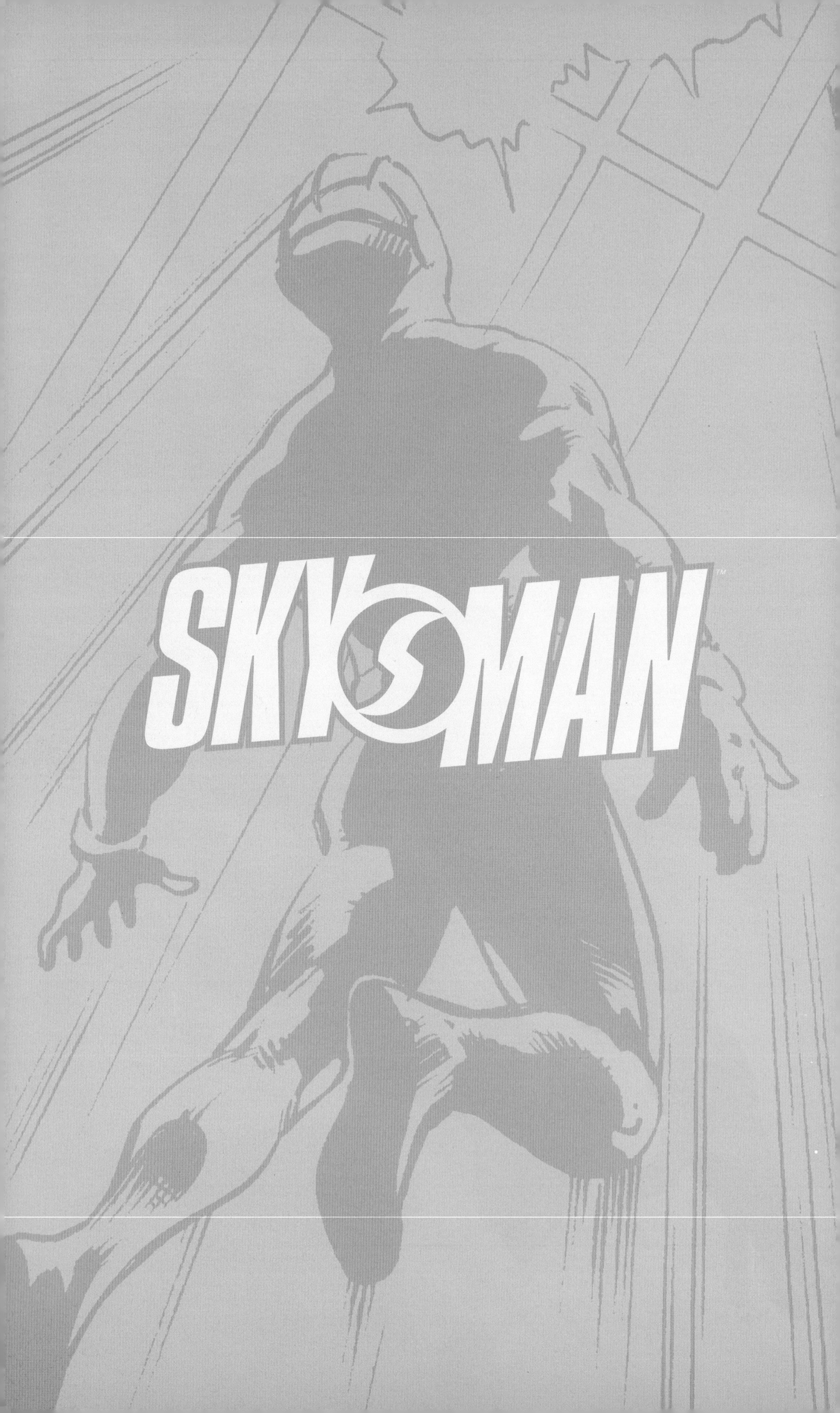
SKYMAN™

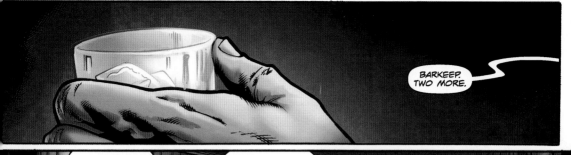

BARKEEP. TWO MORE.

I THINK YOU'VE HAD TOO MUCH, MAN.

FINE. THEN IT'S NOT FOR ME. IT'S FOR HER.

I'M FINE. THANK YOU.

WHAT'S WRONG? DON'T LIKE WHAT YOU SEE? YOU AIN'T MUCH TO LOOK AT--

HEY!

I THINK YOU NEED TO GO. NOW.

I THINK YOU NEED TO TAKE YOUR GODDAMN HAND OFFA ME.

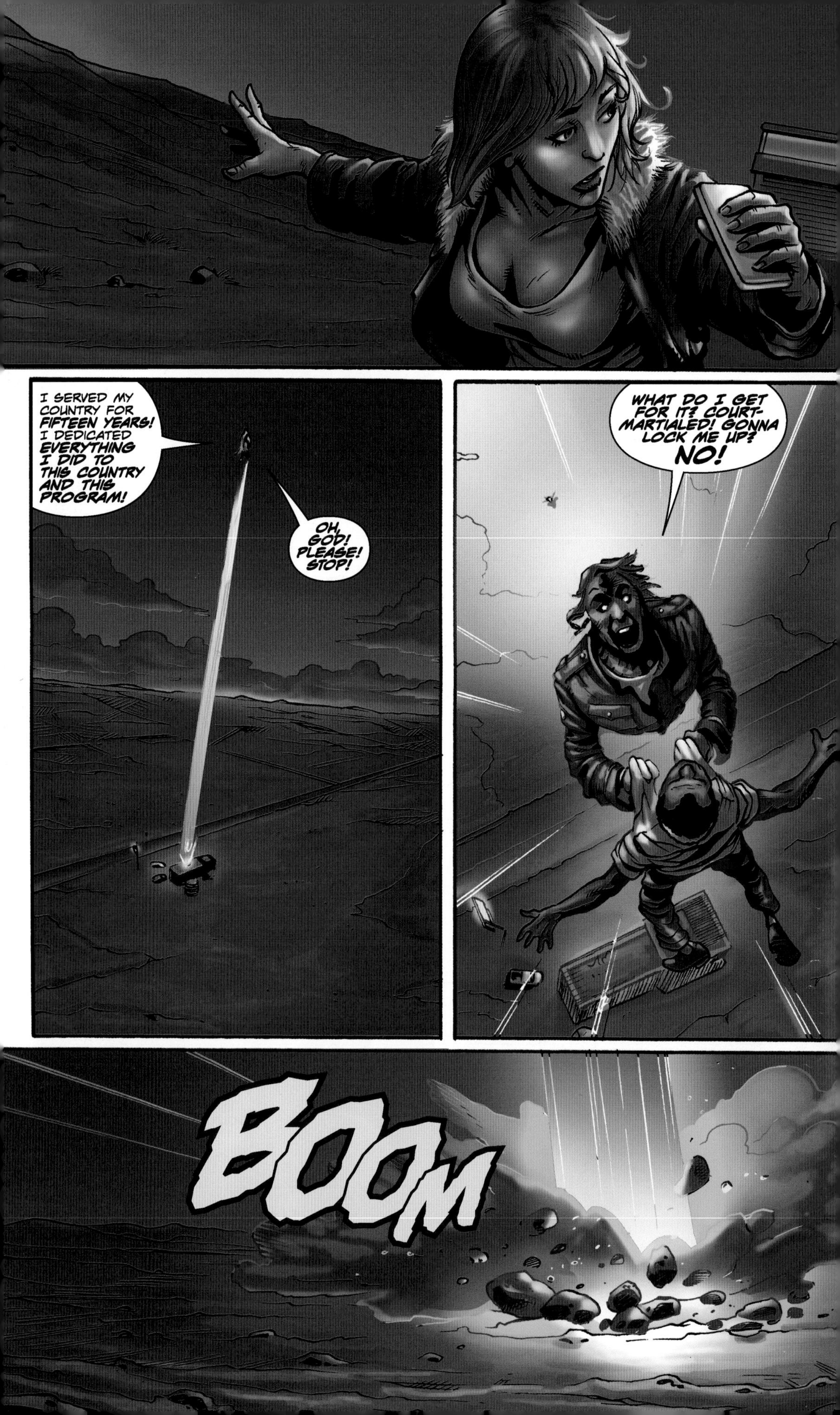
I SERVED MY COUNTRY FOR FIFTEEN YEARS! I DEDICATED EVERYTHING I DID TO THIS COUNTRY AND THIS PROGRAM!
OH, GOD! PLEASE! STOP!
WHAT DO I GET FOR IT? COURT-MARTIALED! GONNA LOCK ME UP? NO!
BOOM

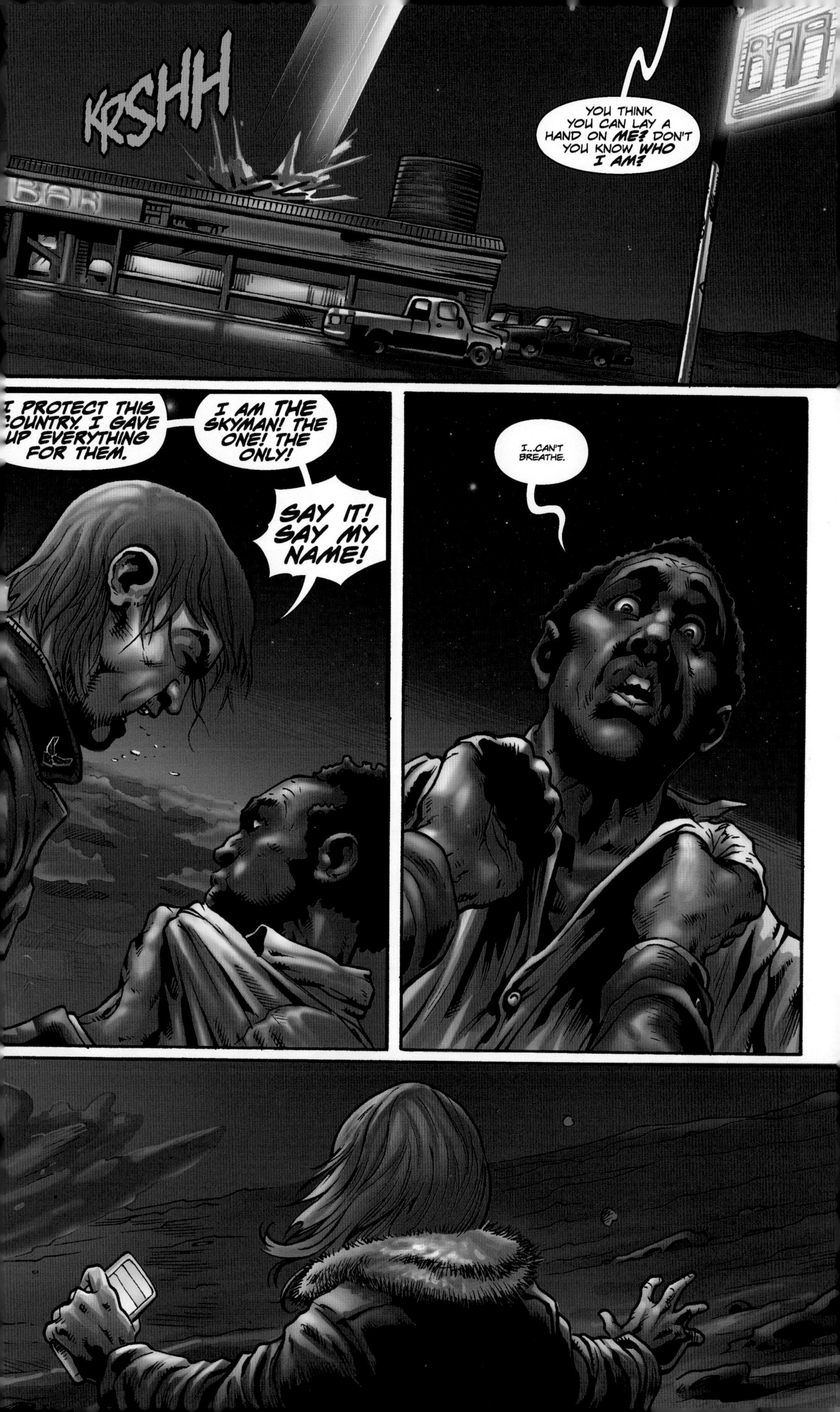
KRSHH
YOU THINK YOU CAN LAY A HAND ON ME? DON'T YOU KNOW WHO I AM?
I PROTECT THIS COUNTRY. I GAVE UP EVERYTHING FOR THEM.
I AM THE SKYMAN! THE ONE! THE ONLY!
SAY IT! SAY MY NAME!
I...CAN'T BREATHE.

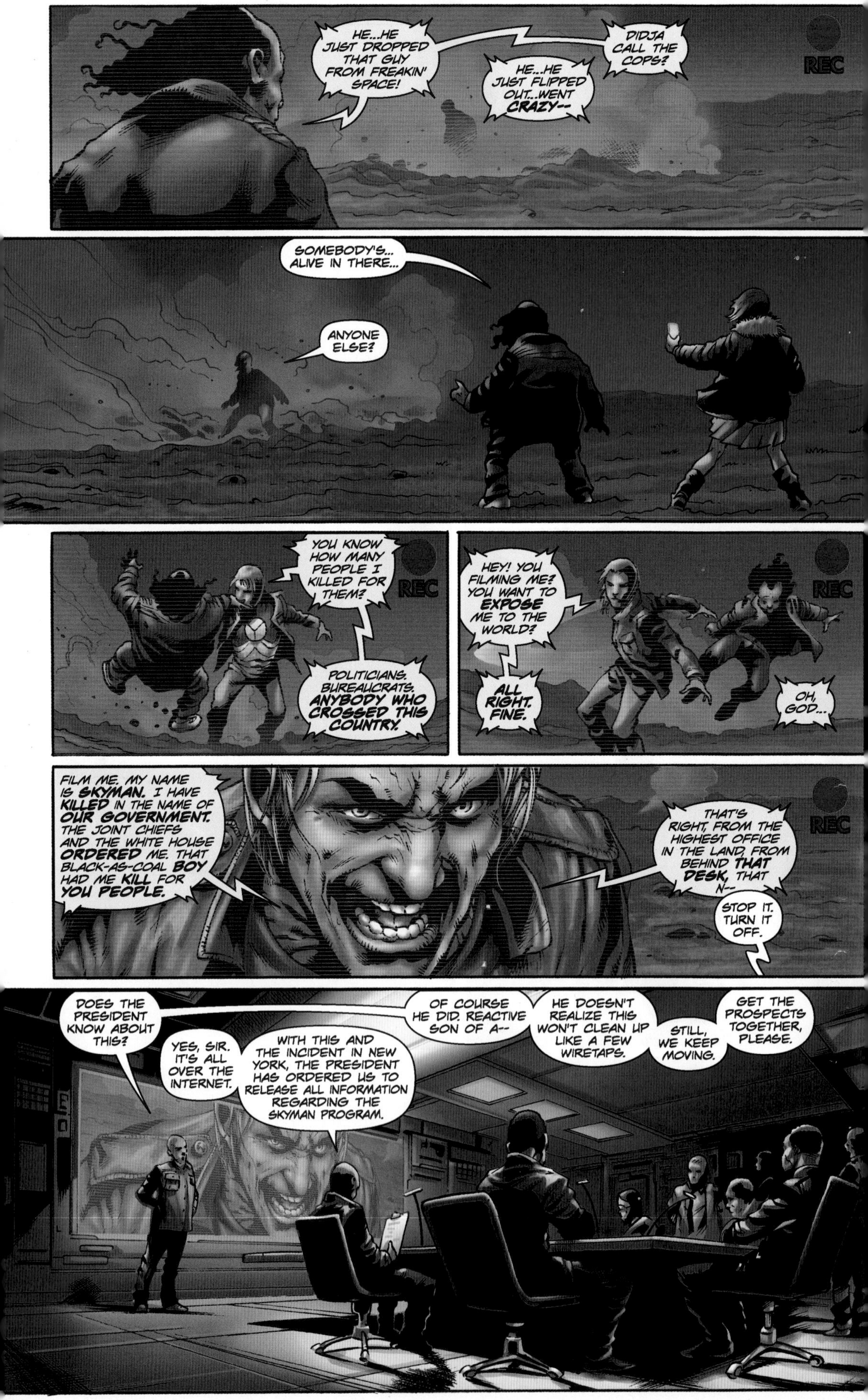

REC
HE...HE JUST DROPPED THAT GUY FROM FREAKIN' SPACE!
DIDJA CALL THE COPS?
HE...HE JUST FLIPPED OUT...WENT CRAZY--
SOMEBODY'S... ALIVE IN THERE...
ANYONE ELSE?
REC
YOU KNOW HOW MANY PEOPLE I KILLED FOR THEM?
POLITICIANS. BUREAUCRATS. ANYBODY WHO CROSSED THIS COUNTRY.
REC
HEY! YOU FILMING ME? YOU WANT TO EXPOSE ME TO THE WORLD?
ALL RIGHT. FINE.
OH, GOD...
REC
FILM ME. MY NAME IS SKYMAN. I HAVE KILLED IN THE NAME OF OUR GOVERNMENT. THE JOINT CHIEFS AND THE WHITE HOUSE ORDERED ME. THAT BLACK-AS-COAL BOY HAD ME KILL FOR YOU PEOPLE.
THAT'S RIGHT, FROM THE HIGHEST OFFICE IN THE LAND, FROM BEHIND THAT DESK, THAT N--
STOP IT. TURN IT OFF.
DOES THE PRESIDENT KNOW ABOUT THIS?
YES, SIR. IT'S ALL OVER THE INTERNET.
WITH THIS AND THE INCIDENT IN NEW YORK, THE PRESIDENT HAS ORDERED US TO RELEASE ALL INFORMATION REGARDING THE SKYMAN PROGRAM.
OF COURSE HE DID. REACTIVE SON OF A--
HE DOESN'T REALIZE THIS WON'T CLEAN UP LIKE A FEW WIRETAPS.
STILL, WE KEEP MOVING.
GET THE PROSPECTS TOGETHER, PLEASE.

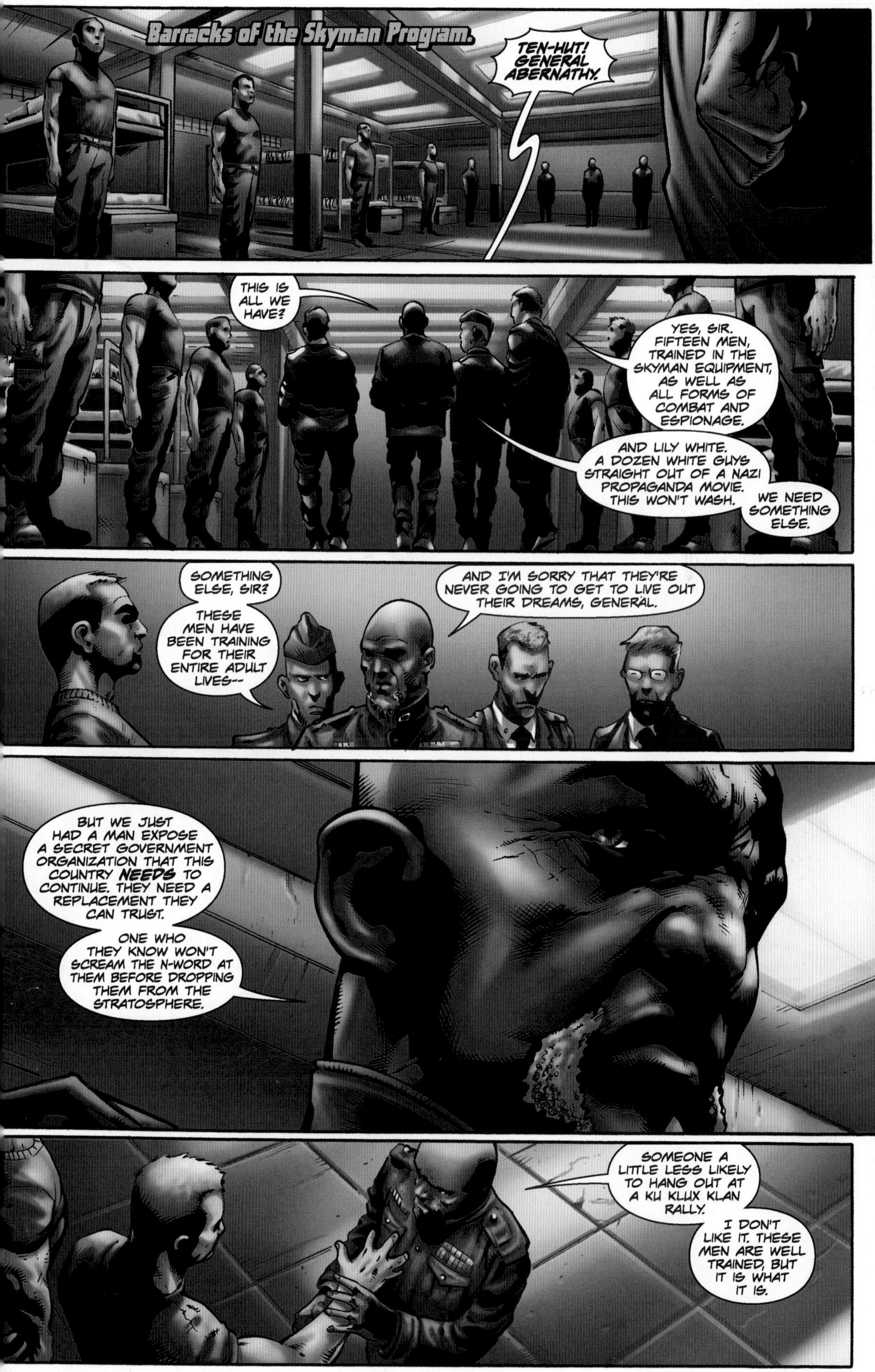
Barracks of the Skyman Program.
TEN-HUT! GENERAL ABERNATHY.
THIS IS ALL WE HAVE?
YES, SIR. FIFTEEN MEN, TRAINED IN THE SKYMAN EQUIPMENT, AS WELL AS ALL FORMS OF COMBAT AND ESPIONAGE.
AND LILY WHITE. A DOZEN WHITE GUYS STRAIGHT OUT OF A NAZI PROPAGANDA MOVIE. THIS WON'T WASH.
WE NEED SOMETHING ELSE.
SOMETHING ELSE, SIR?
THESE MEN HAVE BEEN TRAINING FOR THEIR ENTIRE ADULT LIVES--
AND I'M SORRY THAT THEY'RE NEVER GOING TO GET TO LIVE OUT THEIR DREAMS, GENERAL.
BUT WE JUST HAD A MAN EXPOSE A SECRET GOVERNMENT ORGANIZATION THAT THIS COUNTRY NEEDS TO CONTINUE. THEY NEED A REPLACEMENT THEY CAN TRUST.
ONE WHO THEY KNOW WON'T SCREAM THE N-WORD AT THEM BEFORE DROPPING THEM FROM THE STRATOSPHERE.
SOMEONE A LITTLE LESS LIKELY TO HANG OUT AT A KU KLUX KLAN RALLY.
I DON'T LIKE IT. THESE MEN ARE WELL TRAINED, BUT IT IS WHAT IT IS.

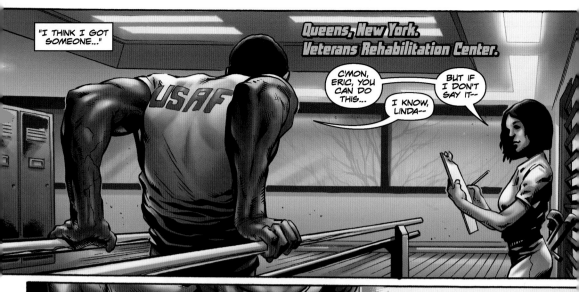

"I THINK I GOT SOMEONE..."
Queens, New York.
Veterans Rehabilitation Center.
C'MON, ERIC, YOU CAN DO THIS...
BUT IF I DON'T SAY IT--
I KNOW, LINDA--
USAF
ALL RIGHT, TIME TO STOP DICKING AROUND.
ERIC, TOO MUCH--
LIKE HELL.
ERIC! THAT WAS AMAZING!
THANKS, MA'AM.
I THINK I'M GONNA PUKE--

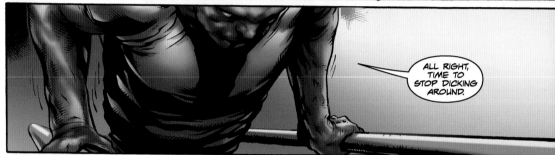

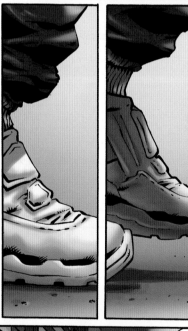

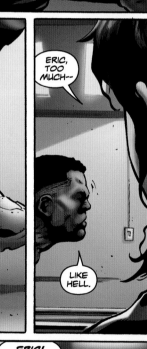

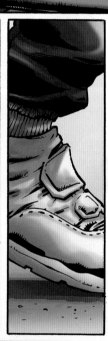

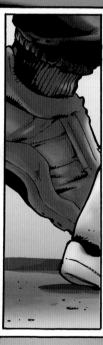

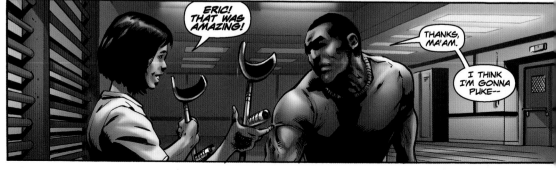

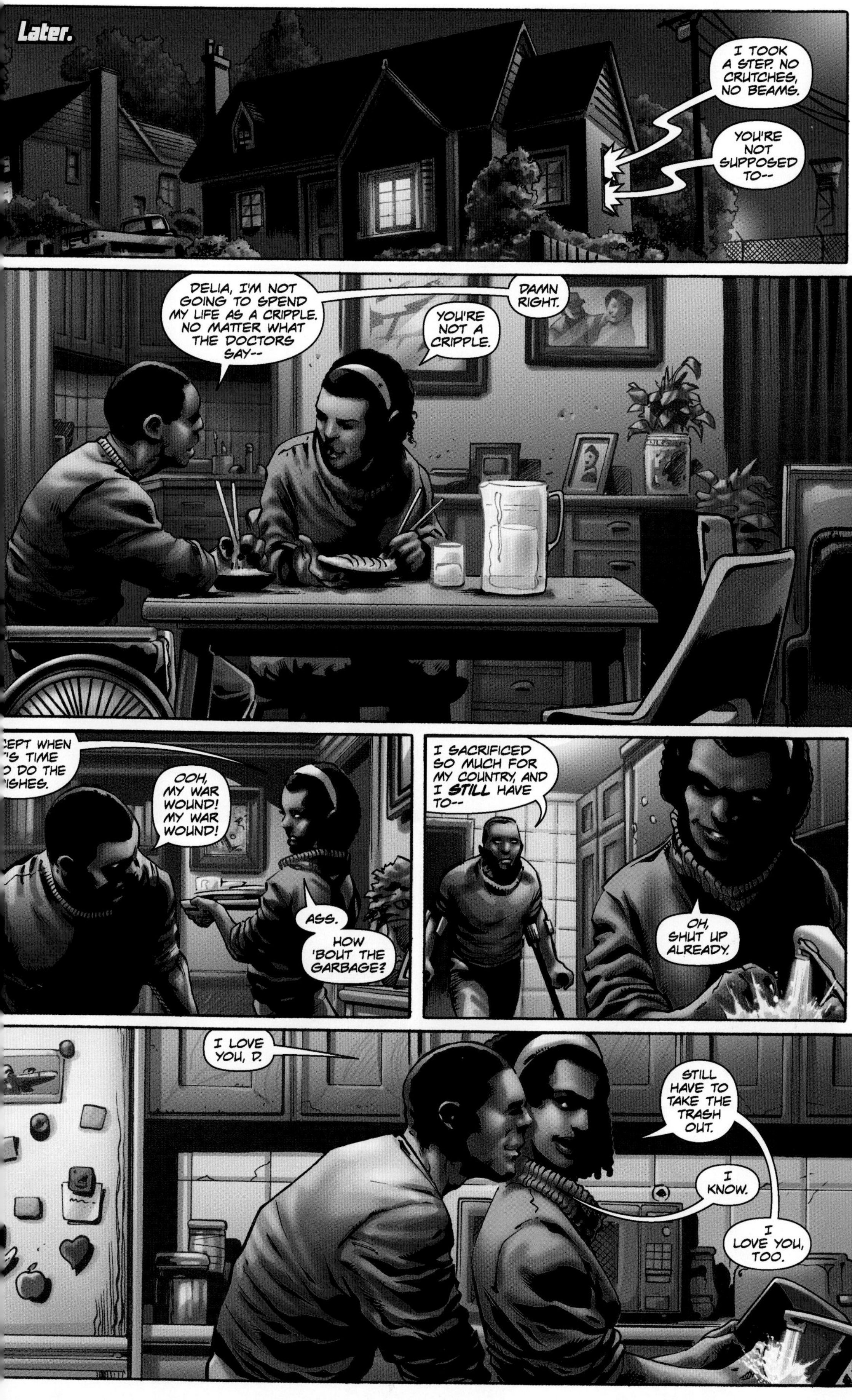
Later.
I TOOK A STEP. NO CRUTCHES, NO BEAMS.
YOU'RE NOT SUPPOSED TO--
DELIA, I'M NOT GOING TO SPEND MY LIFE AS A CRIPPLE. NO MATTER WHAT THE DOCTORS SAY--
YOU'RE NOT A CRIPPLE.
DAMN RIGHT.
CEPT WHEN 'S TIME O DO THE ISHES.
OOH, MY WAR WOUND! MY WAR WOUND!
ASS.
HOW 'BOUT THE GARBAGE?
I SACRIFICED SO MUCH FOR MY COUNTRY, AND I STILL HAVE TO--
OH, SHUT UP ALREADY.
I LOVE YOU, D.
STILL HAVE TO TAKE THE TRASH OUT.
I KNOW.
I LOVE YOU, TOO.

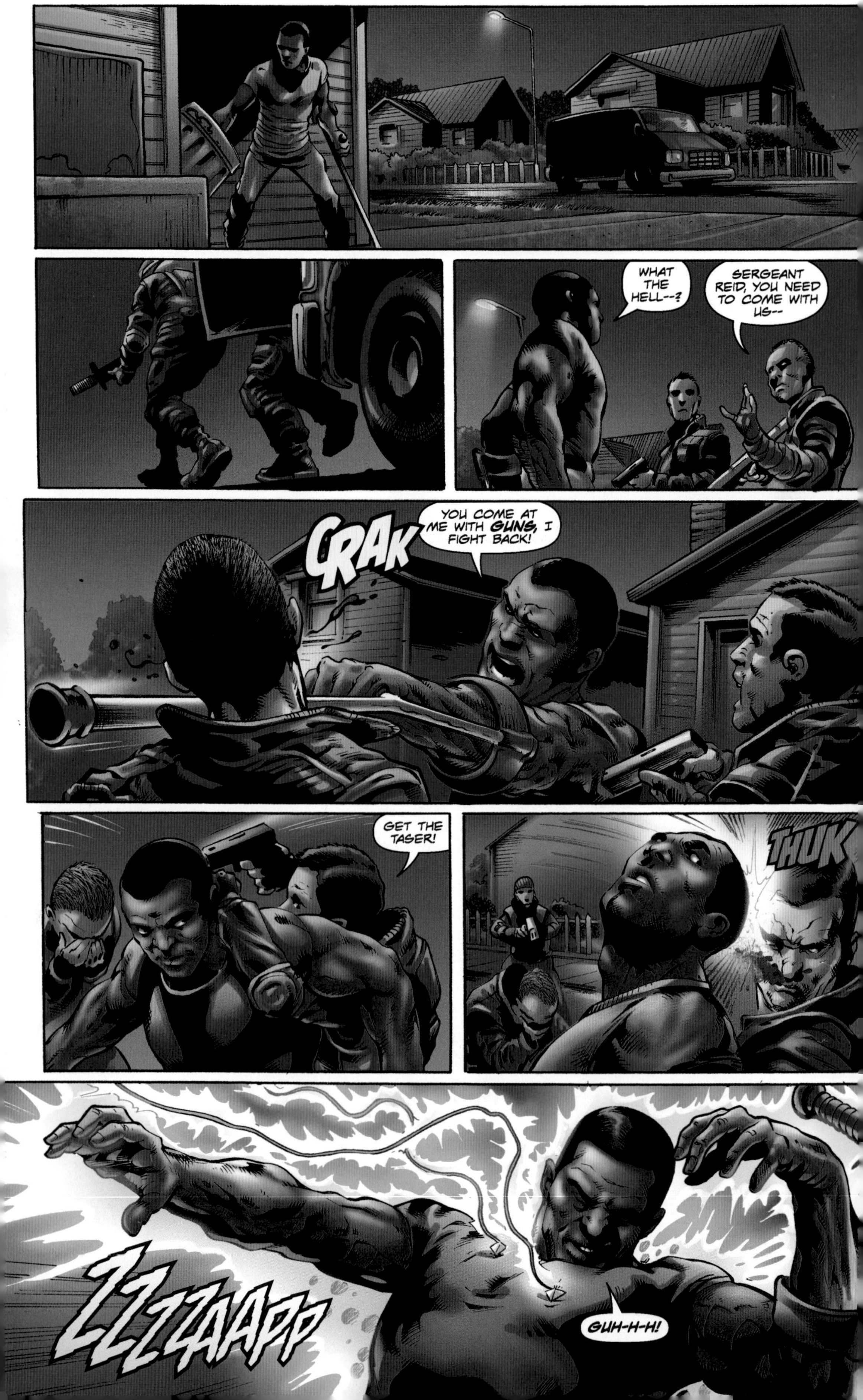

WHAT THE HELL--?
SERGEANT REID, YOU NEED TO COME WITH US--
CRAK
YOU COME AT ME WITH **GUNS**, I FIGHT BACK!
GET THE TASER!
THUK
ZZZZAAPP
GUH-H-H!

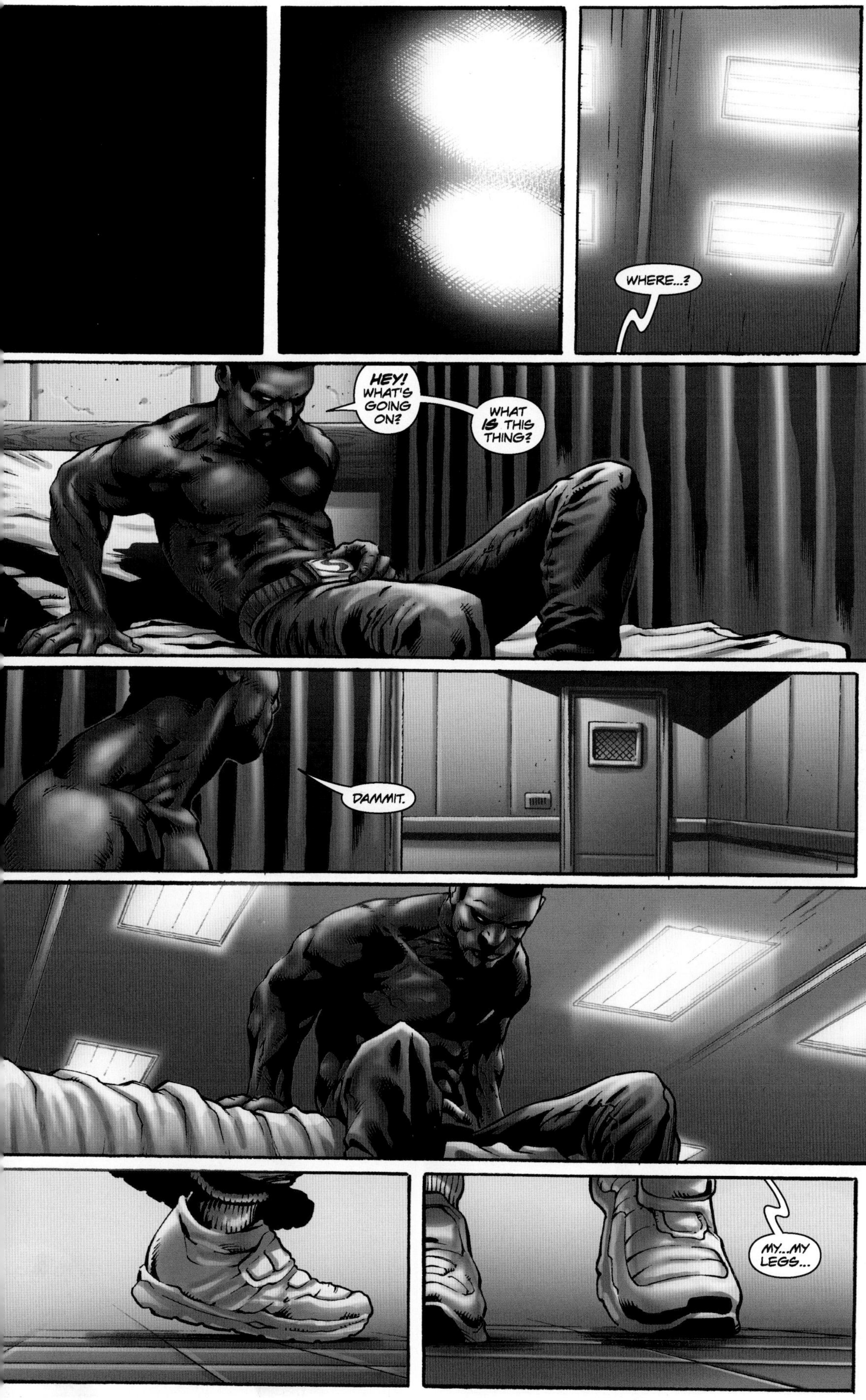
WHERE...?
HEY! WHAT'S GOING ON?
WHAT IS THIS THING?
DAMMIT.
MY...MY LEGS...

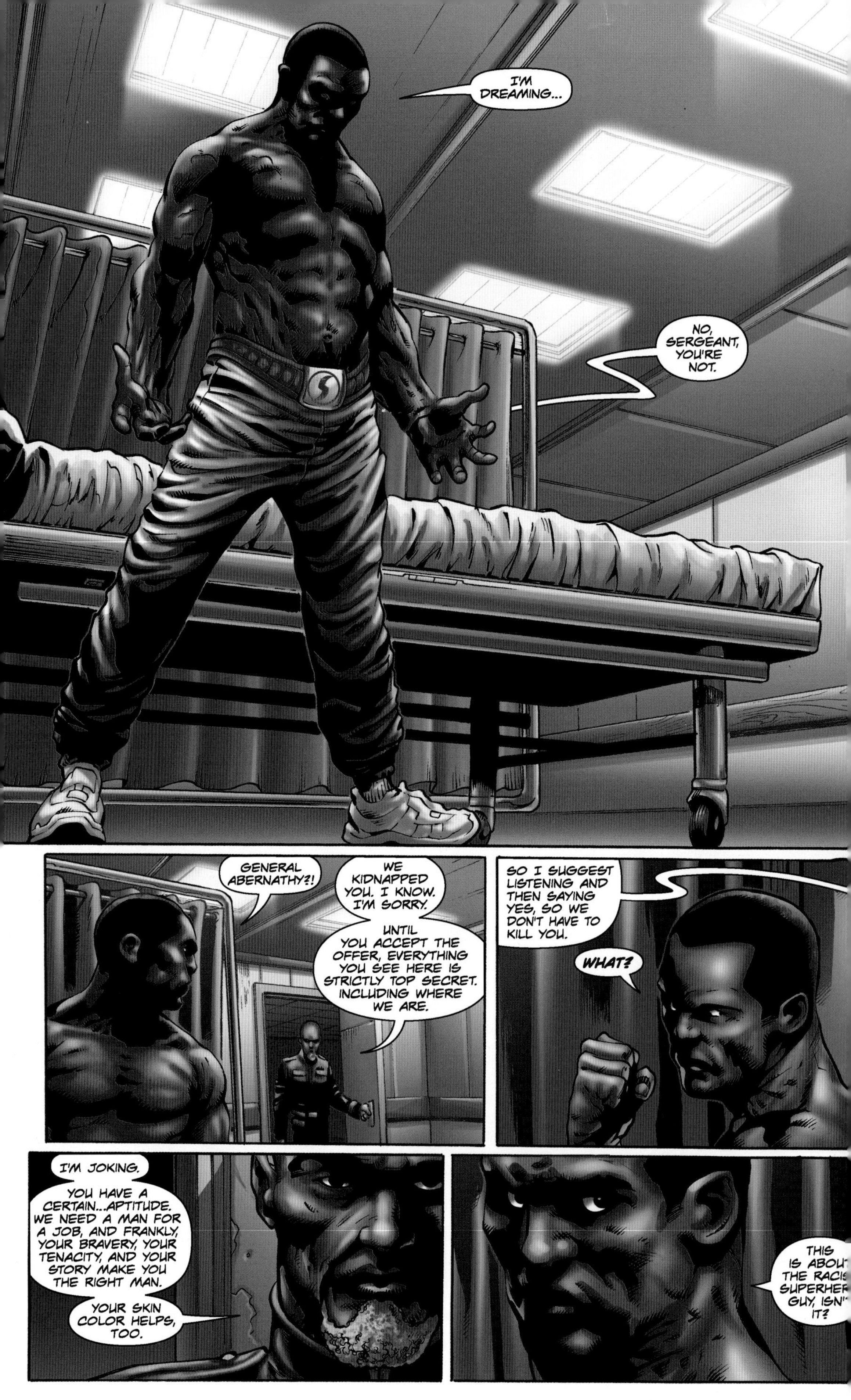

I'M DREAMING...
NO, SERGEANT, YOU'RE NOT.
GENERAL ABERNATHY?!
WE KIDNAPPED YOU. I KNOW. I'M SORRY.
UNTIL YOU ACCEPT THE OFFER, EVERYTHING YOU SEE HERE IS STRICTLY TOP SECRET. INCLUDING WHERE WE ARE.
SO I SUGGEST LISTENING AND THEN SAYING YES, SO WE DON'T HAVE TO KILL YOU.
WHAT?
I'M JOKING.
YOU HAVE A CERTAIN...APTITUDE. WE NEED A MAN FOR A JOB, AND FRANKLY, YOUR BRAVERY, YOUR TENACITY, AND YOUR STORY MAKE YOU THE RIGHT MAN.
YOUR SKIN COLOR HELPS, TOO.
THIS IS ABOU THE RACIS SUPERHER GUY, ISN' IT?

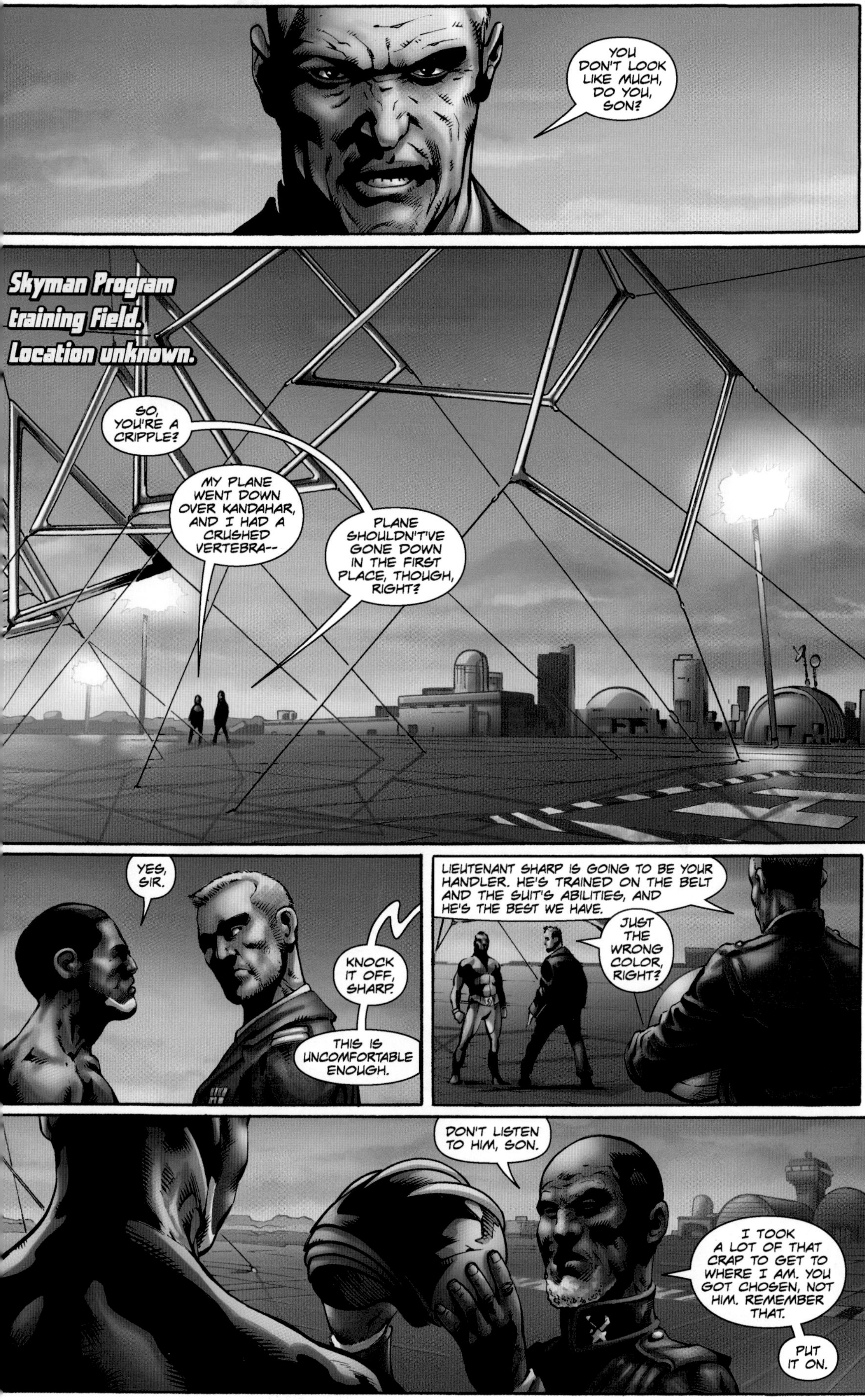
YOU DON'T LOOK LIKE MUCH, DO YOU, SON?
Skyman Program training Field. Location unknown.
SO, YOU'RE A CRIPPLE?
MY PLANE WENT DOWN OVER KANDAHAR, AND I HAD A CRUSHED VERTEBRA--
PLANE SHOULDN'T'VE GONE DOWN IN THE FIRST PLACE, THOUGH, RIGHT?
YES, SIR.
KNOCK IT OFF, SHARP.
THIS IS UNCOMFORTABLE ENOUGH.
LIEUTENANT SHARP IS GOING TO BE YOUR HANDLER. HE'S TRAINED ON THE BELT AND THE SUIT'S ABILITIES, AND HE'S THE BEST WE HAVE.
JUST THE WRONG COLOR, RIGHT?
DON'T LISTEN TO HIM, SON.
I TOOK A LOT OF THAT CRAP TO GET TO WHERE I AM. YOU GOT CHOSEN, NOT HIM. REMEMBER THAT.
PUT IT ON.

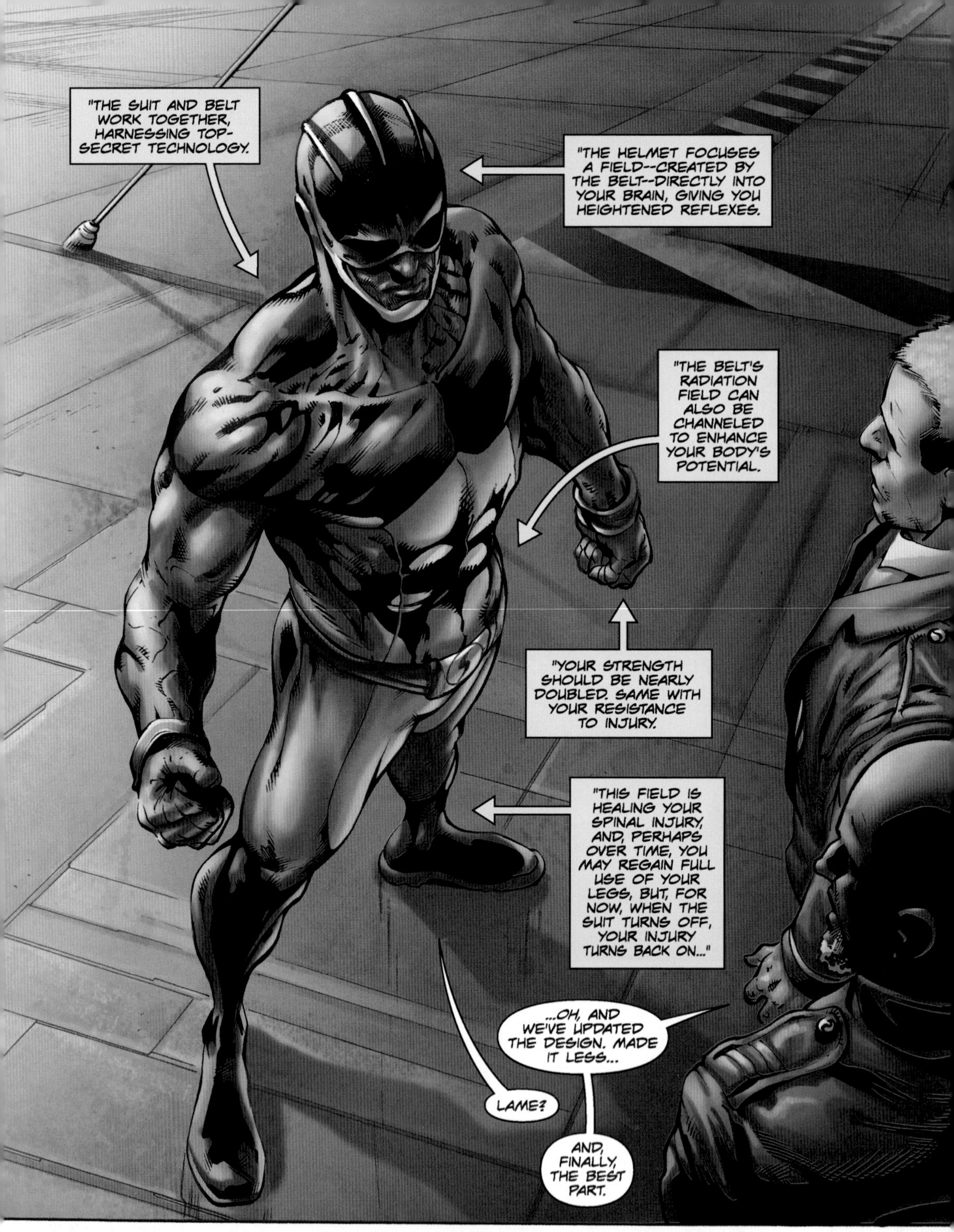
"THE SUIT AND BELT WORK TOGETHER, HARNESSING TOP-SECRET TECHNOLOGY.
"THE HELMET FOCUSES A FIELD--CREATED BY THE BELT--DIRECTLY INTO YOUR BRAIN, GIVING YOU HEIGHTENED REFLEXES.
"THE BELT'S RADIATION FIELD CAN ALSO BE CHANNELED TO ENHANCE YOUR BODY'S POTENTIAL.
"YOUR STRENGTH SHOULD BE NEARLY DOUBLED. SAME WITH YOUR RESISTANCE TO INJURY.
"THIS FIELD IS HEALING YOUR SPINAL INJURY, AND, PERHAPS OVER TIME, YOU MAY REGAIN FULL USE OF YOUR LEGS, BUT, FOR NOW, WHEN THE SUIT TURNS OFF, YOUR INJURY TURNS BACK ON..."
...OH, AND WE'VE UPDATED THE DESIGN. MADE IT LESS...
LAME?
AND, FINALLY, THE BEST PART.
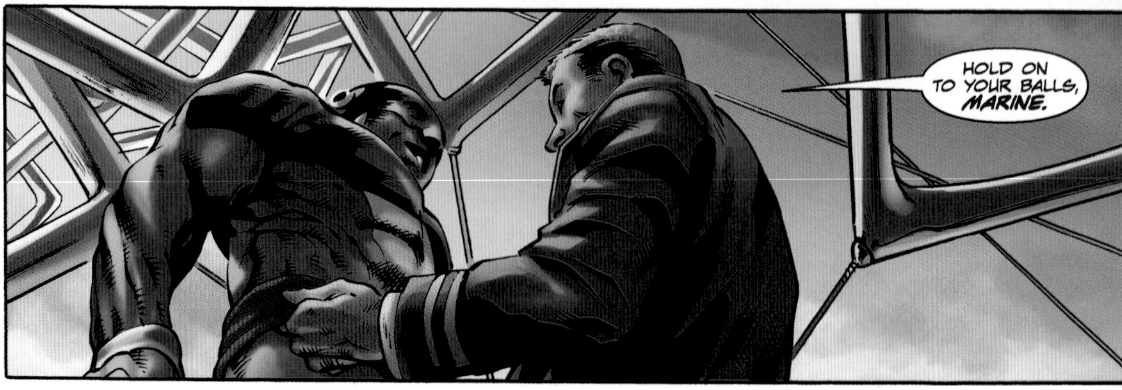
HOLD ON TO YOUR BALLS, ***MARINE.***

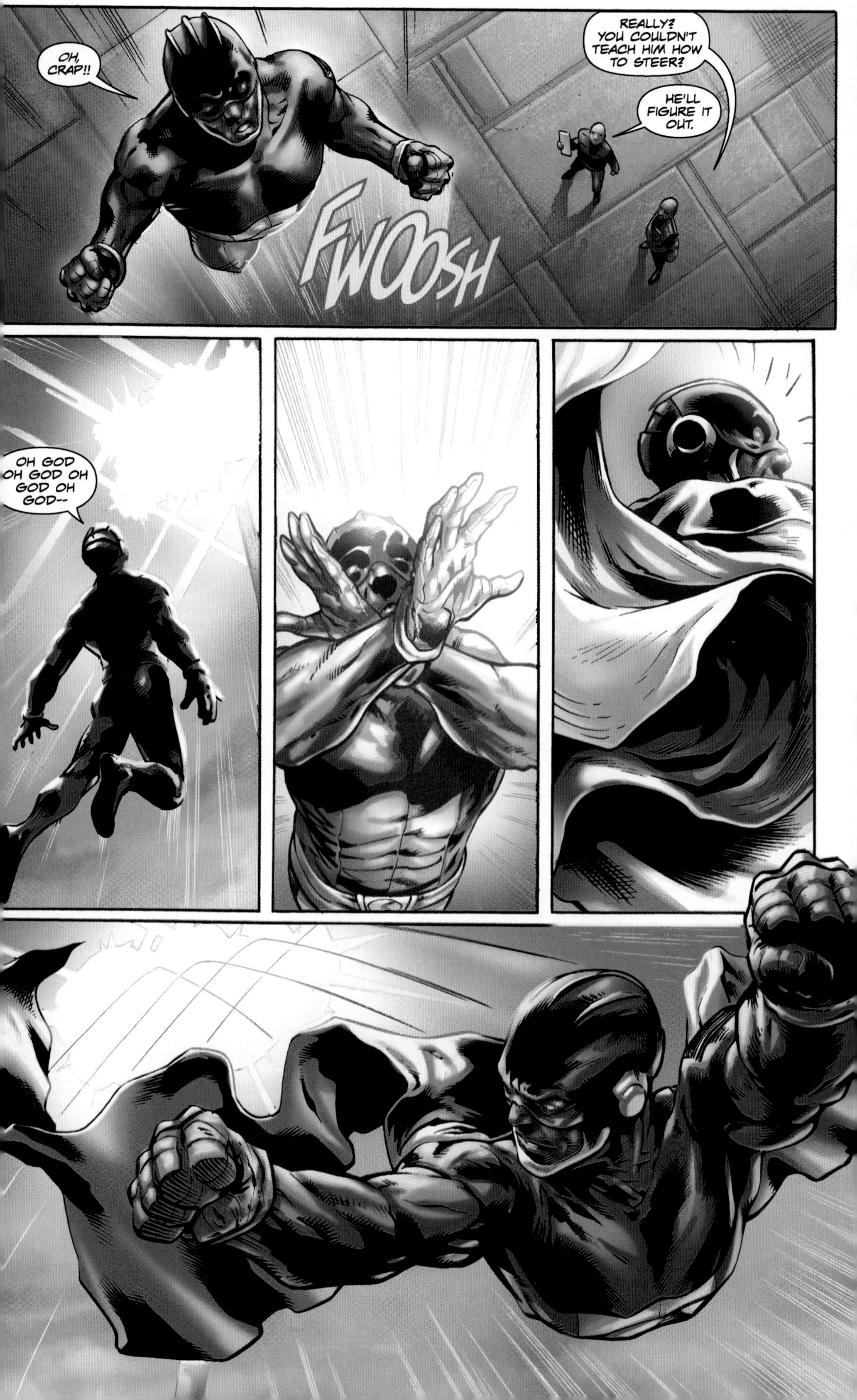
OH, CRAP!!
FWOOSH
REALLY? YOU COULDN'T TEACH HIM HOW TO STEER?
HE'LL FIGURE IT OUT.
OH GOD OH GOD OH GOD OH GOD--

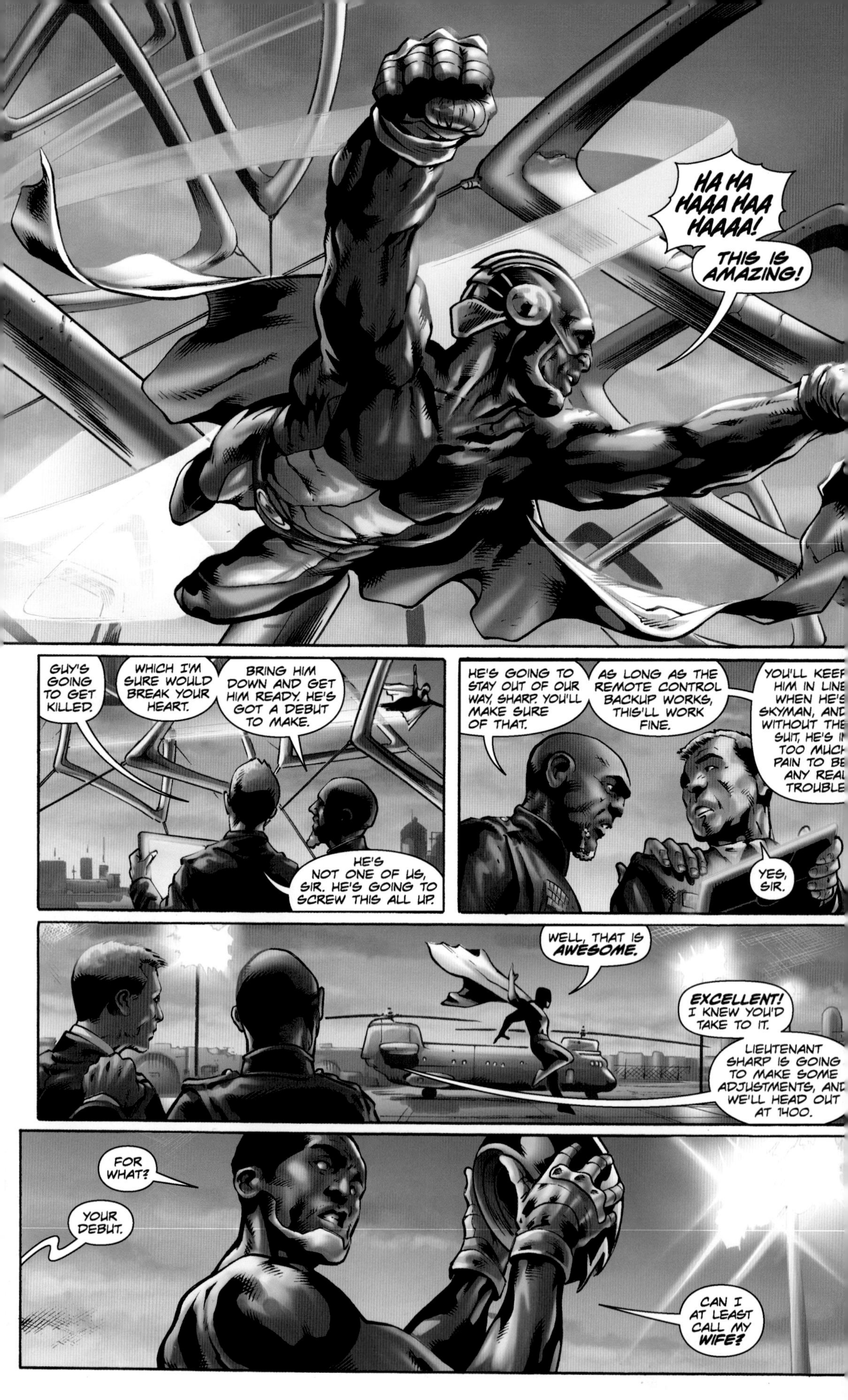

HA HA HAAA HAA HAAAA!
THIS IS AMAZING!
GUY'S GOING TO GET KILLED.
WHICH I'M SURE WOULD BREAK YOUR HEART.
BRING HIM DOWN AND GET HIM READY. HE'S GOT A DEBUT TO MAKE.
HE'S NOT ONE OF US, SIR. HE'S GOING TO SCREW THIS ALL UP.
HE'S GOING TO STAY OUT OF OUR WAY, SHARP. YOU'LL MAKE SURE OF THAT.
AS LONG AS THE REMOTE CONTROL BACKUP WORKS, THIS'LL WORK FINE.
YOU'LL KEEP HIM IN LINE WHEN HE'S SKYMAN, AND WITHOUT THE SUIT, HE'S IN TOO MUCH PAIN TO BE ANY REAL TROUBLE.
YES, SIR.
WELL, THAT IS AWESOME.
EXCELLENT! I KNEW YOU'D TAKE TO IT.
LIEUTENANT SHARP IS GOING TO MAKE SOME ADJUSTMENTS, AND WE'LL HEAD OUT AT 1400.
FOR WHAT?
YOUR DEBUT.
CAN I AT LEAST CALL MY WIFE?

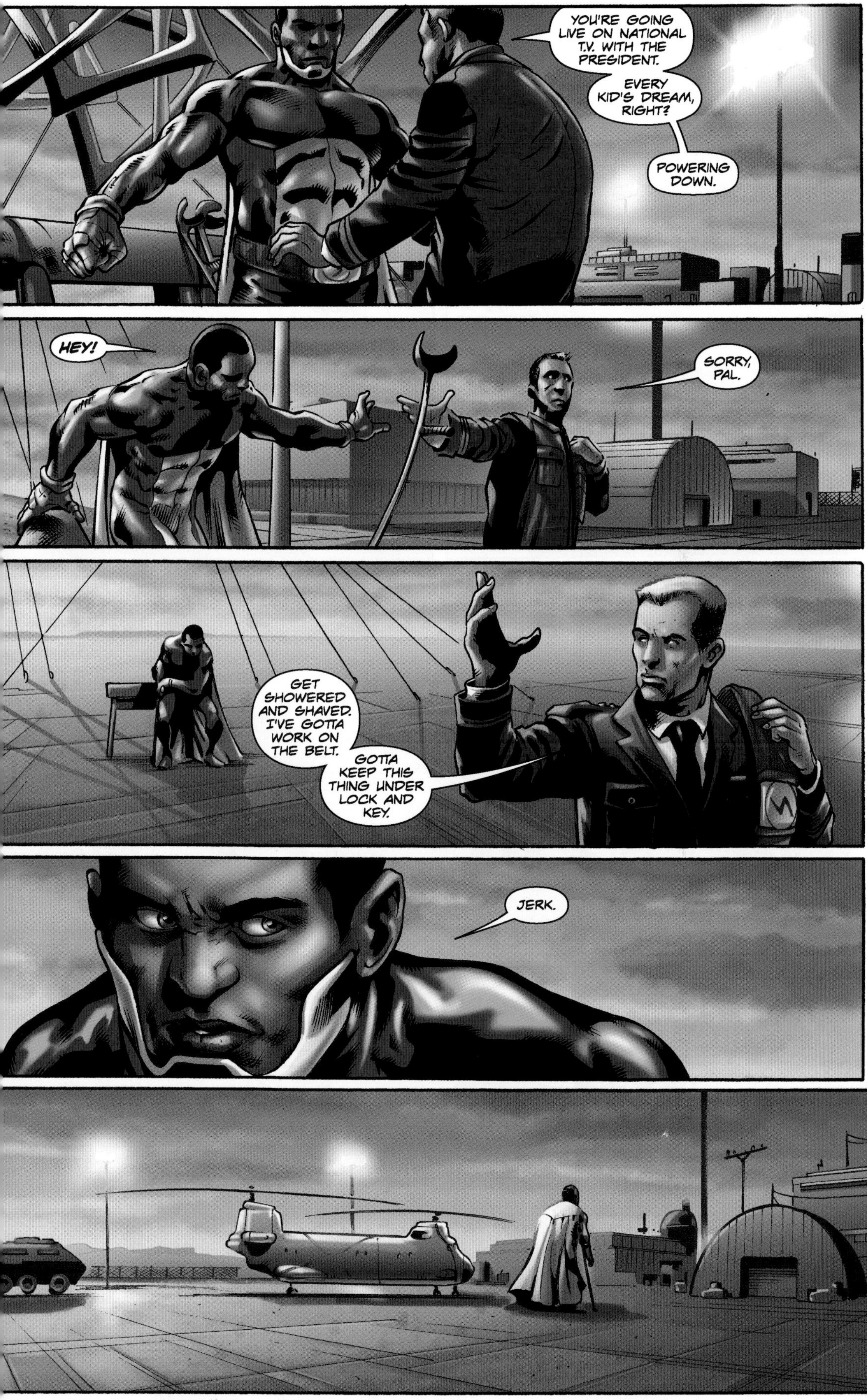
YOU'RE GOING LIVE ON NATIONAL T.V. WITH THE PRESIDENT.
EVERY KID'S DREAM, RIGHT?
POWERING DOWN.
HEY!
SORRY, PAL.
GET SHOWERED AND SHAVED. I'VE GOTTA WORK ON THE BELT.
GOTTA KEEP THIS THING UNDER LOCK AND KEY.
JERK.

Later.

THE STABILATOR GOT STUCK, RIGHT?

JESUS. YOU SCARED ME--

THE STABILATOR GOT STUCK. THAT'S WHAT YOU SAID ON THE REPORT.

YOU HAD TO BAIL.

WHAT'S YOUR PROBLEM, MAN?

MY PROBLEM IS I THINK YOU'RE A LIAR, AND A COWARD, AND I THINK YOU GOT YOUR SQUAD SHOT DOWN.

BUT YOU KNOW WHAT? I'LL MAKE YOU A PROMISE. AFTER YOU CRASH AND BURN, I CAN GO VISIT THAT PRETTY LITTLE WIFE OF YOURS--

WHFF

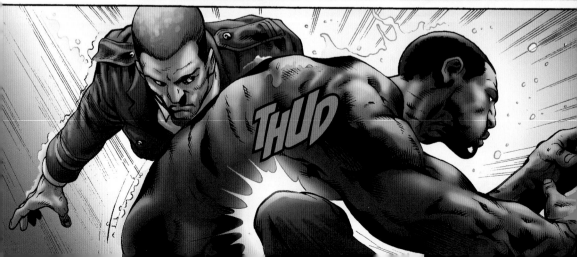

THUD

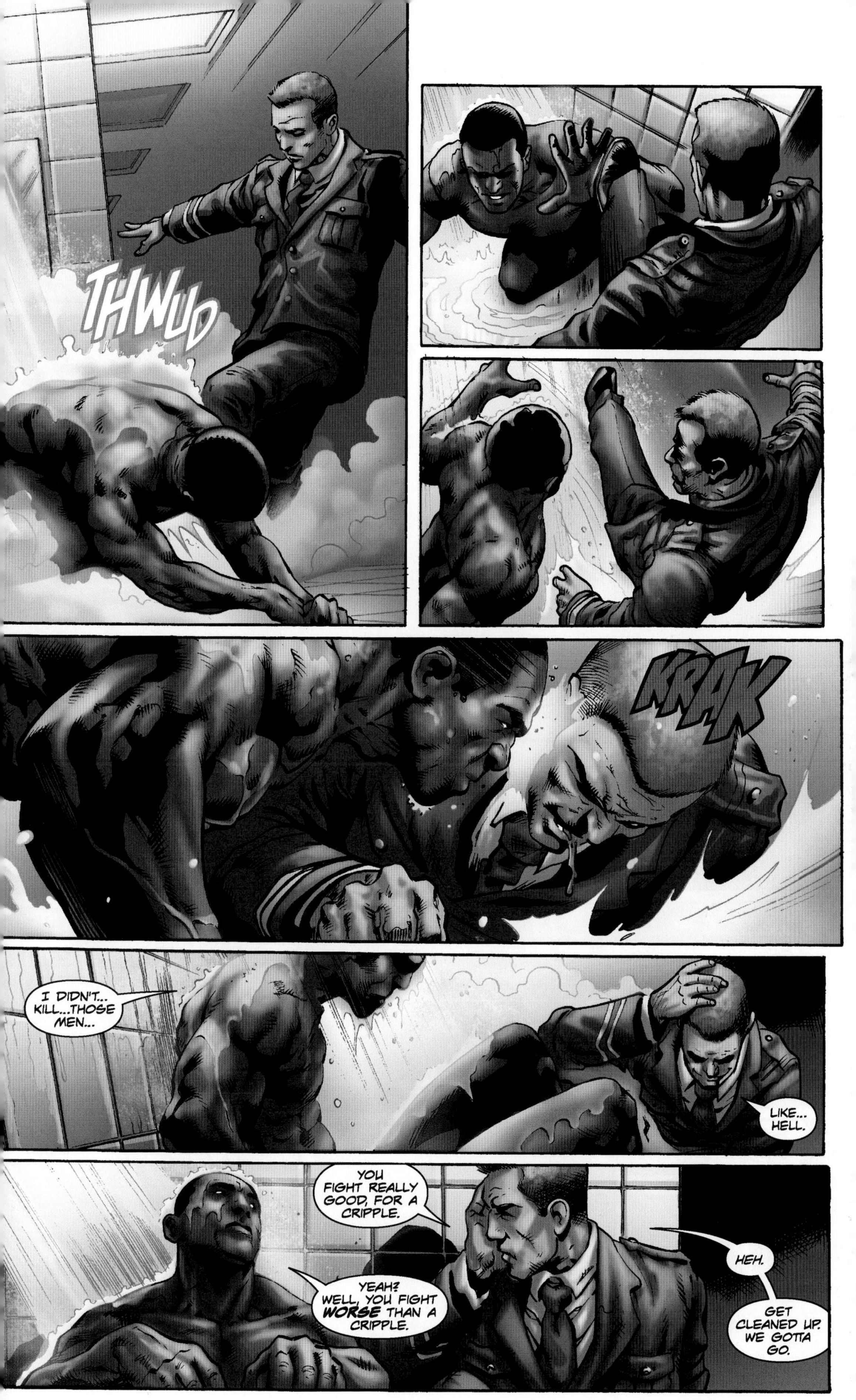
THWUD
KRAK
I DIDN'T... KILL...THOSE MEN...
LIKE... HELL.
YOU FIGHT REALLY GOOD, FOR A CRIPPLE.
YEAH? WELL, YOU FIGHT WORSE THAN A CRIPPLE.
HEH.
GET CLEANED UP. WE GOTTA GO.

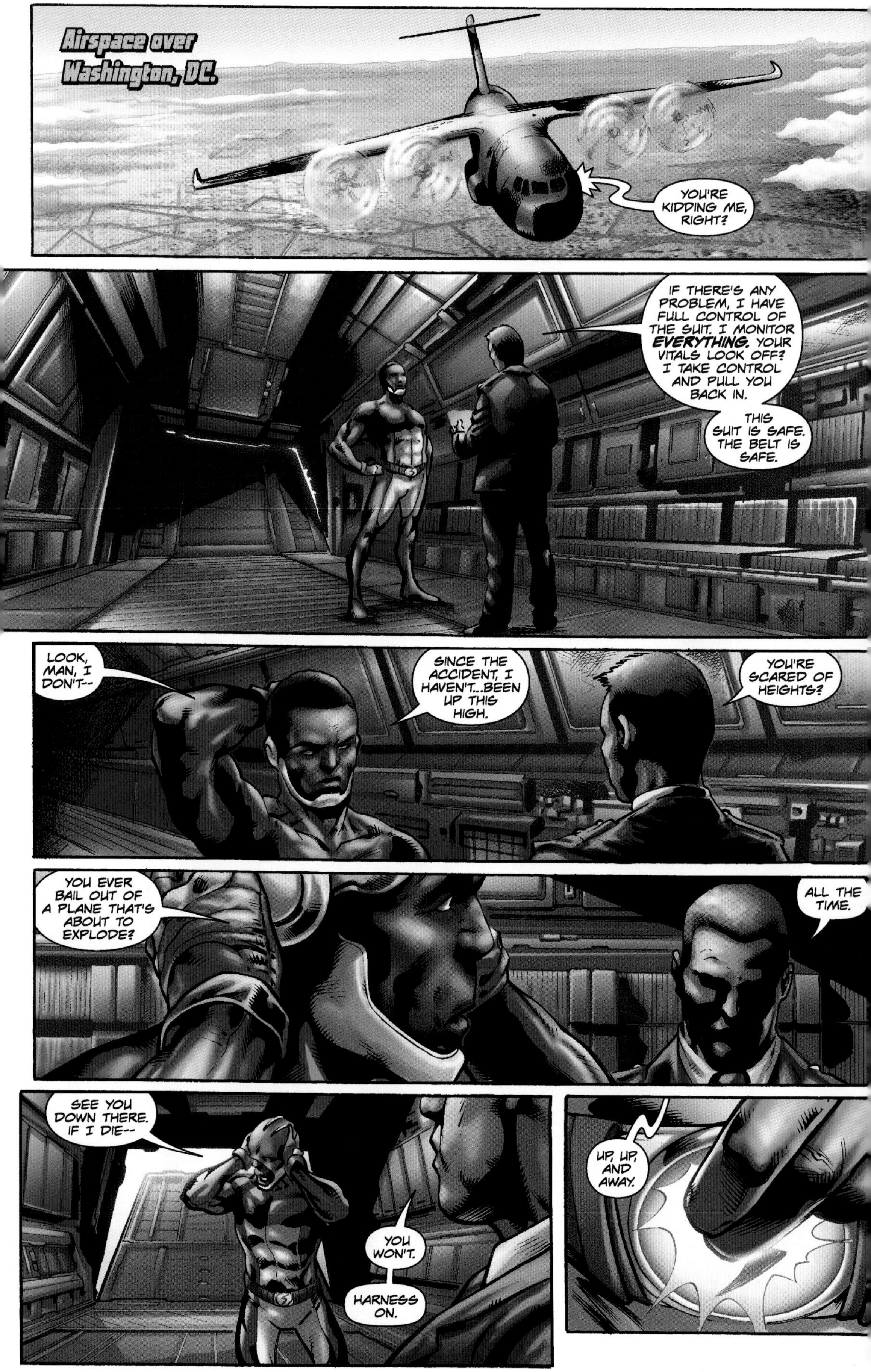
Airspace over Washington, DC.
YOU'RE KIDDING ME, RIGHT?
IF THERE'S ANY PROBLEM, I HAVE FULL CONTROL OF THE SUIT. I MONITOR EVERYTHING. YOUR VITALS LOOK OFF? I TAKE CONTROL AND PULL YOU BACK IN.
THIS SUIT IS SAFE. THE BELT IS SAFE.
LOOK, MAN, I DON'T--
SINCE THE ACCIDENT, I HAVEN'T...BEEN UP THIS HIGH.
YOU'RE SCARED OF HEIGHTS?
YOU EVER BAIL OUT OF A PLANE THAT'S ABOUT TO EXPLODE?
ALL THE TIME.
SEE YOU DOWN THERE. IF I DIE--
YOU WON'T.
HARNESS ON.
UP, UP, AND AWAY.

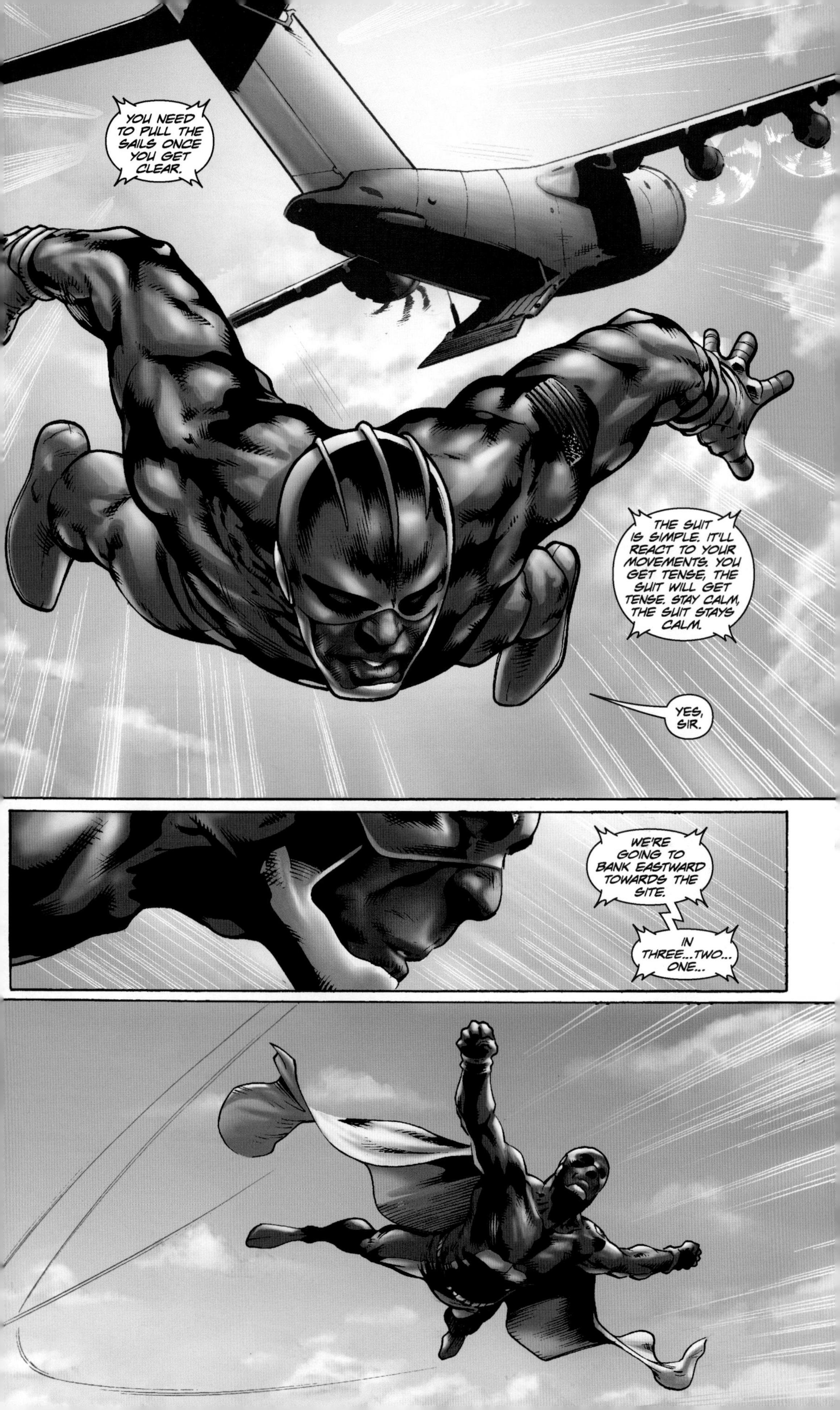
YOU NEED TO PULL THE SAILS ONCE YOU GET CLEAR.
THE SUIT IS SIMPLE. IT'LL REACT TO YOUR MOVEMENTS. YOU GET TENSE, THE SUIT WILL GET TENSE. STAY CALM, THE SUIT STAYS CALM.
YES, SIR.
WE'RE GOING TO BANK EASTWARD TOWARDS THE SITE.
IN THREE...TWO... ONE...

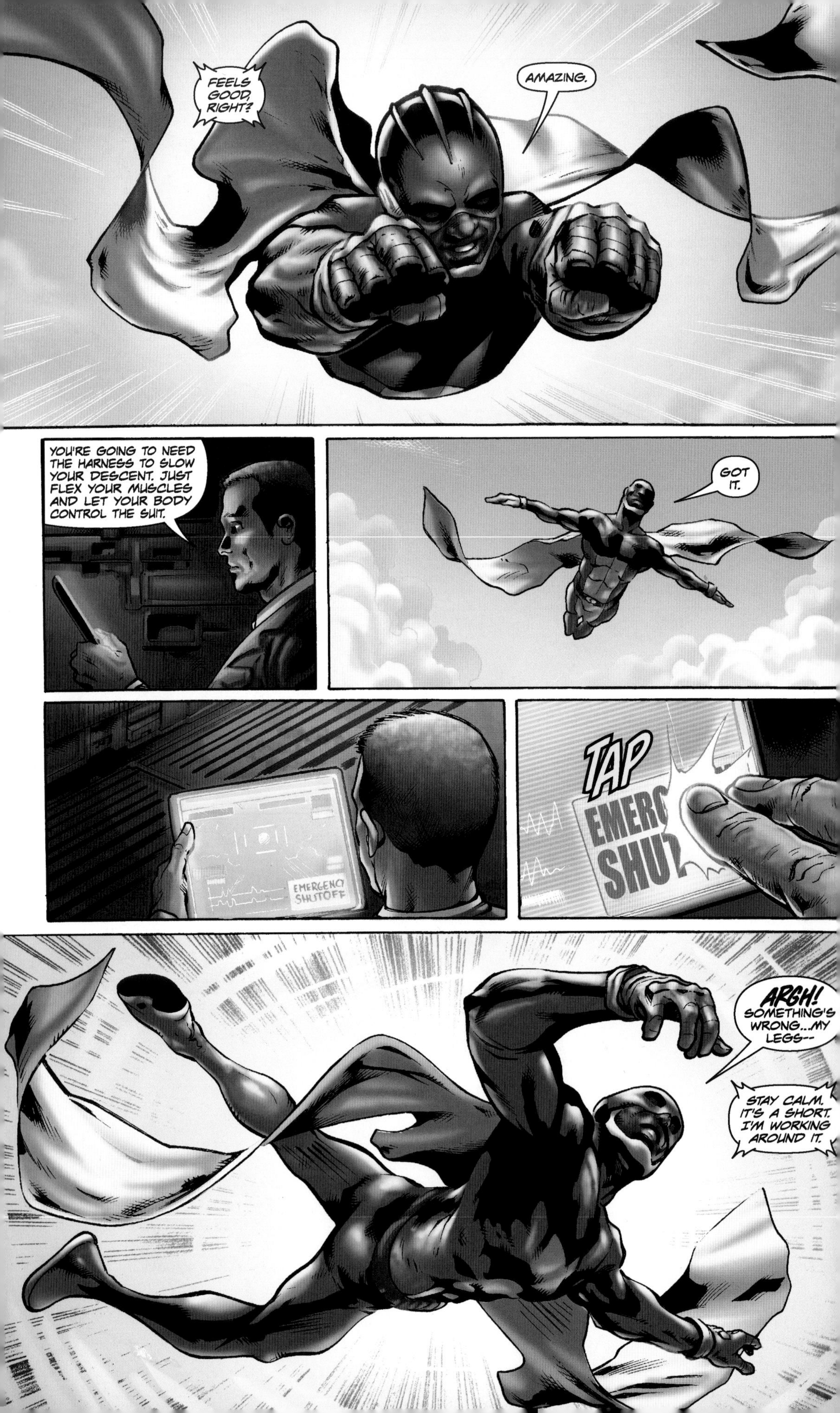
FEELS GOOD, RIGHT?
AMAZING.
YOU'RE GOING TO NEED THE HARNESS TO SLOW YOUR DESCENT. JUST FLEX YOUR MUSCLES AND LET YOUR BODY CONTROL THE SUIT.
GOT IT.
EMERGENCY SHUTOFF
TAP
ARGH! SOMETHING'S WRONG...MY LEGS--
STAY CALM. IT'S A SHORT. I'M WORKING AROUND IT.

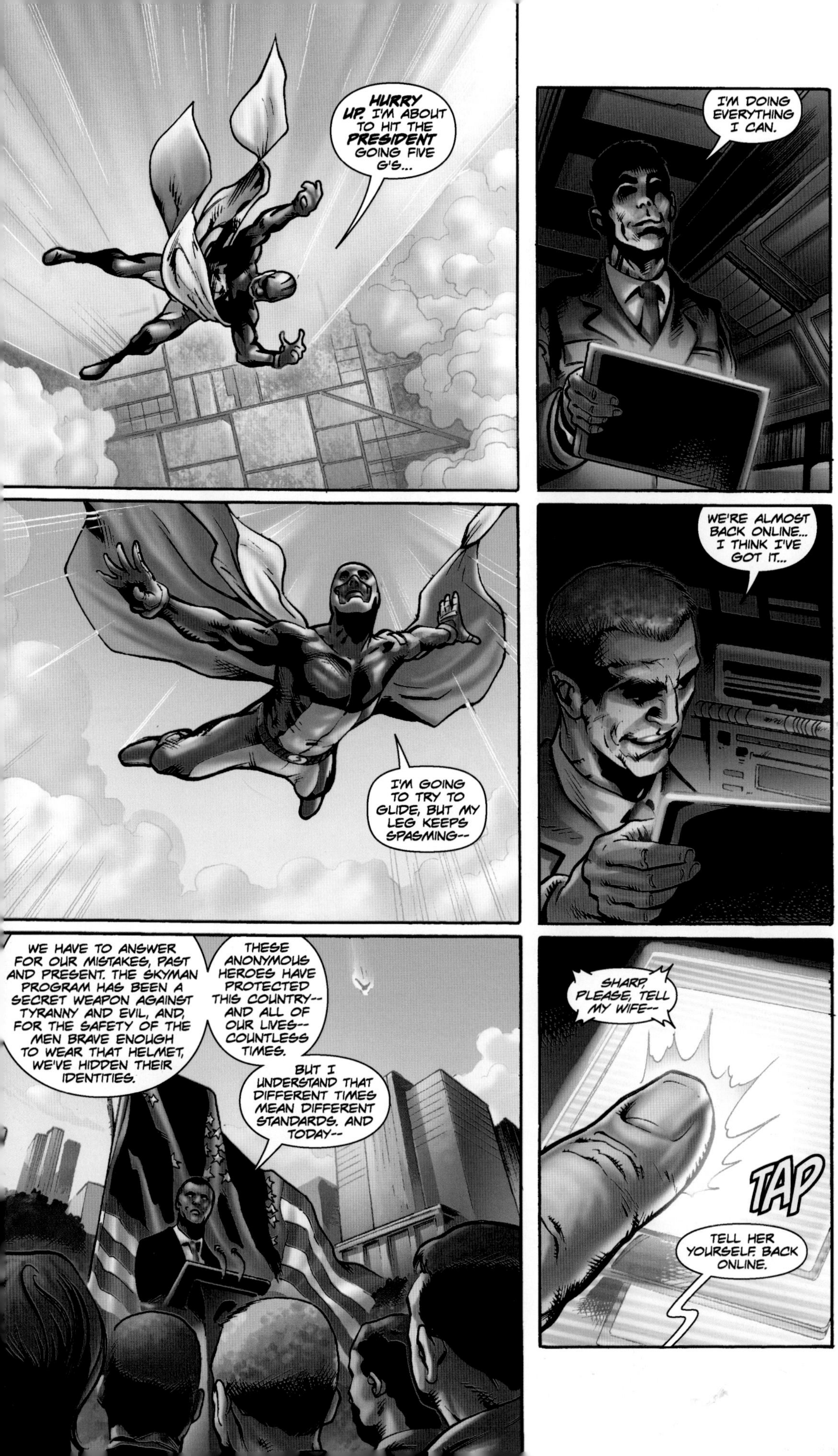
HURRY UP. I'M ABOUT TO HIT THE PRESIDENT GOING FIVE G'S...
I'M DOING EVERYTHING I CAN.
I'M GOING TO TRY TO GLIDE, BUT MY LEG KEEPS SPASMING--
WE'RE ALMOST BACK ONLINE... I THINK I'VE GOT IT...
WE HAVE TO ANSWER FOR OUR MISTAKES, PAST AND PRESENT. THE SKYMAN PROGRAM HAS BEEN A SECRET WEAPON AGAINST TYRANNY AND EVIL, AND, FOR THE SAFETY OF THE MEN BRAVE ENOUGH TO WEAR THAT HELMET, WE'VE HIDDEN THEIR IDENTITIES.
THESE ANONYMOUS HEROES HAVE PROTECTED THIS COUNTRY-- AND ALL OF OUR LIVES-- COUNTLESS TIMES.
BUT I UNDERSTAND THAT DIFFERENT TIMES MEAN DIFFERENT STANDARDS. AND TODAY--
SHARP, PLEASE, TELL MY WIFE--
TAP
TELL HER YOURSELF. BACK ONLINE.

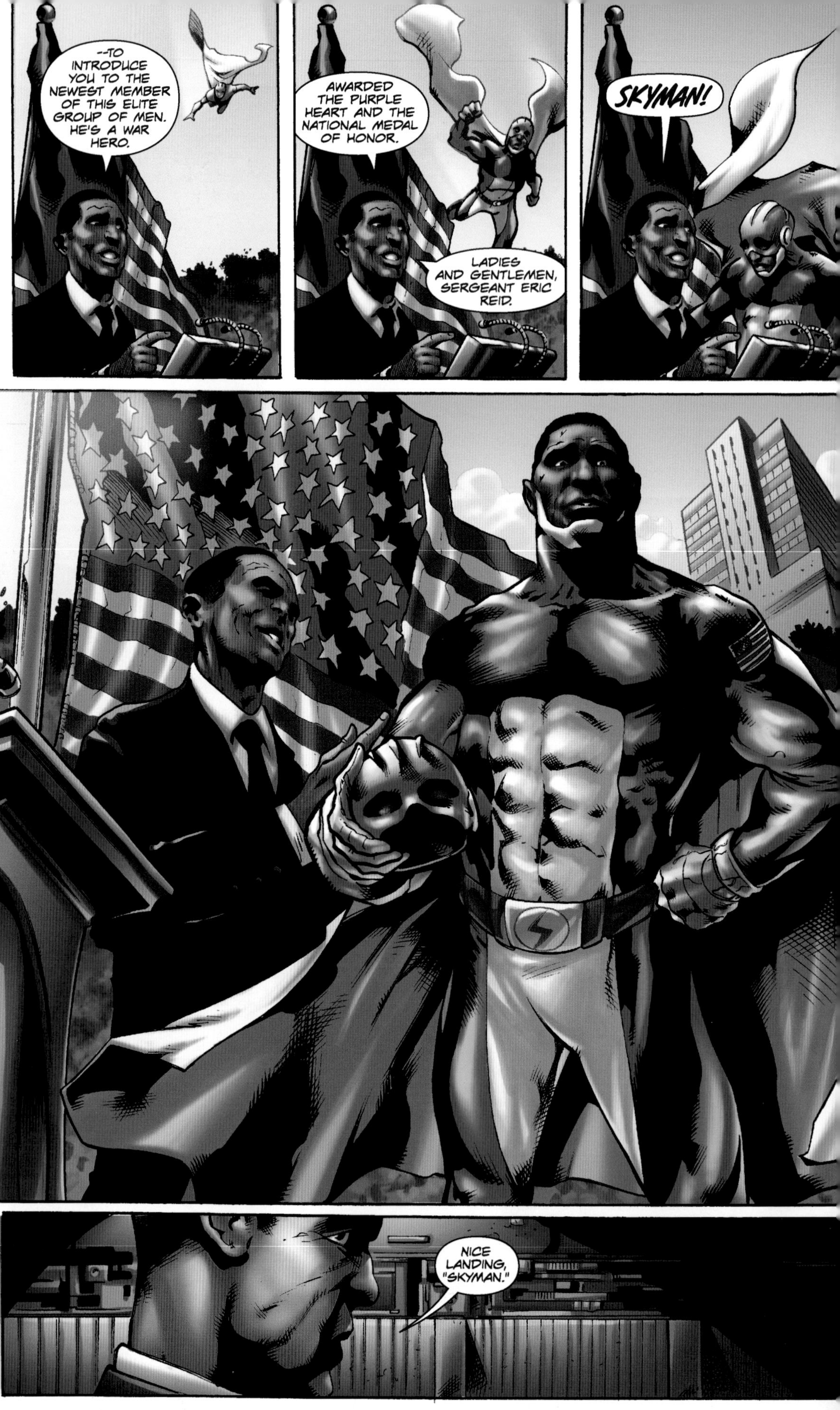
--TO INTRODUCE YOU TO THE NEWEST MEMBER OF THIS ELITE GROUP OF MEN. HE'S A WAR HERO.
AWARDED THE PURPLE HEART AND THE NATIONAL MEDAL OF HONOR.
LADIES AND GENTLEMEN, SERGEANT ERIC REID.
SKYMAN!
NICE LANDING, "SKYMAN."

# CHAPTER 2

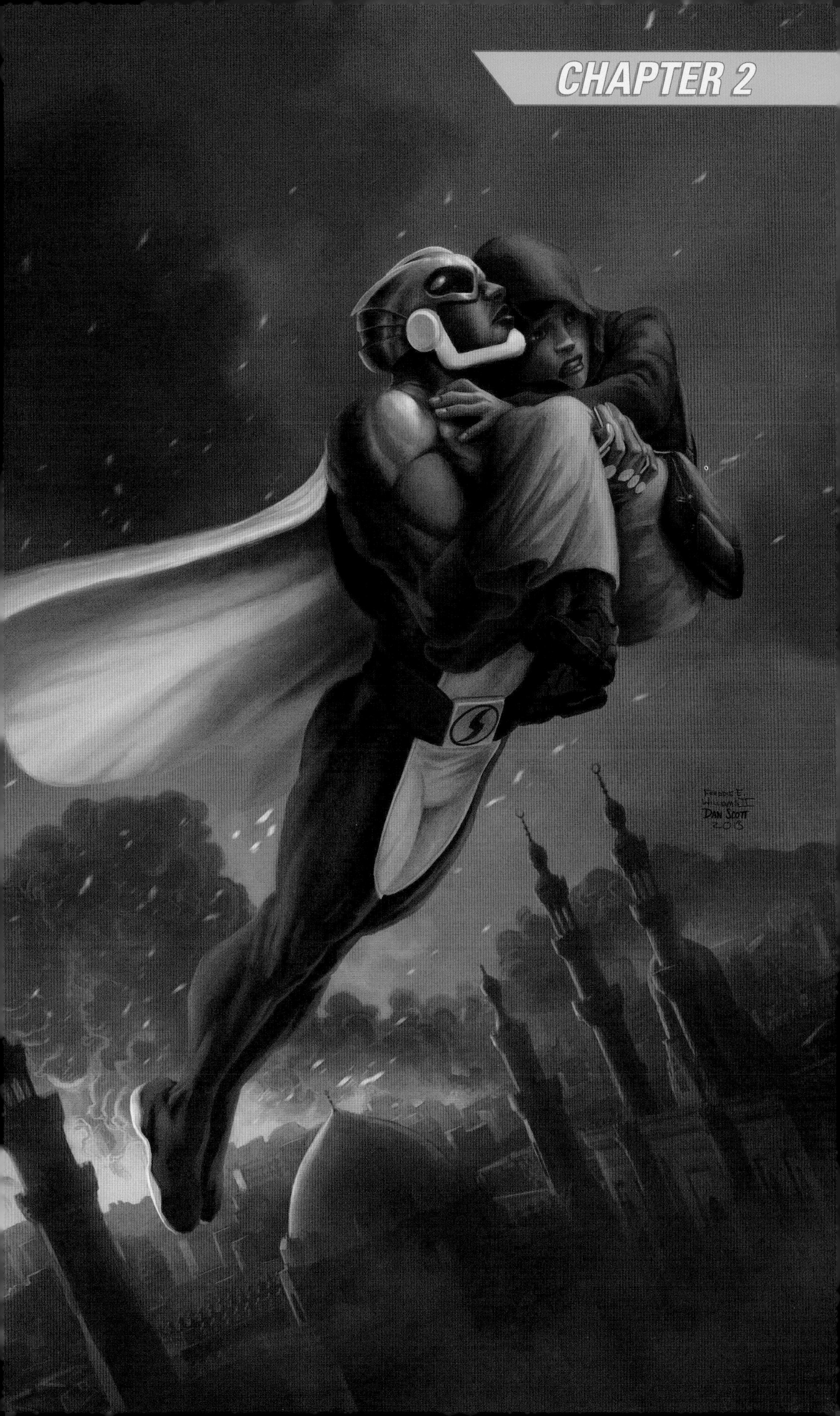
DAN SCOTT

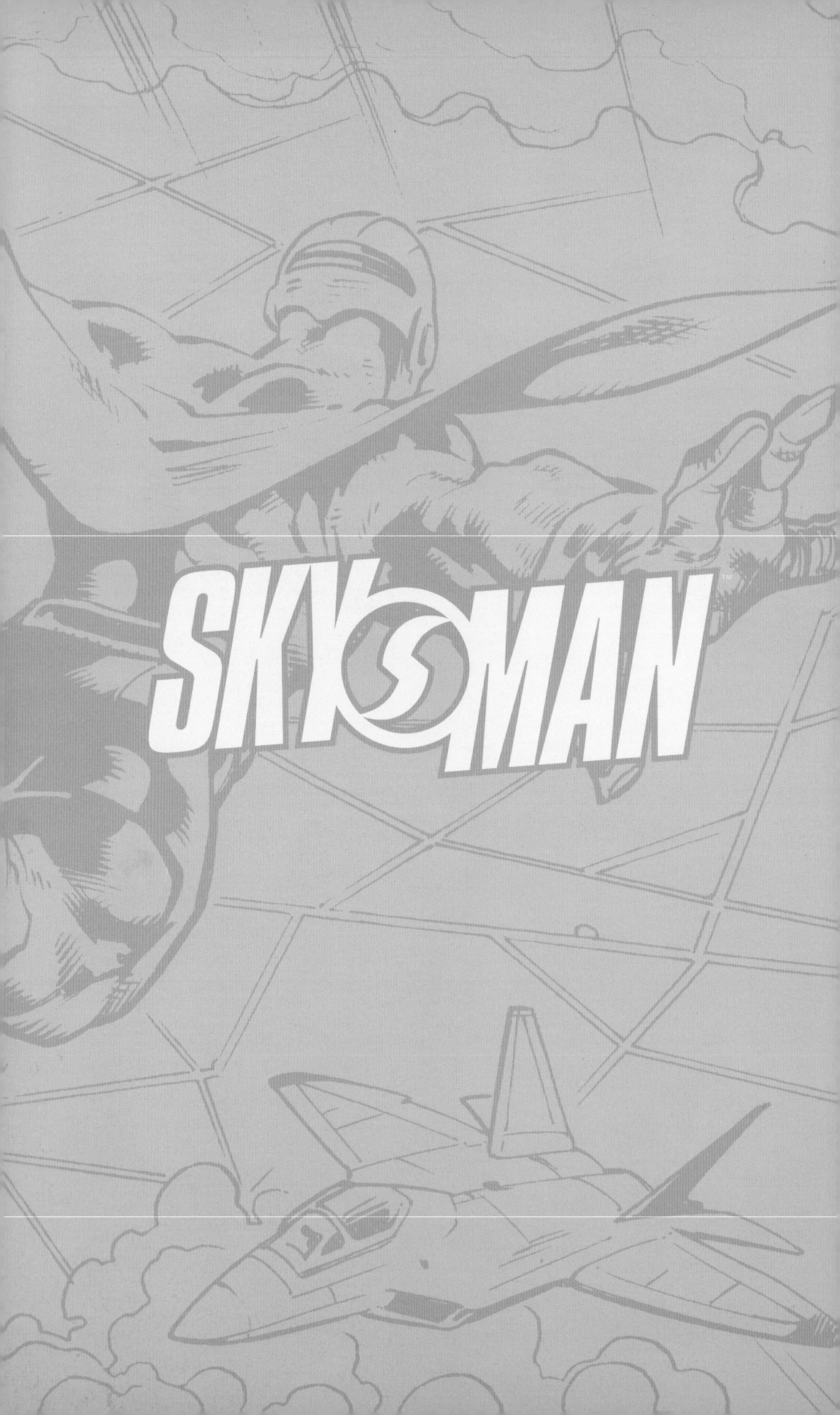
SKYMAN™

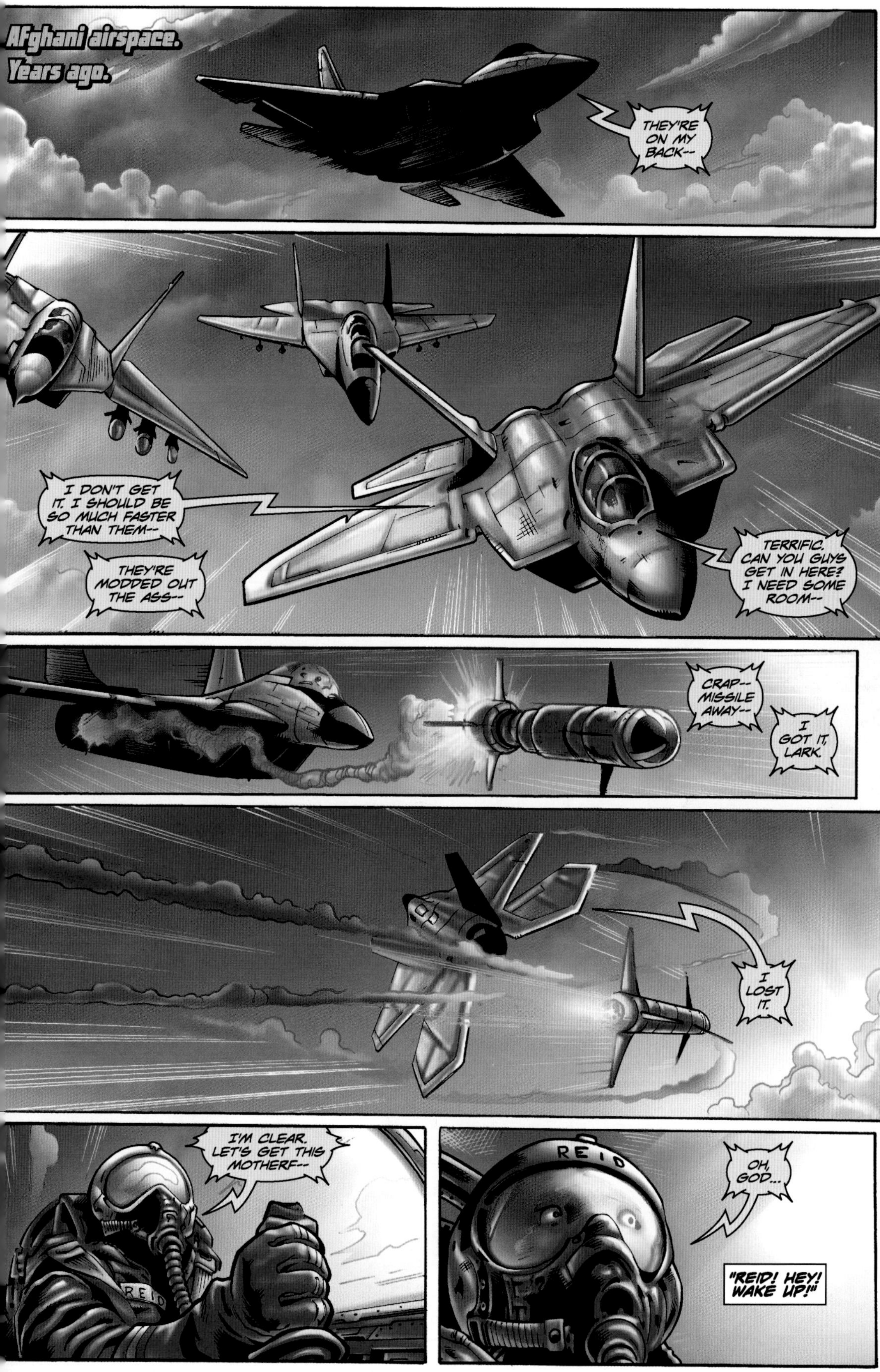

Afghani airspace. Years ago.
THEY'RE ON MY BACK--
I DON'T GET IT. I SHOULD BE SO MUCH FASTER THAN THEM--
THEY'RE MODDED OUT THE ASS--
TERRIFIC. CAN YOU GUYS GET IN HERE? I NEED SOME ROOM--
CRAP-- MISSILE AWAY--
I GOT IT, LARK.
I LOST IT.
I'M CLEAR. LET'S GET THIS MOTHERF--
REID
REID
OH, GOD...
"REID! HEY! WAKE UP!"

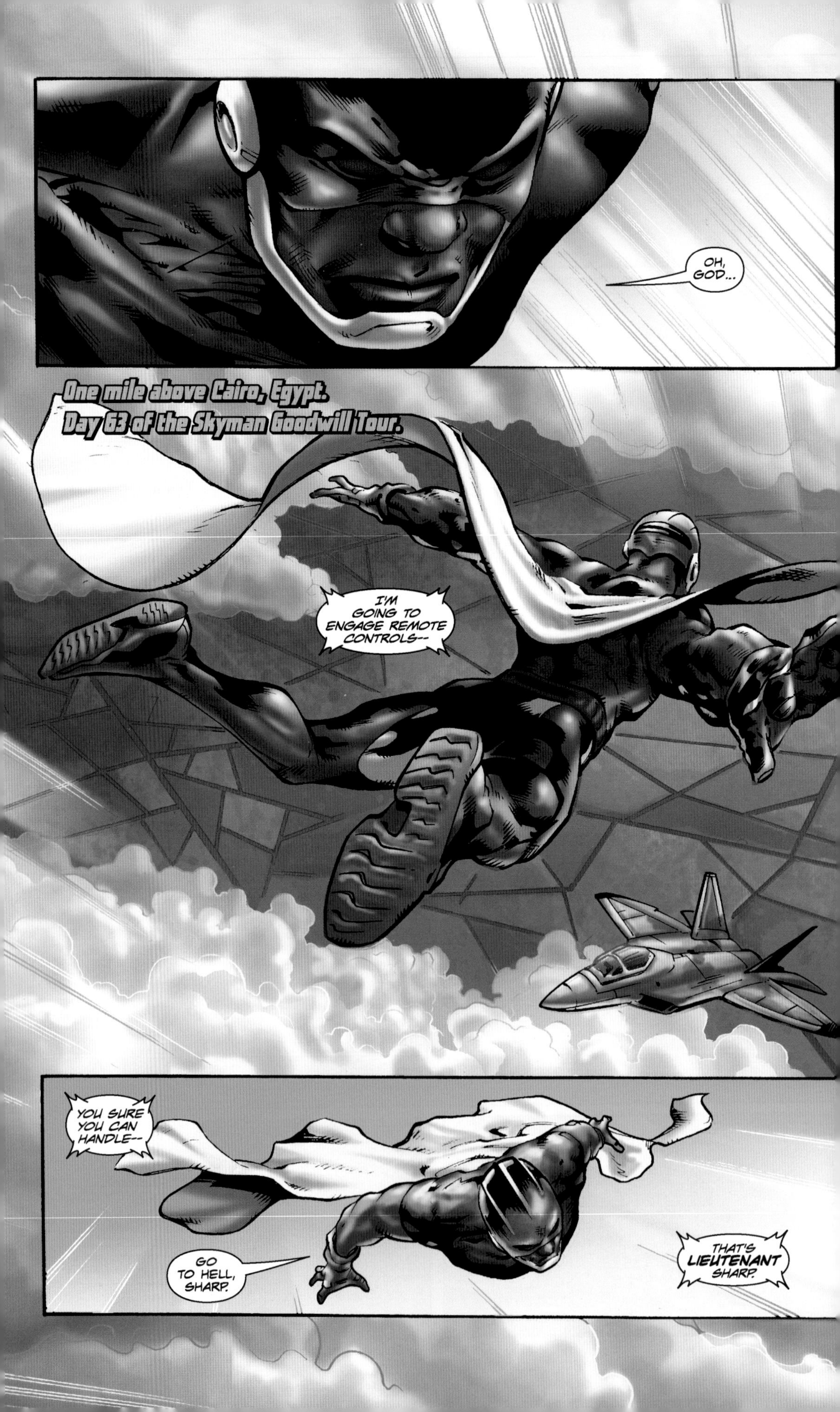
OH, GOD...
One mile above Cairo, Egypt.
Day 63 of the Skyman Goodwill Tour.
I'M GOING TO ENGAGE REMOTE CONTROLS--
YOU SURE YOU CAN HANDLE--
GO TO HELL, SHARP.
THAT'S LIEUTENANT SHARP.

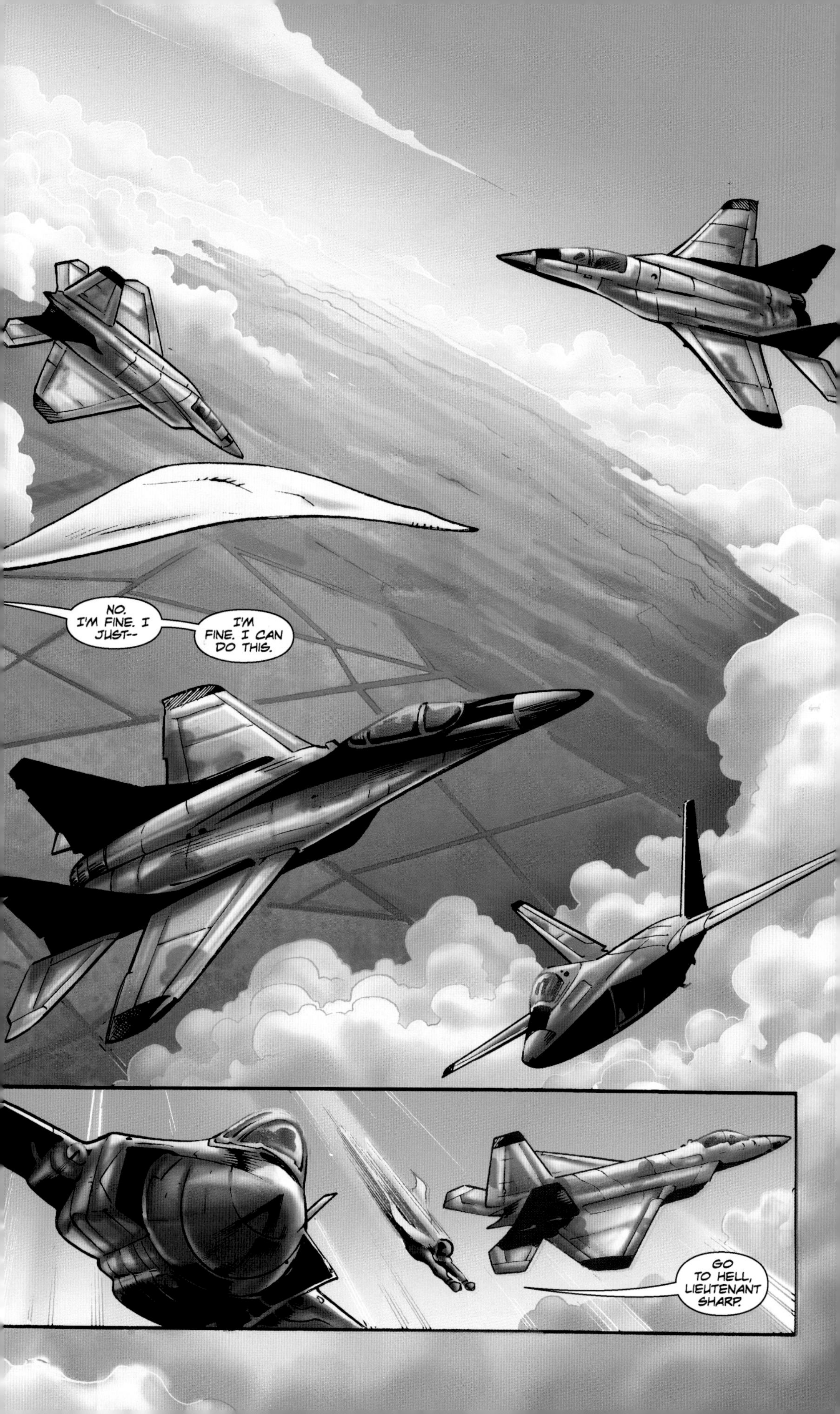
NO. I'M FINE. I JUST--
I'M FINE. I CAN DO THIS.
GO TO HELL, LIEUTENANT SHARP.

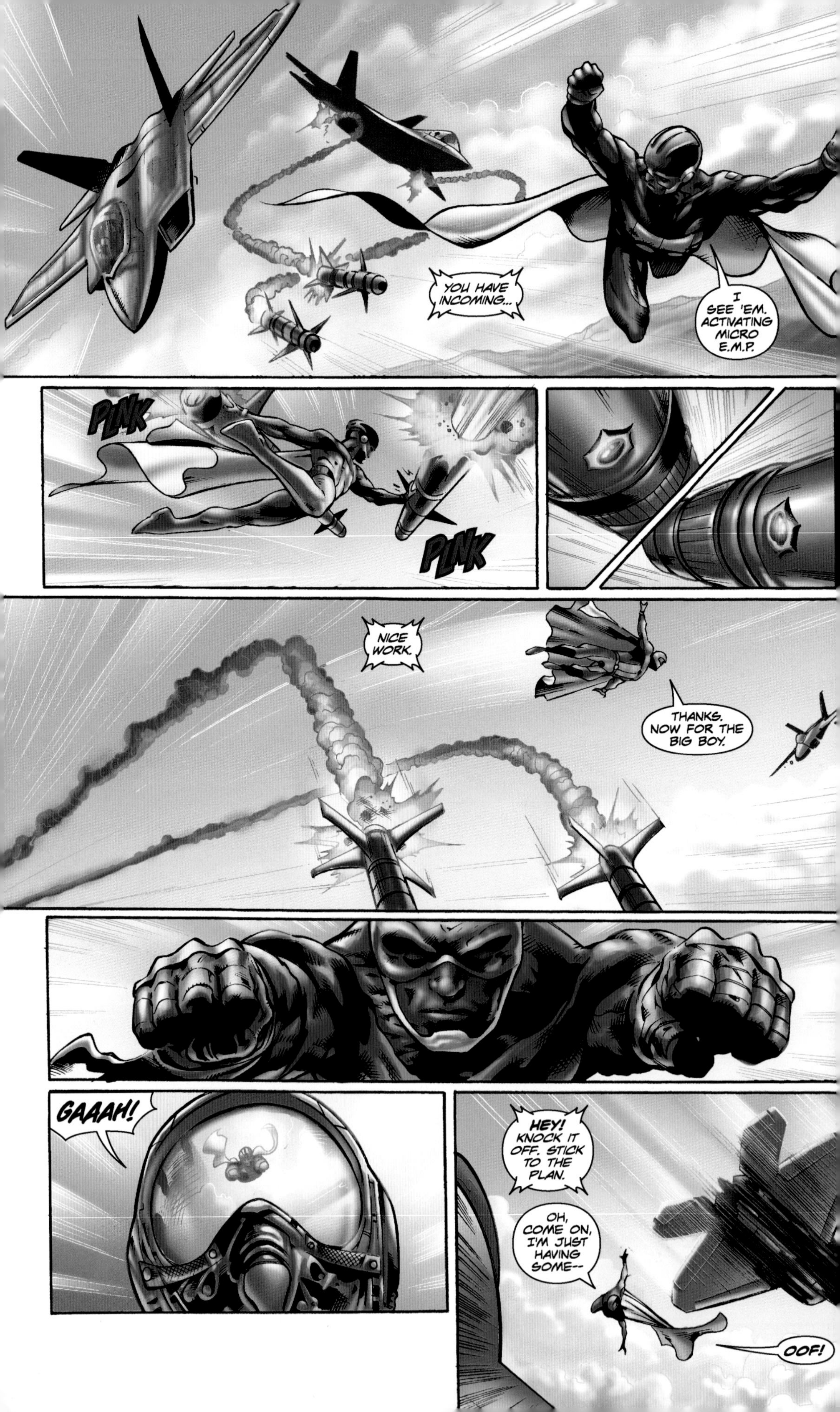
YOU HAVE INCOMING...
I SEE 'EM. ACTIVATING MICRO E.M.P.
PLNK
PLNK
NICE WORK.
THANKS. NOW FOR THE BIG BOY.
GAAAH!
HEY! KNOCK IT OFF. STICK TO THE PLAN.
OH, COME ON, I'M JUST HAVING SOME--
OOF!

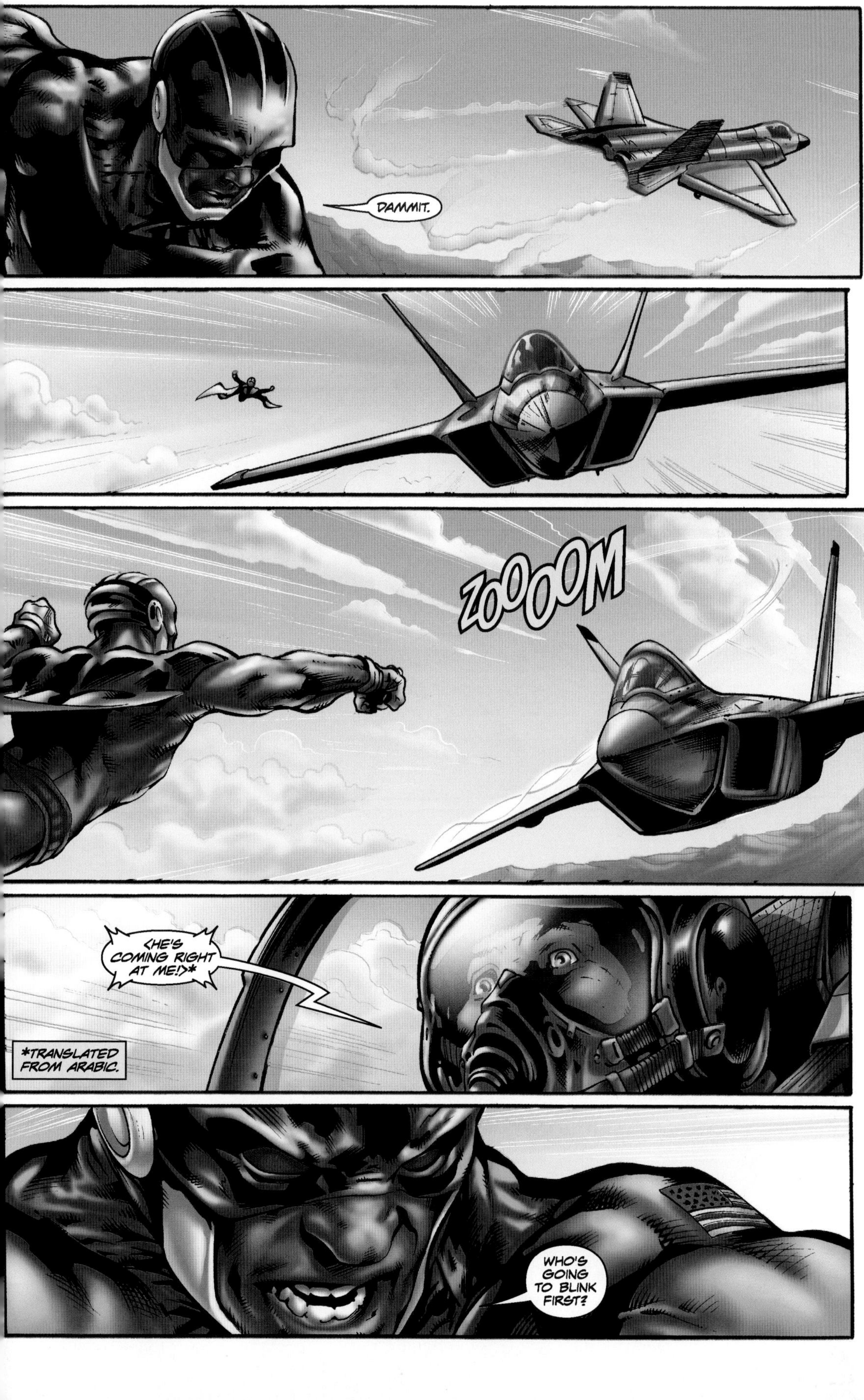
DAMMIT.
ZOOOOM
<HE'S COMING RIGHT AT ME!>*
*TRANSLATED FROM ARABIC.
WHO'S GOING TO BLINK FIRST?

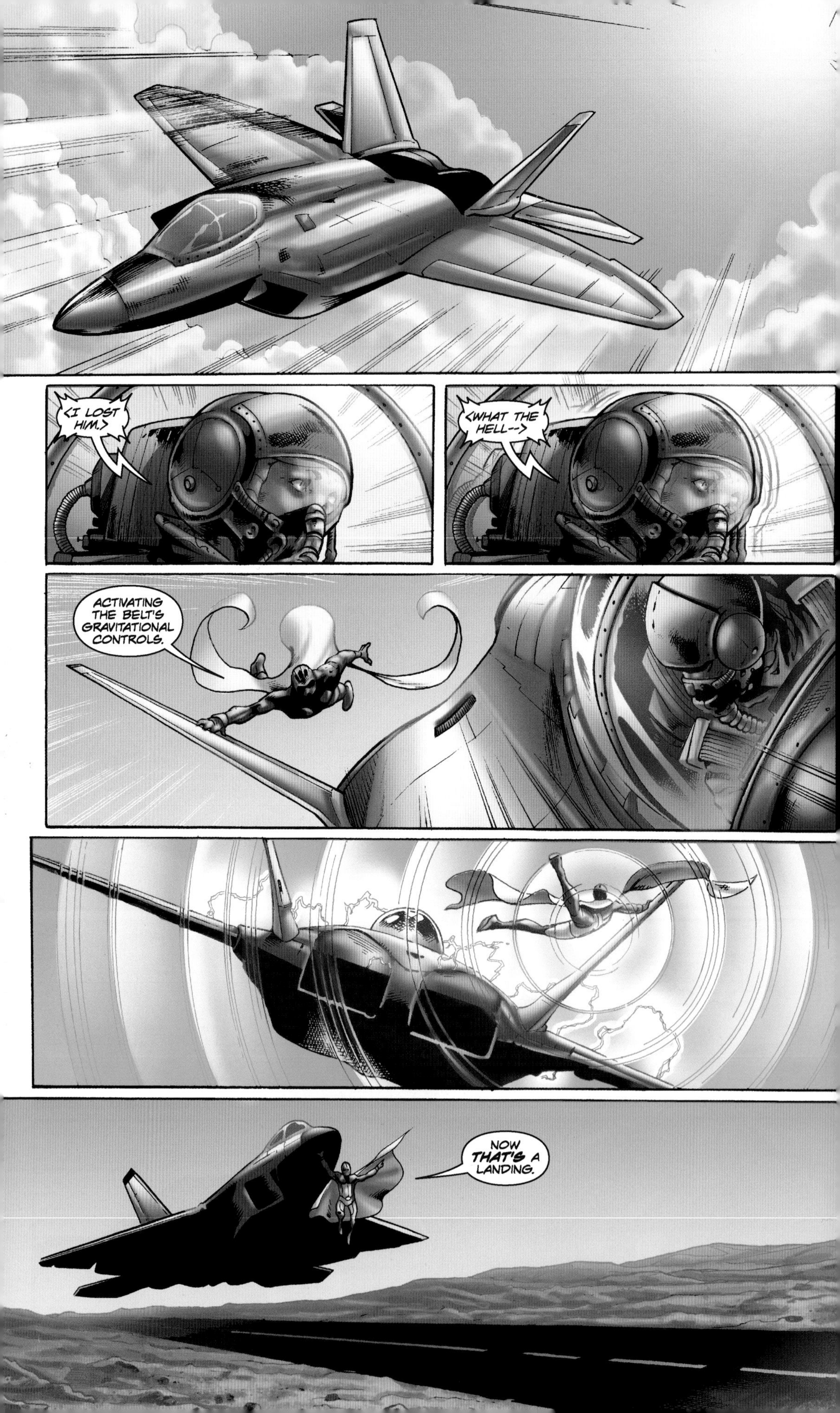
<I LOST HIM.>
<WHAT THE HELL-->
ACTIVATING THE BELT'S GRAVITATIONAL CONTROLS.
NOW **THAT'S** A LANDING.

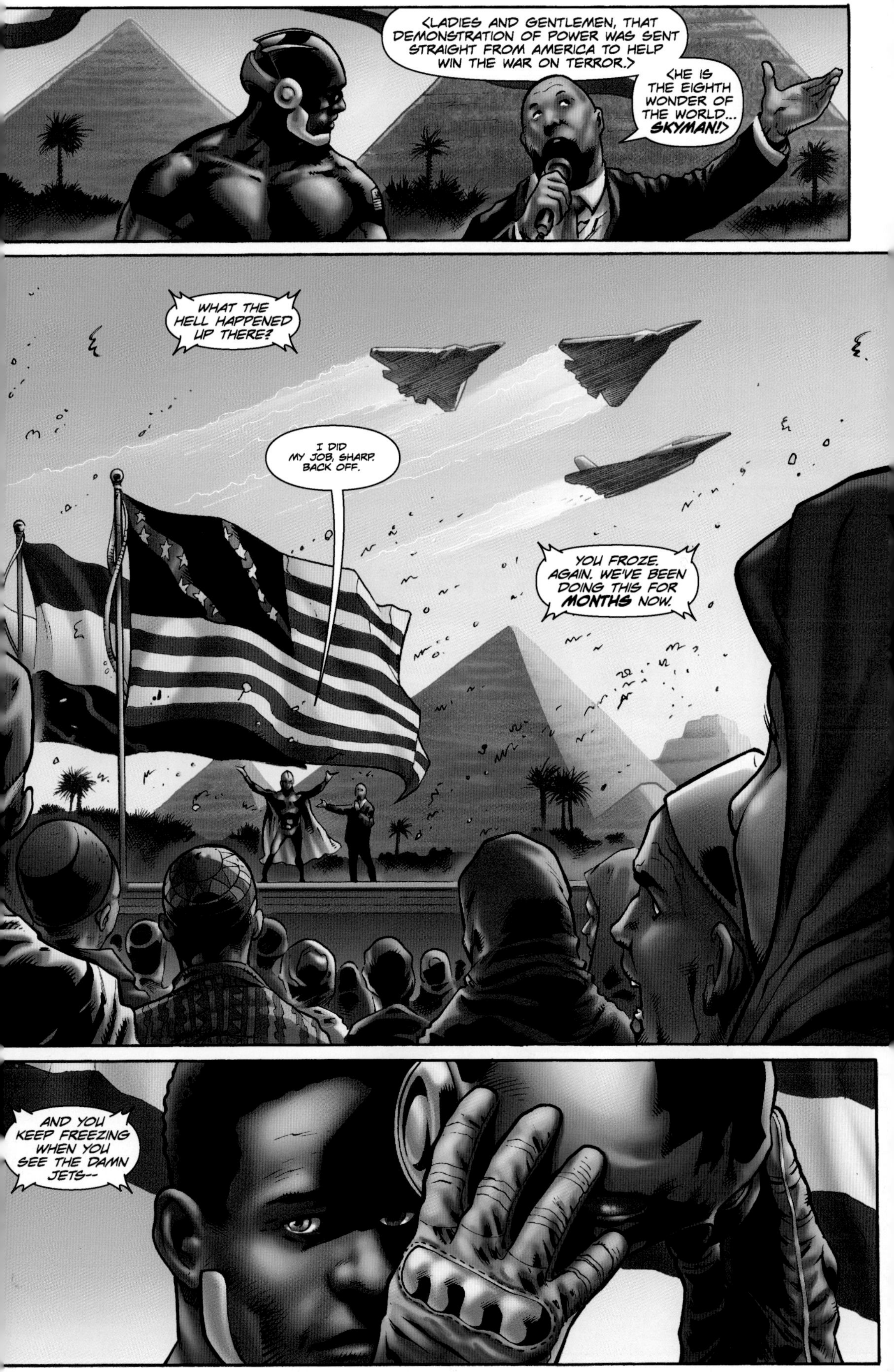
<LADIES AND GENTLEMEN, THAT DEMONSTRATION OF POWER WAS SENT STRAIGHT FROM AMERICA TO HELP WIN THE WAR ON TERROR.>
<HE IS THE EIGHTH WONDER OF THE WORLD... SKYMAN!>
WHAT THE HELL HAPPENED UP THERE?
I DID MY JOB, SHARP. BACK OFF.
YOU FROZE. AGAIN. WE'VE BEEN DOING THIS FOR MONTHS NOW.
AND YOU KEEP FREEZING WHEN YOU SEE THE DAMN JETS--

WHAT DO YOU WANT FROM ME? I'M YOUR GODDAMN PERFORMING DOG, DAY AFTER DAY.

WHY GIVE ME THE SUIT AND THEN HAVE ME JUST SCREW AROUND AT AIR SHOWS, ANYWAY?

THE U.N. WANTS THE PRESIDENT TO TURN OVER THE SKYMAN TECH, AS DOES THE REST OF THE SECURITY COUNCIL.

YOU THINK WE'RE JUST GOING TO HAND IT OVER TO CHINA AND RUSSIA? HELL, NO.

SO WE GOTTA MAKE NICE, SHOW W CAN PLAY ALON AND AREN'T THREAT...

YOU'RE KEEPING WORLD WAR III AT BAY, REID. ONE AIR SHOW AT A TIME.

I THOUGHT I WAS SUPPOSED TO BE A HERO.

YEAH, WELL, I KNOW HOW THAT FEELS.

BE BACK IN AN HOUR. WE'RE MOVING OUT.

I'M GONNA GO CALL MY WIFE.

SUIT UP. WE HAVE THE TARGET.

YES, SIR, GENERAL ABERNATHY.

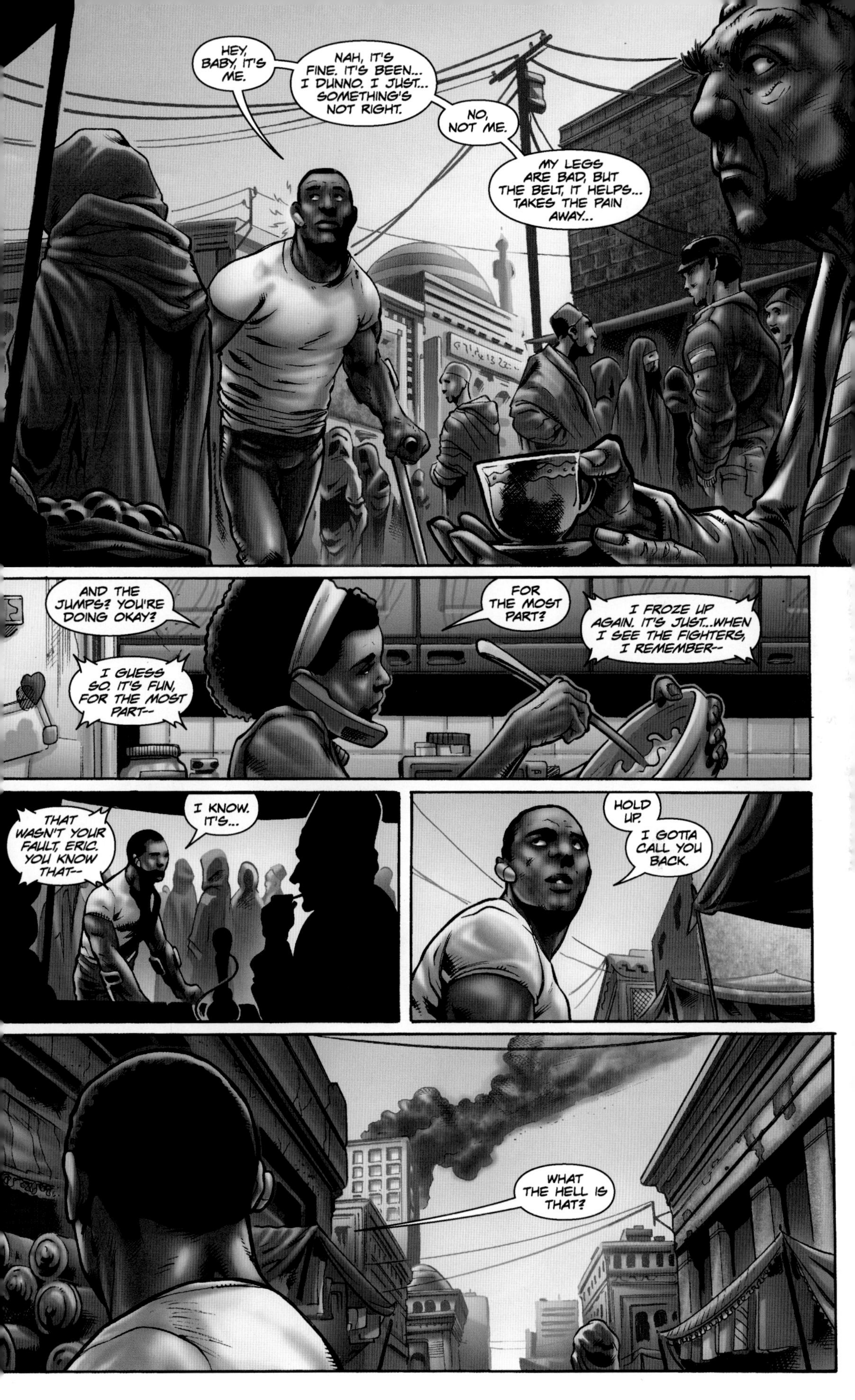
HEY, BABY, IT'S ME.
NAH, IT'S FINE. IT'S BEEN... I DUNNO. I JUST... SOMETHING'S NOT RIGHT.
NO, NOT ME.
MY LEGS ARE BAD, BUT THE BELT, IT HELPS... TAKES THE PAIN AWAY...
AND THE JUMPS? YOU'RE DOING OKAY?
I GUESS SO. IT'S FUN, FOR THE MOST PART--
FOR THE MOST PART?
I FROZE UP AGAIN. IT'S JUST...WHEN I SEE THE FIGHTERS, I REMEMBER--
THAT WASN'T YOUR FAULT, ERIC. YOU KNOW THAT--
I KNOW. IT'S...
HOLD UP.
I GOTTA CALL YOU BACK.
WHAT THE HELL IS THAT?

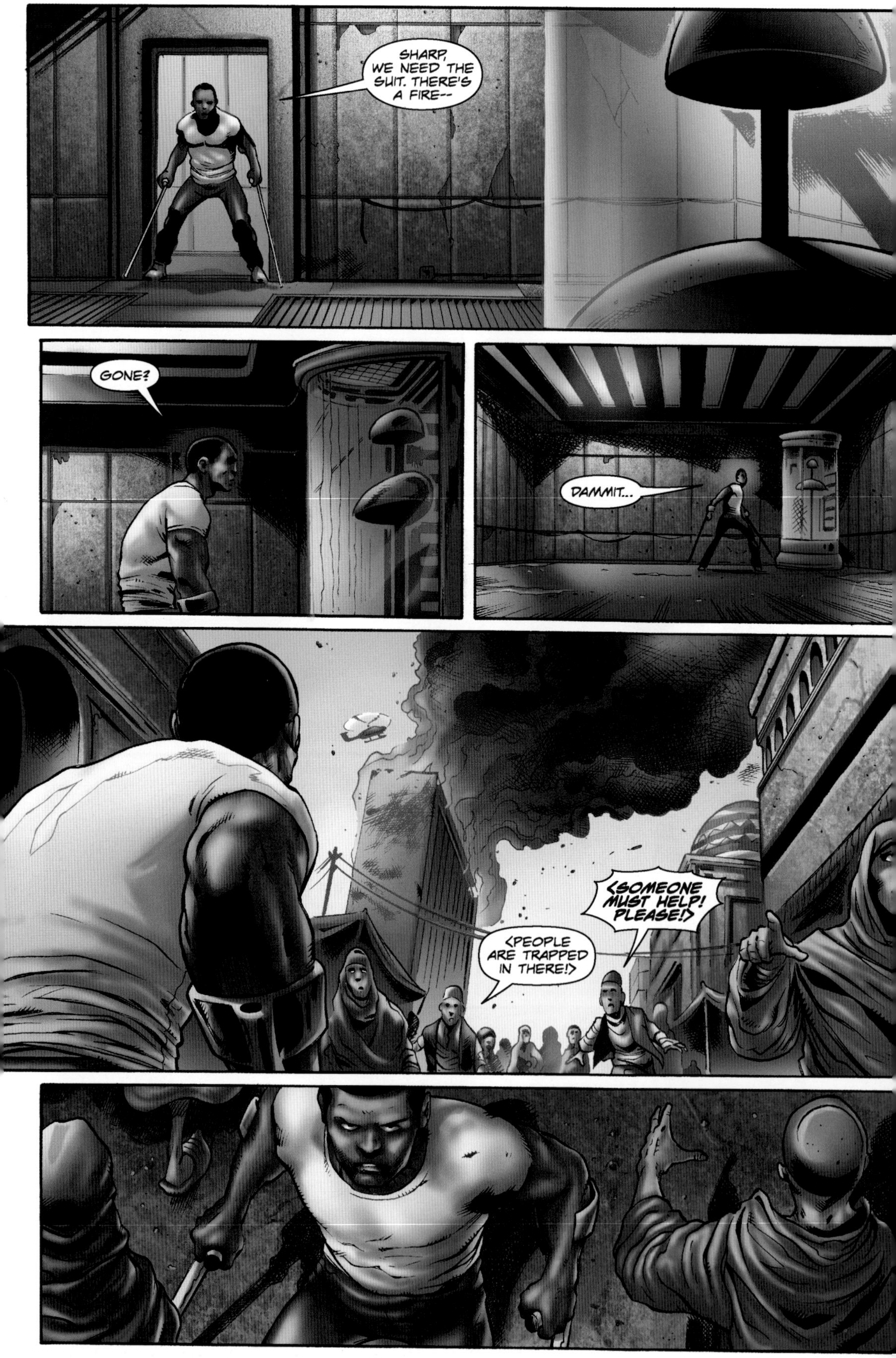
SHARP, WE NEED THE SUIT. THERE'S A FIRE--
GONE?
DAMMIT...
<SOMEONE MUST HELP! PLEASE!>
<PEOPLE ARE TRAPPED IN THERE!>

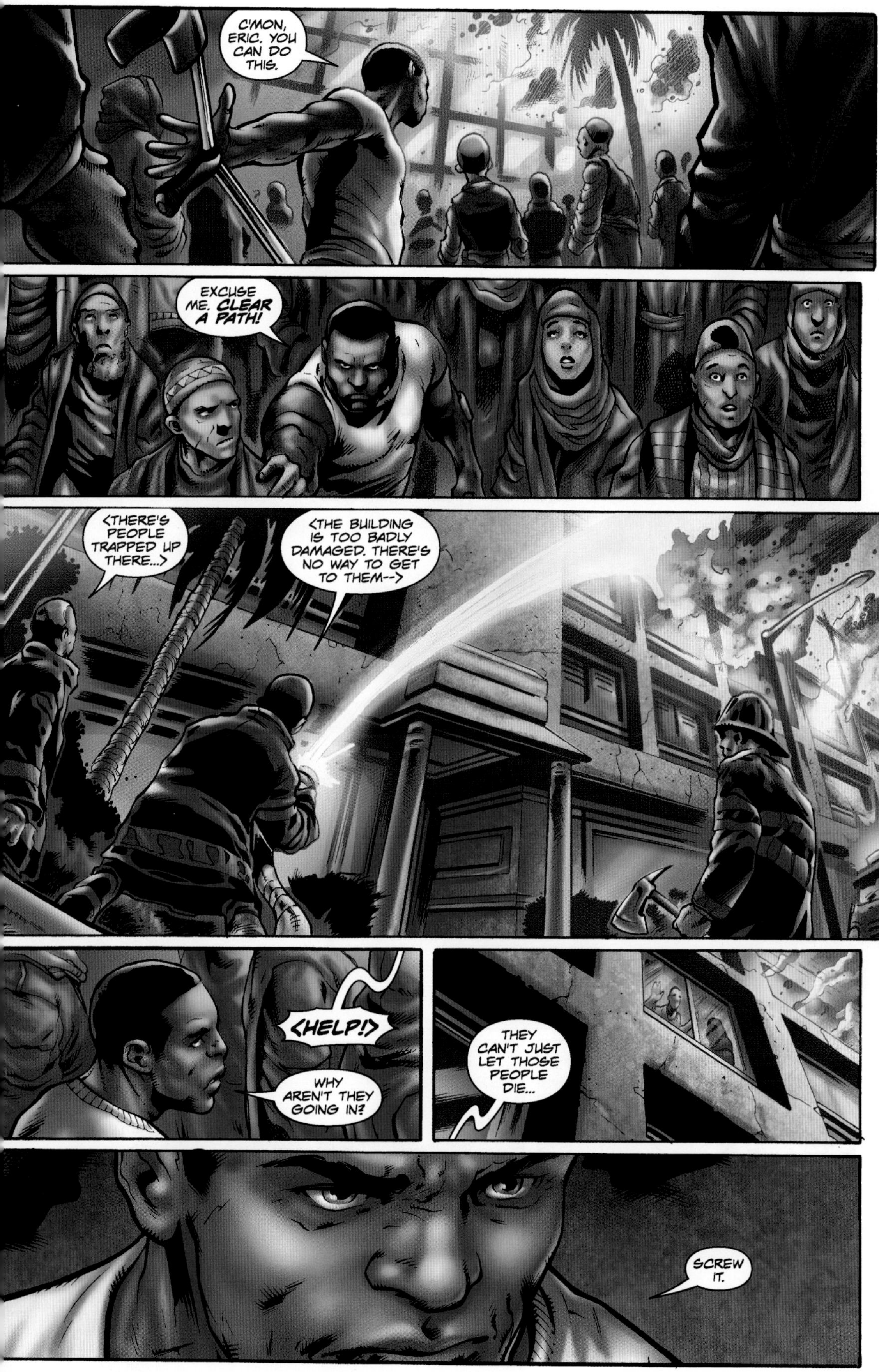
C'MON, ERIC. YOU CAN DO THIS.
EXCUSE ME. CLEAR A PATH!
<THERE'S PEOPLE TRAPPED UP THERE...>
<THE BUILDING IS TOO BADLY DAMAGED. THERE'S NO WAY TO GET TO THEM-->
<HELP!>
WHY AREN'T THEY GOING IN?
THEY CAN'T JUST LET THOSE PEOPLE DIE...
SCREW IT.

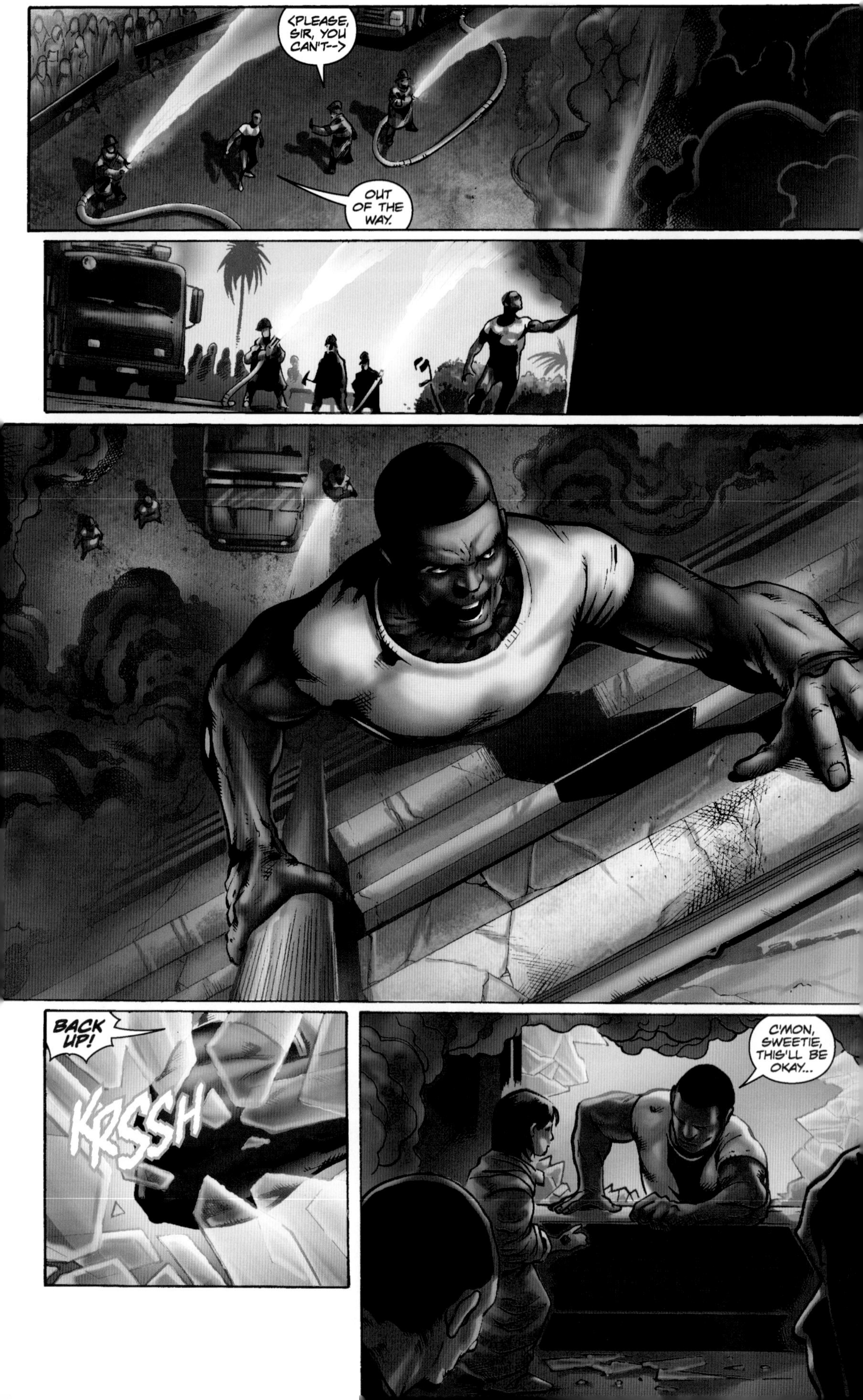
<PLEASE, SIR, YOU CAN'T-->
OUT OF THE WAY.
BACK UP!
KRSSH
C'MON, SWEETIE, THIS'LL BE OKAY...

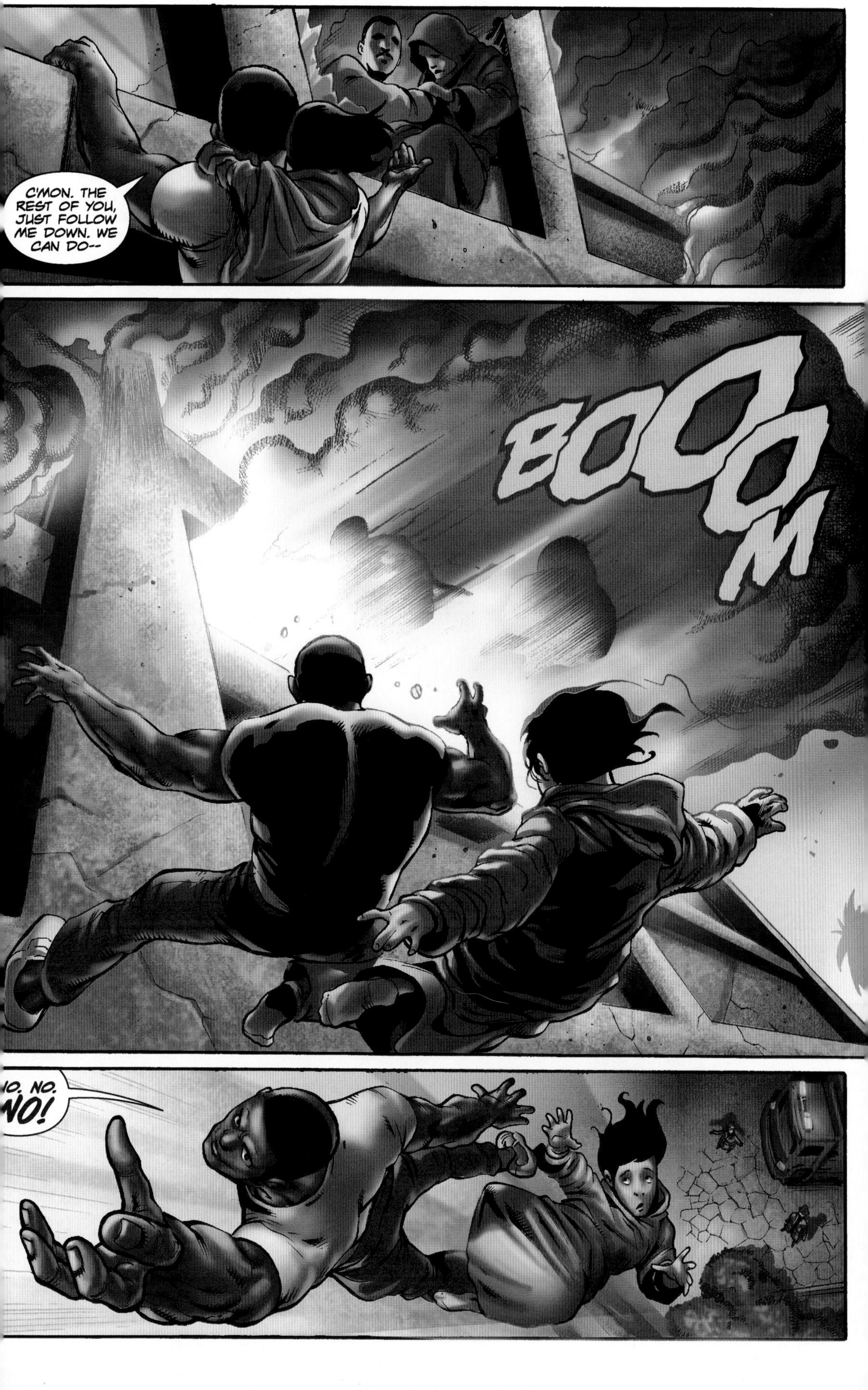
C'MON. THE REST OF YOU, JUST FOLLOW ME DOWN. WE CAN DO--
BOOOM
NO!

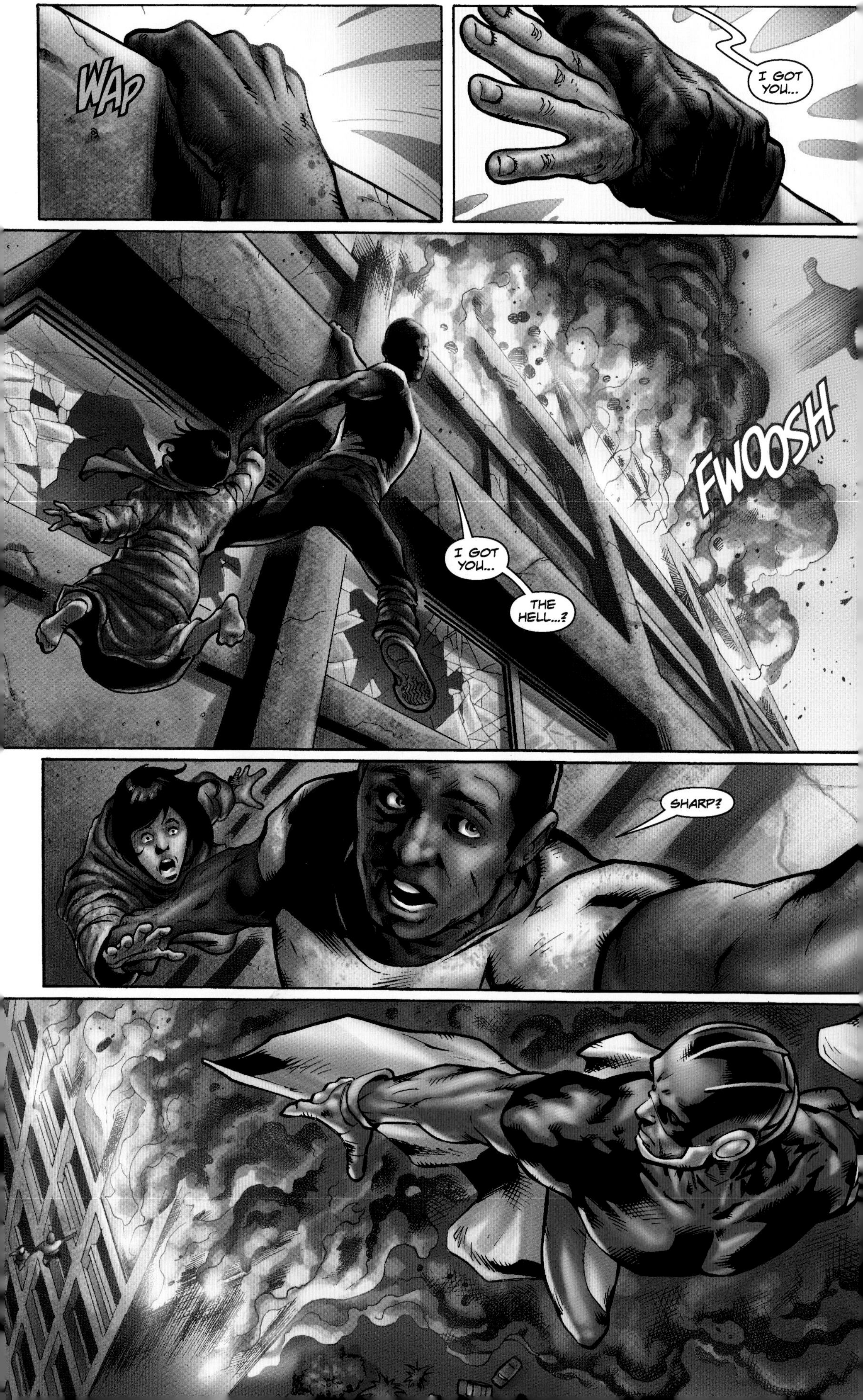
WAP
I GOT YOU...
FWOOSH
I GOT YOU...
THE HELL...?
SHARP?

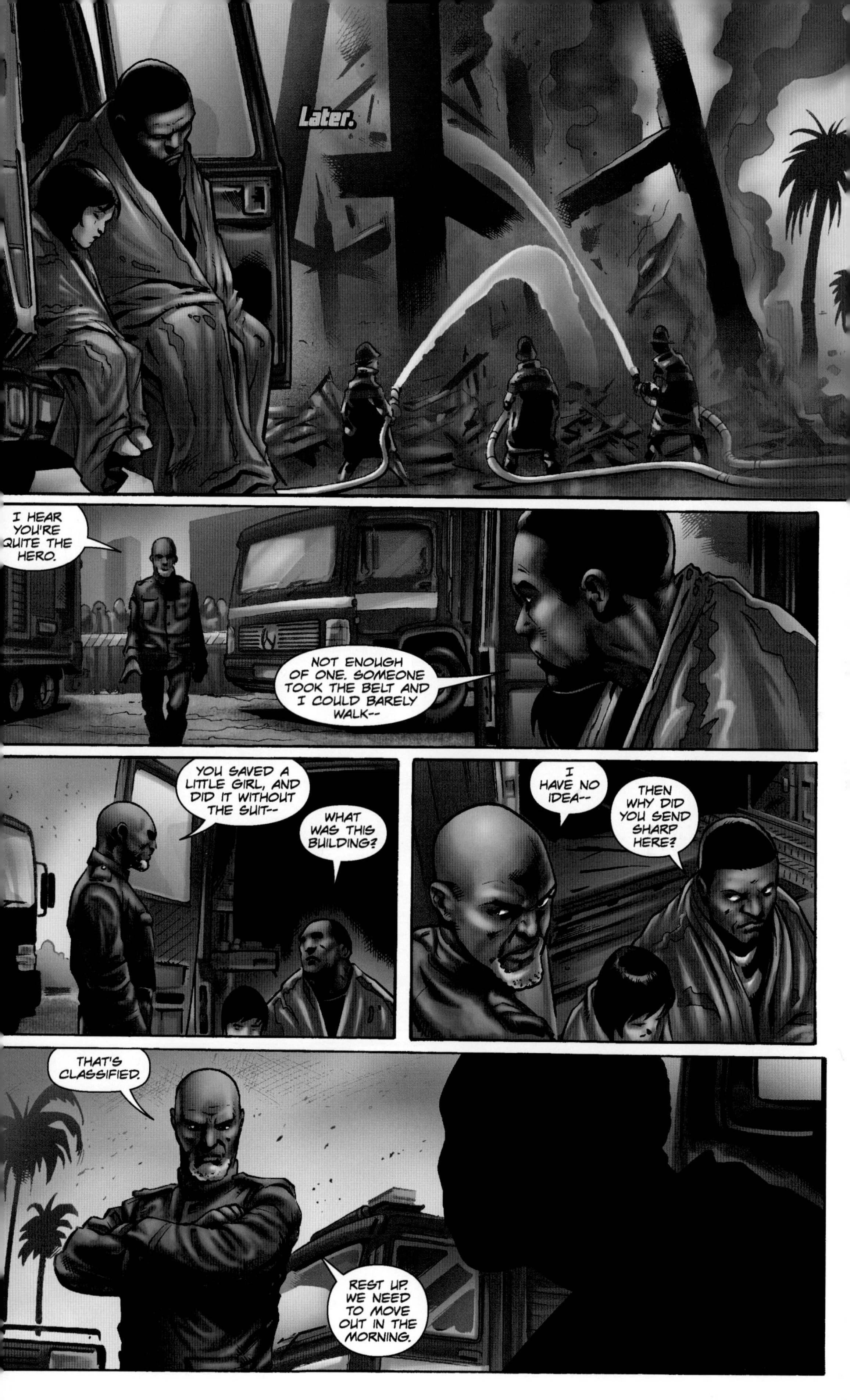
Later.
I HEAR YOU'RE QUITE THE HERO.
NOT ENOUGH OF ONE. SOMEONE TOOK THE BELT AND I COULD BARELY WALK--
YOU SAVED A LITTLE GIRL, AND DID IT WITHOUT THE SUIT--
WHAT WAS THIS BUILDING?
I HAVE NO IDEA--
THEN WHY DID YOU SEND SHARP HERE?
THAT'S CLASSIFIED.
REST UP. WE NEED TO MOVE OUT IN THE MORNING.

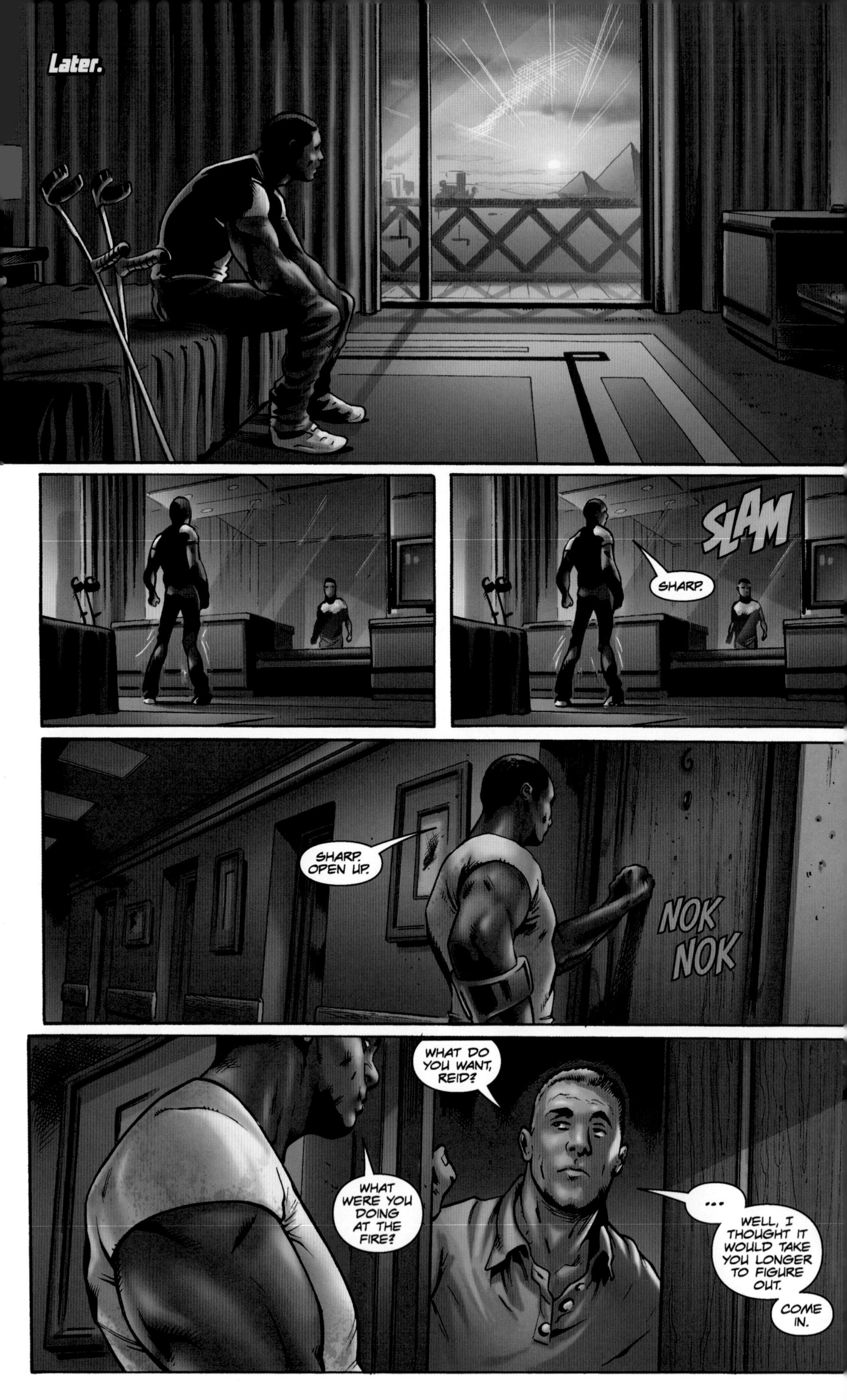
Later.
SLAM
SHARP.
SHARP. OPEN UP.
NOK NOK
WHAT DO YOU WANT, REID?
WHAT WERE YOU DOING AT THE FIRE?
...
WELL, I THOUGHT IT WOULD TAKE YOU LONGER TO FIGURE OUT.
COME IN.

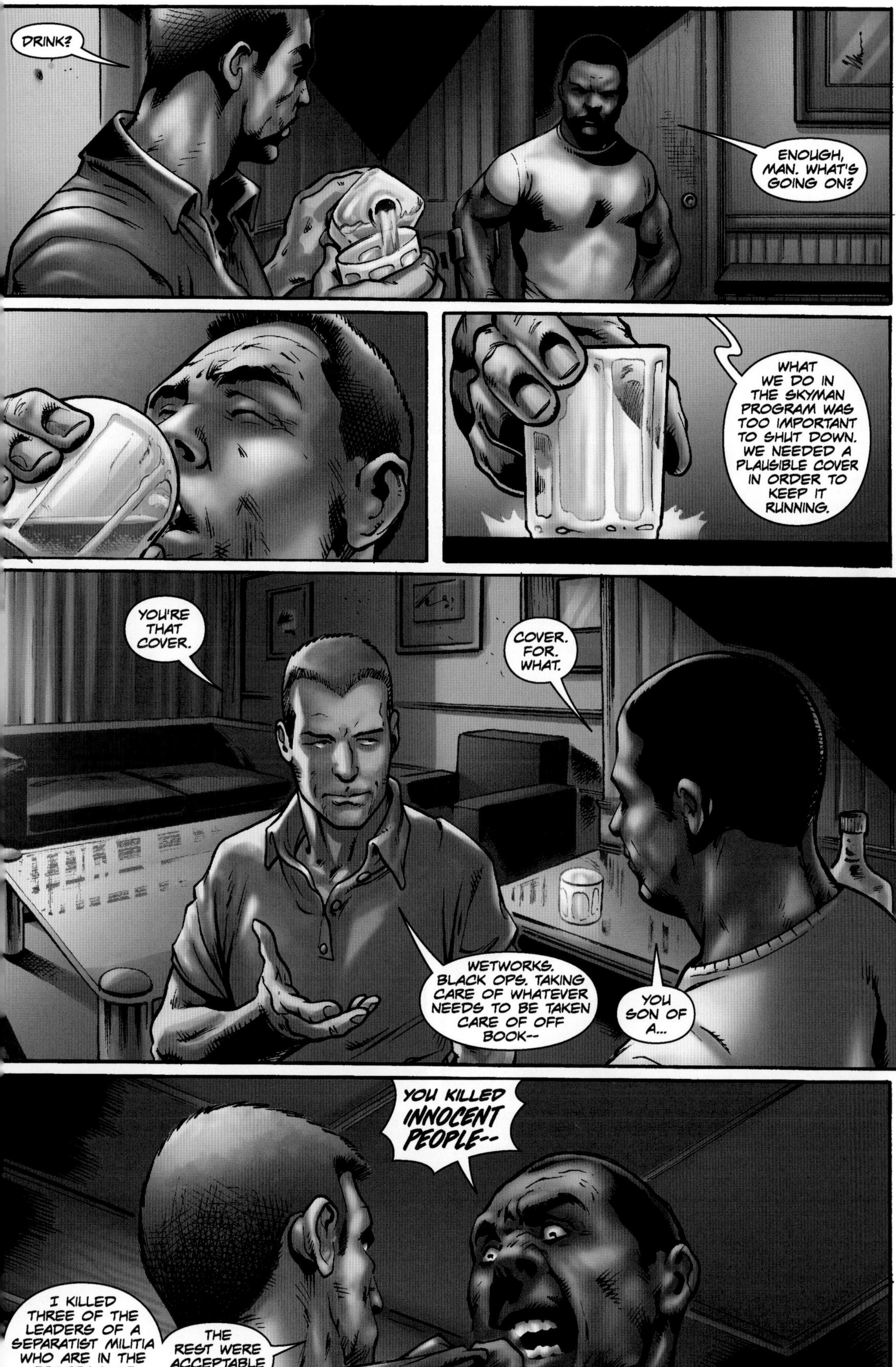

DRINK?
ENOUGH, MAN. WHAT'S GOING ON?
WHAT WE DO IN THE SKYMAN PROGRAM WAS TOO IMPORTANT TO SHUT DOWN. WE NEEDED A PLAUSIBLE COVER IN ORDER TO KEEP IT RUNNING.
YOU'RE THAT COVER.
COVER. FOR. WHAT.
WETWORKS. BLACK OPS. TAKING CARE OF WHATEVER NEEDS TO BE TAKEN CARE OF OFF BOOK--
YOU SON OF A...
YOU KILLED INNOCENT PEOPLE--
I KILLED THREE OF THE LEADERS OF A SEPARATIST MILITIA WHO ARE IN THE PROCESS OF UNDERMINING THIS GOVERNMENT.
THE REST WERE ACCEPTABLE LOSSES--

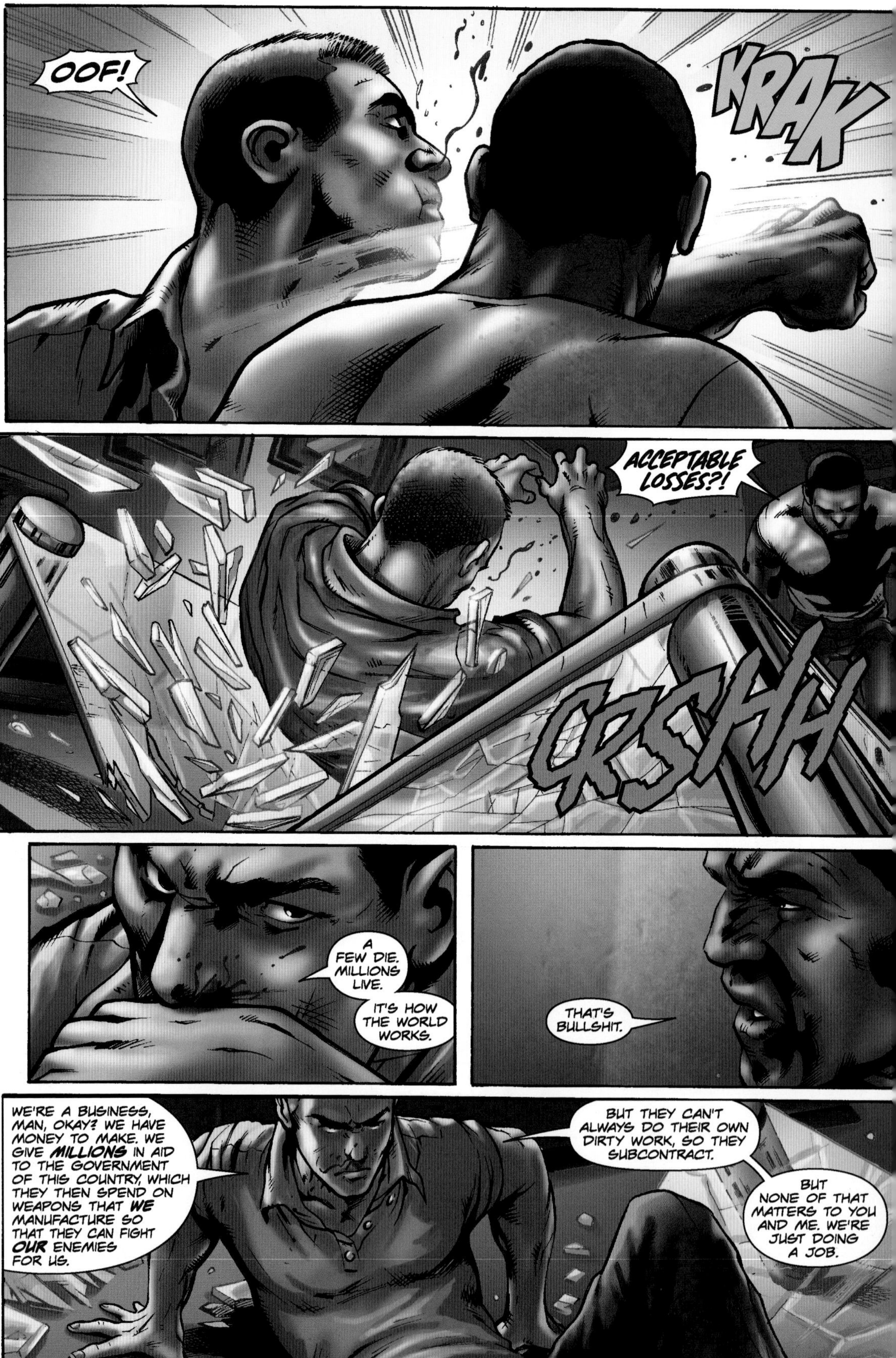
OOF!
KRAK
ACCEPTABLE LOSSES?!
QRSHH
A FEW DIE. MILLIONS LIVE.
IT'S HOW THE WORLD WORKS.
THAT'S BULLSHIT.
WE'RE A BUSINESS, MAN, OKAY? WE HAVE MONEY TO MAKE. WE GIVE MILLIONS IN AID TO THE GOVERNMENT OF THIS COUNTRY, WHICH THEY THEN SPEND ON WEAPONS THAT WE MANUFACTURE SO THAT THEY CAN FIGHT OUR ENEMIES FOR US.
BUT THEY CAN'T ALWAYS DO THEIR OWN DIRTY WORK, SO THEY SUBCONTRACT.
BUT NONE OF THAT MATTERS TO YOU AND ME. WE'RE JUST DOING A JOB.

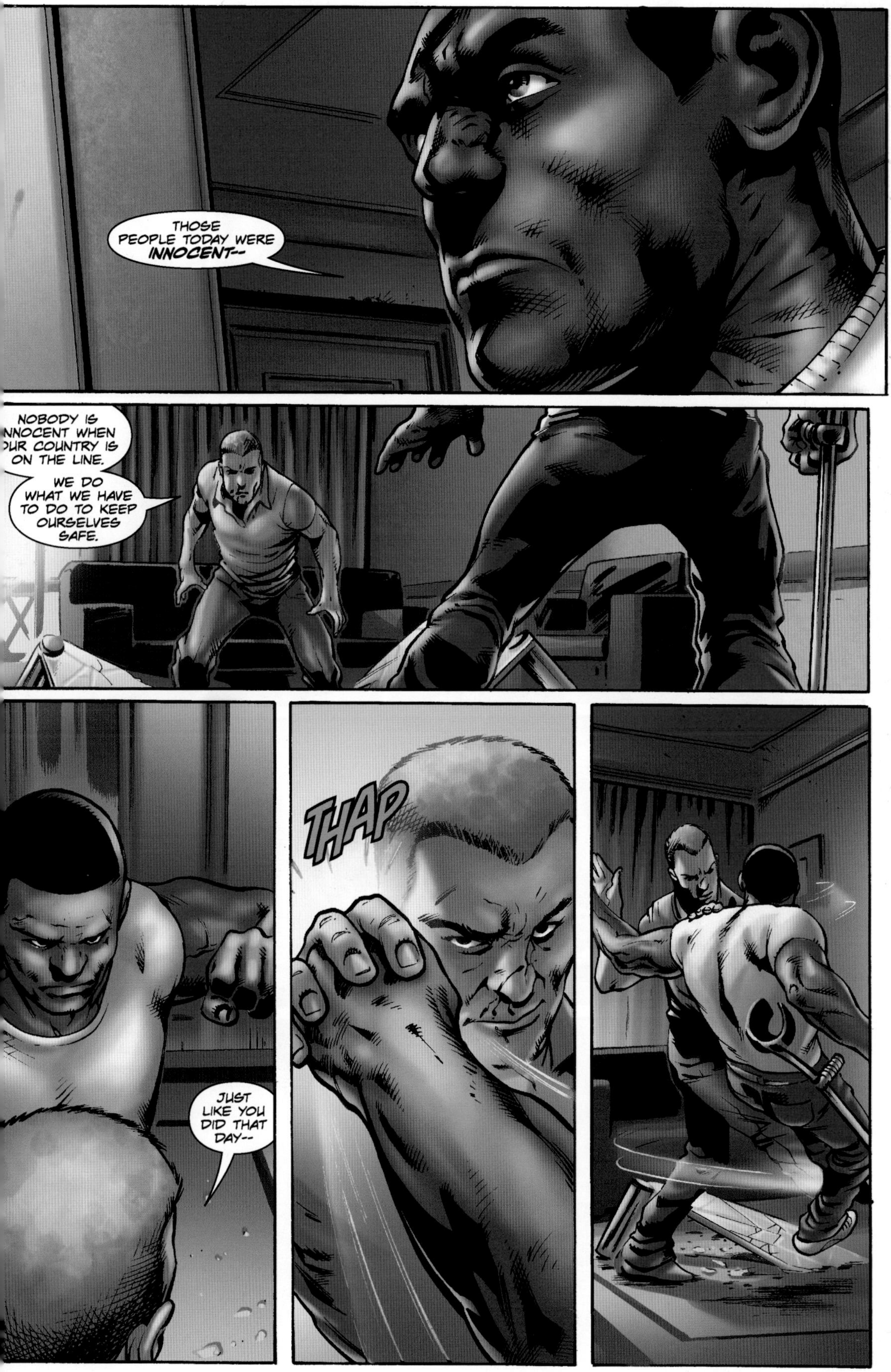
THOSE PEOPLE TODAY WERE INNOCENT--
NOBODY IS INNOCENT WHEN OUR COUNTRY IS ON THE LINE.
WE DO WHAT WE HAVE TO DO TO KEEP OURSELVES SAFE.
JUST LIKE YOU DID THAT DAY--
THAP

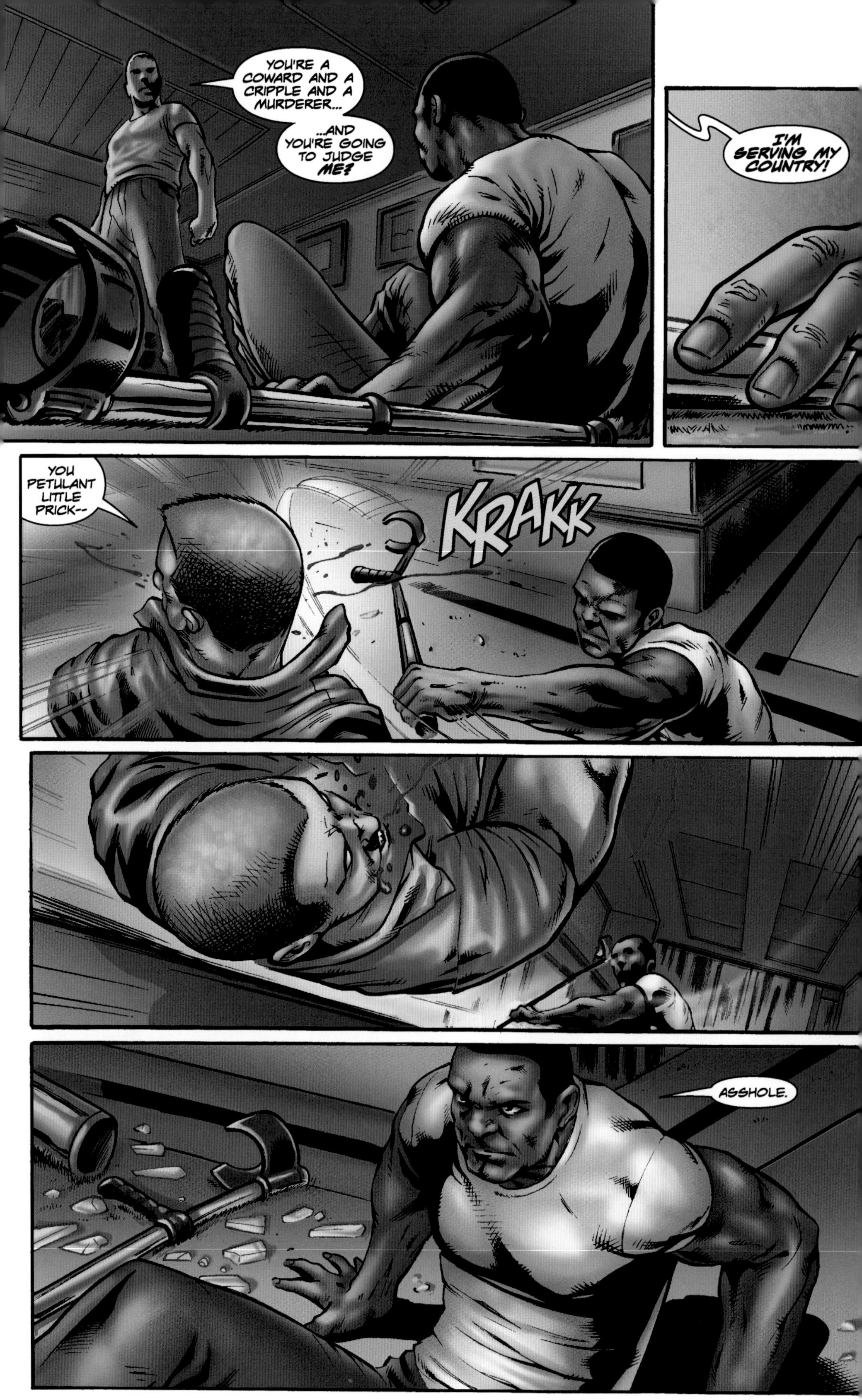
YOU'RE A COWARD AND A CRIPPLE AND A MURDERER...
...AND YOU'RE GOING TO JUDGE ME?
I'M SERVING MY COUNTRY!
YOU PETULANT LITTLE PRICK--
KRAKK
ASSHOLE.

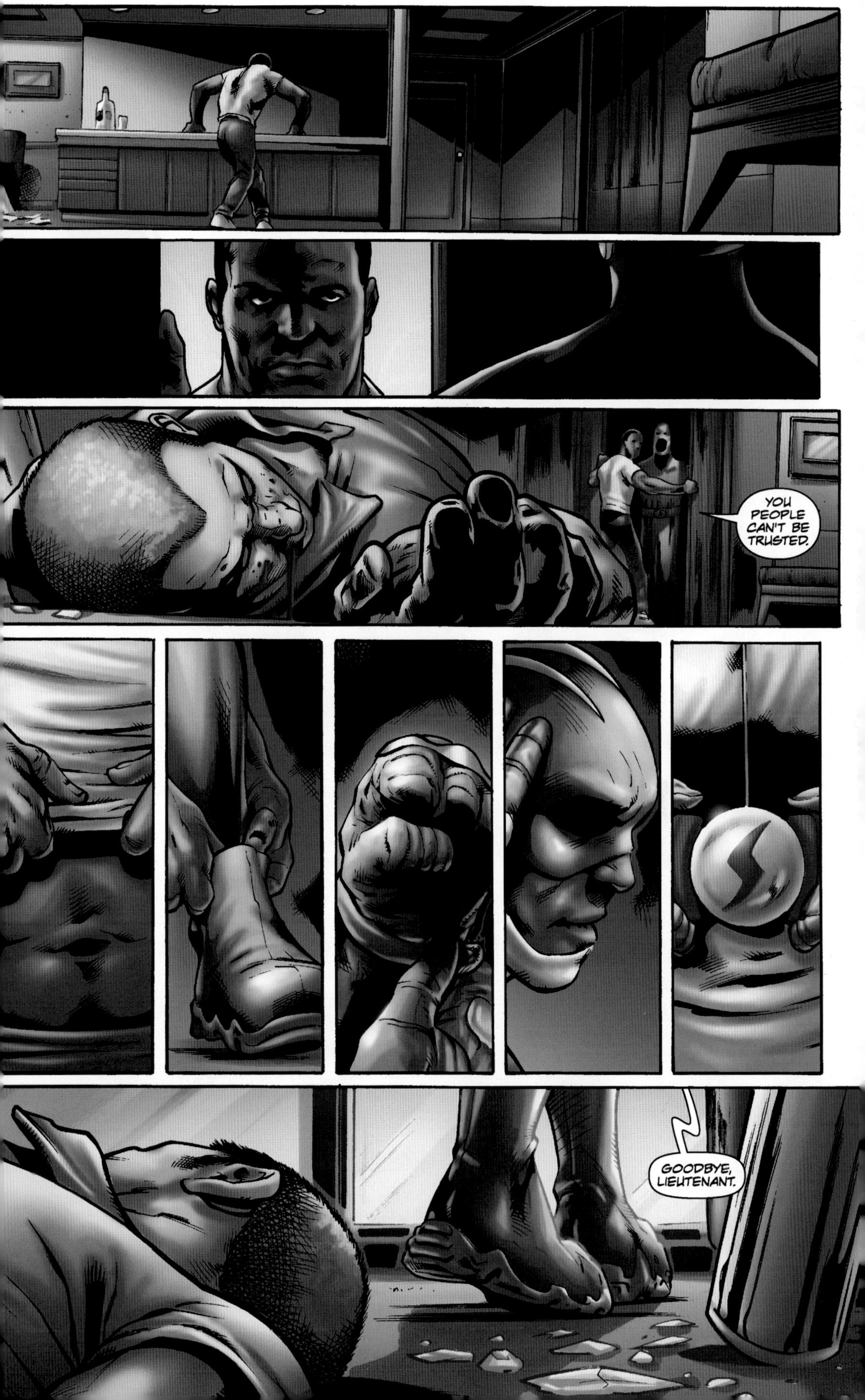
YOU PEOPLE CAN'T BE TRUSTED.
GOODBYE, LIEUTENANT.

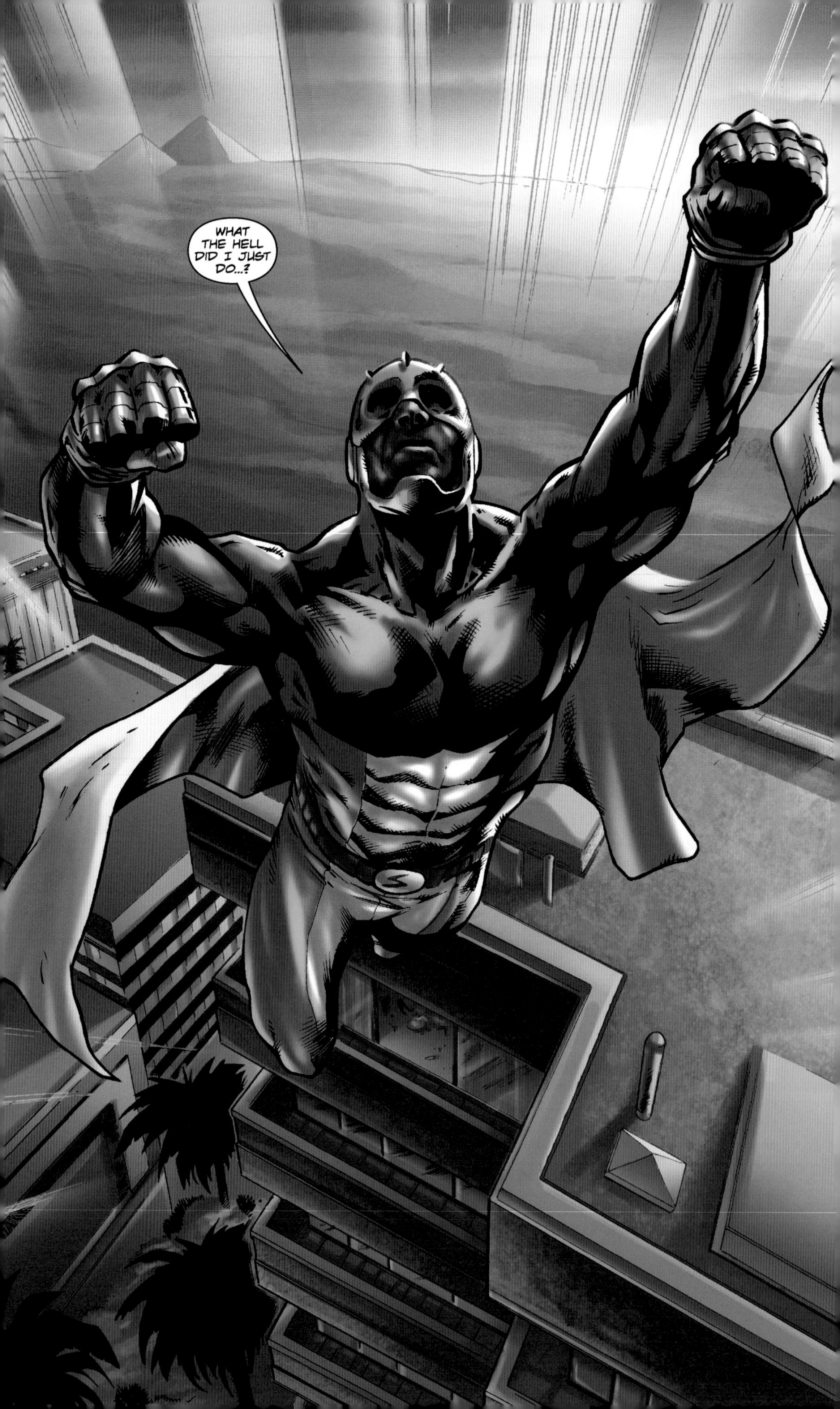
WHAT THE HELL DID I JUST DO...?

# CHAPTER 3

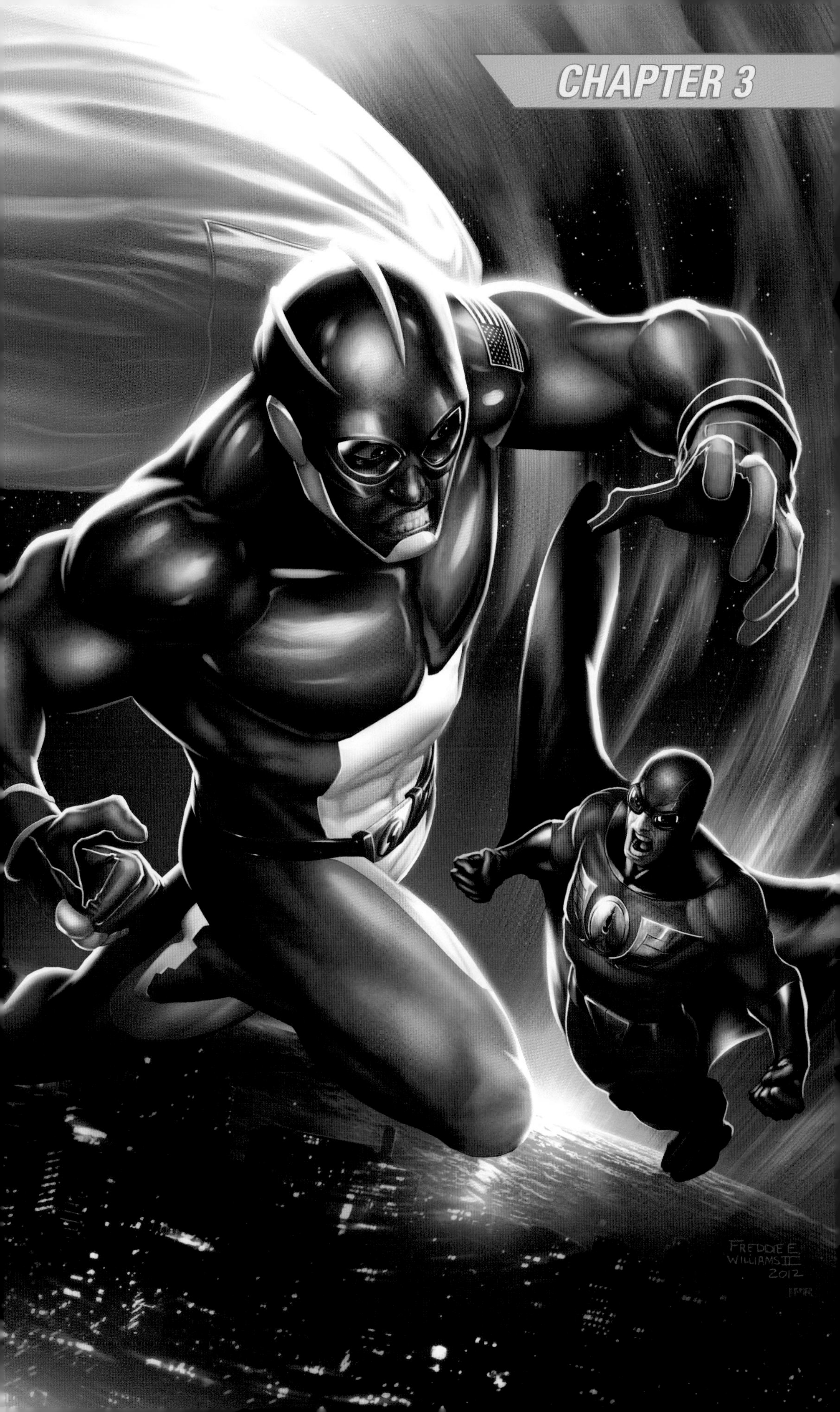
FREDDIE E.
WILLIAMS II
2012

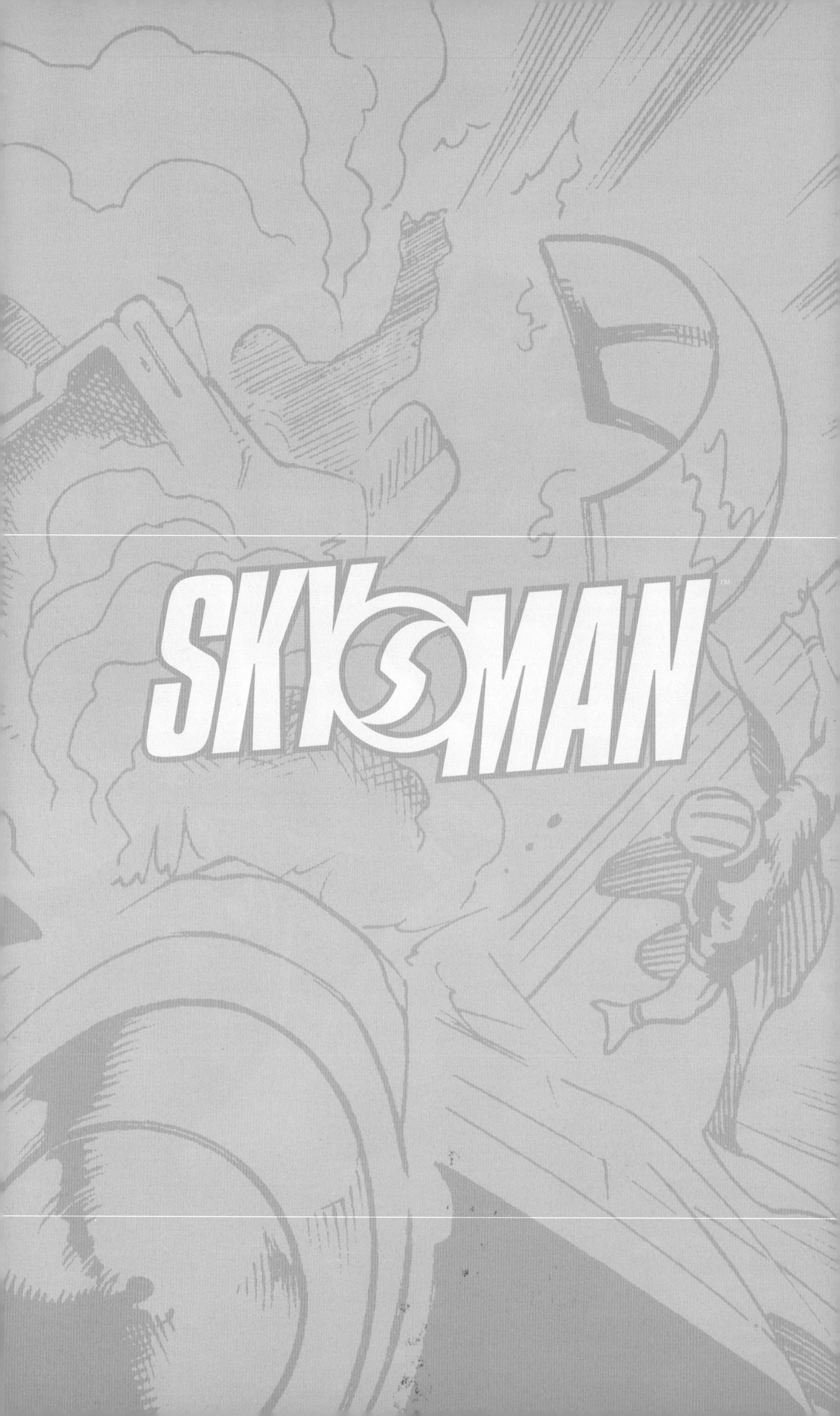
SKYMAN™

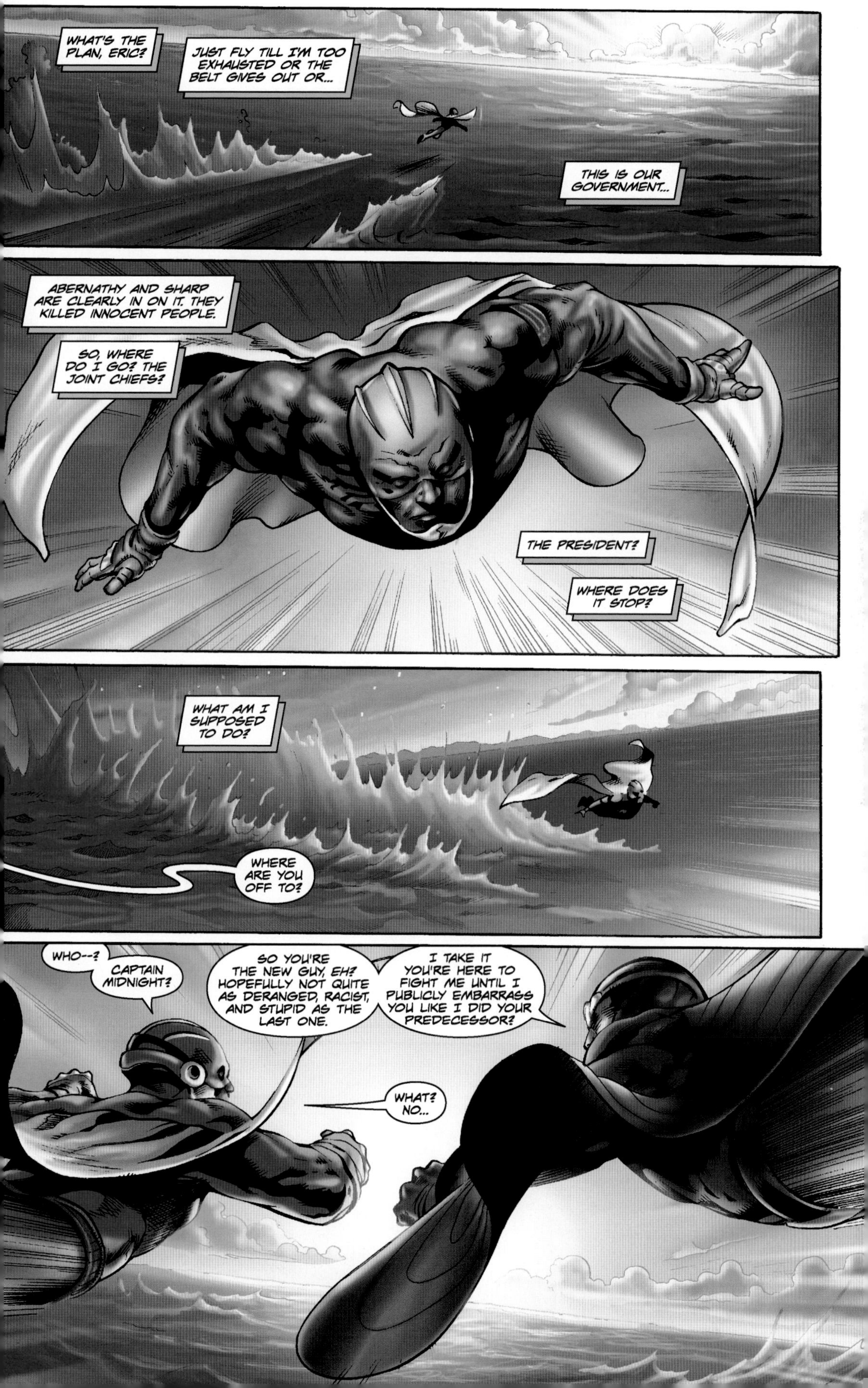
WHAT'S THE PLAN, ERIC?
JUST FLY TILL I'M TOO EXHAUSTED OR THE BELT GIVES OUT OR...
THIS IS OUR GOVERNMENT...
ABERNATHY AND SHARP ARE CLEARLY IN ON IT. THEY KILLED INNOCENT PEOPLE.
SO, WHERE DO I GO? THE JOINT CHIEFS?
THE PRESIDENT?
WHERE DOES IT STOP?
WHAT AM I SUPPOSED TO DO?
WHERE ARE YOU OFF TO?
WHO--?
CAPTAIN MIDNIGHT?
SO YOU'RE THE NEW GUY, EH? HOPEFULLY NOT QUITE AS DERANGED, RACIST, AND STUPID AS THE LAST ONE.
I TAKE IT YOU'RE HERE TO FIGHT ME UNTIL I PUBLICLY EMBARRASS YOU LIKE I DID YOUR PREDECESSOR?
WHAT? NO...

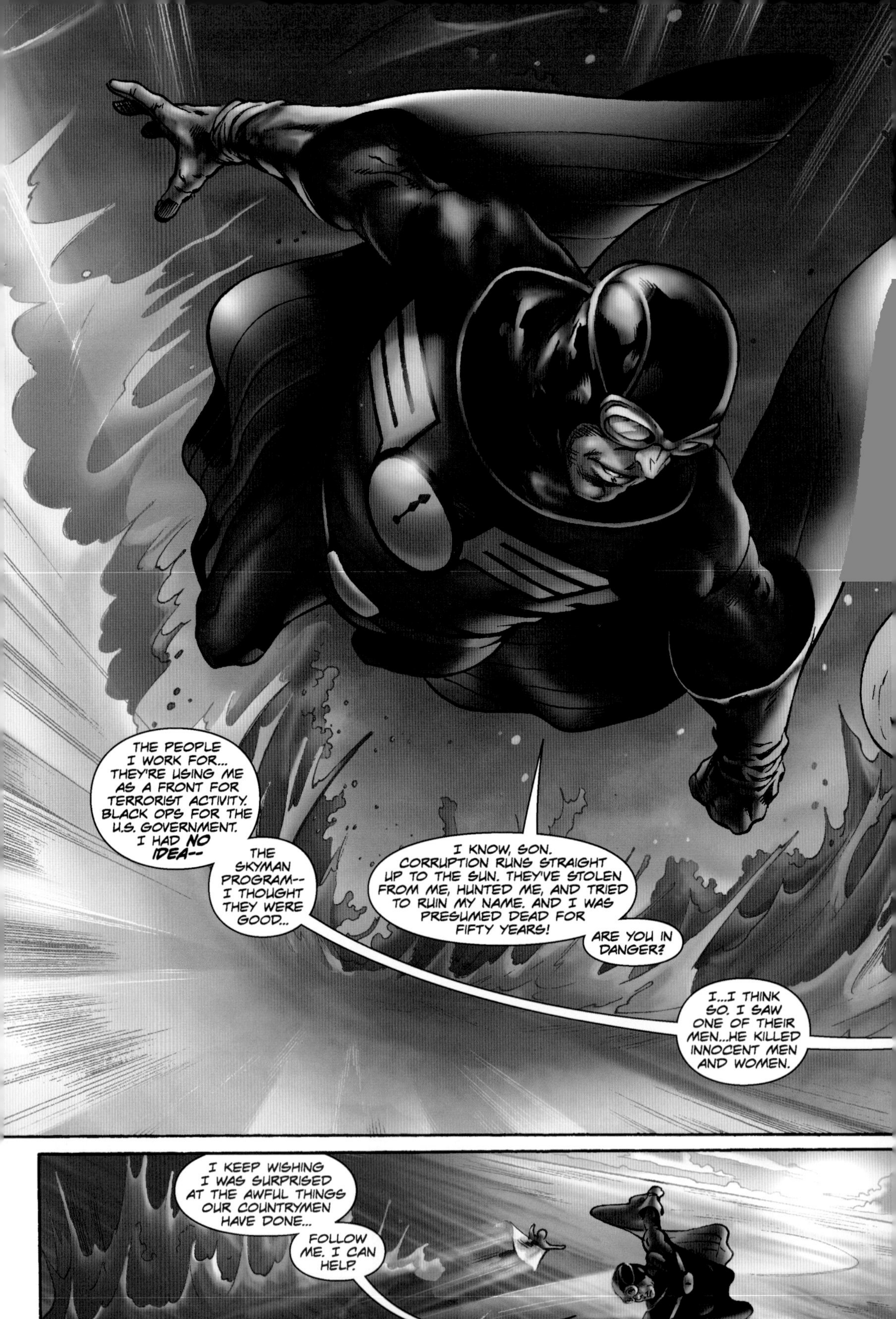
THE PEOPLE I WORK FOR... THEY'RE USING ME AS A FRONT FOR TERRORIST ACTIVITY. BLACK OPS FOR THE U.S. GOVERNMENT. I HAD NO IDEA--
THE SKYMAN PROGRAM-- I THOUGHT THEY WERE GOOD...
I KNOW, SON. CORRUPTION RUNS STRAIGHT UP TO THE SUN. THEY'VE STOLEN FROM ME, HUNTED ME, AND TRIED TO RUIN MY NAME. AND I WAS PRESUMED DEAD FOR FIFTY YEARS!
ARE YOU IN DANGER?
I...I THINK SO. I SAW ONE OF THEIR MEN...HE KILLED INNOCENT MEN AND WOMEN.

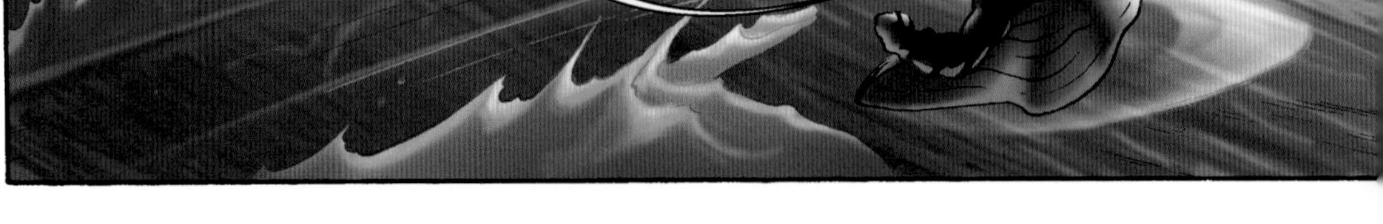
I KEEP WISHING I WAS SURPRISED AT THE AWFUL THINGS OUR COUNTRYMEN HAVE DONE...
FOLLOW ME. I CAN HELP.

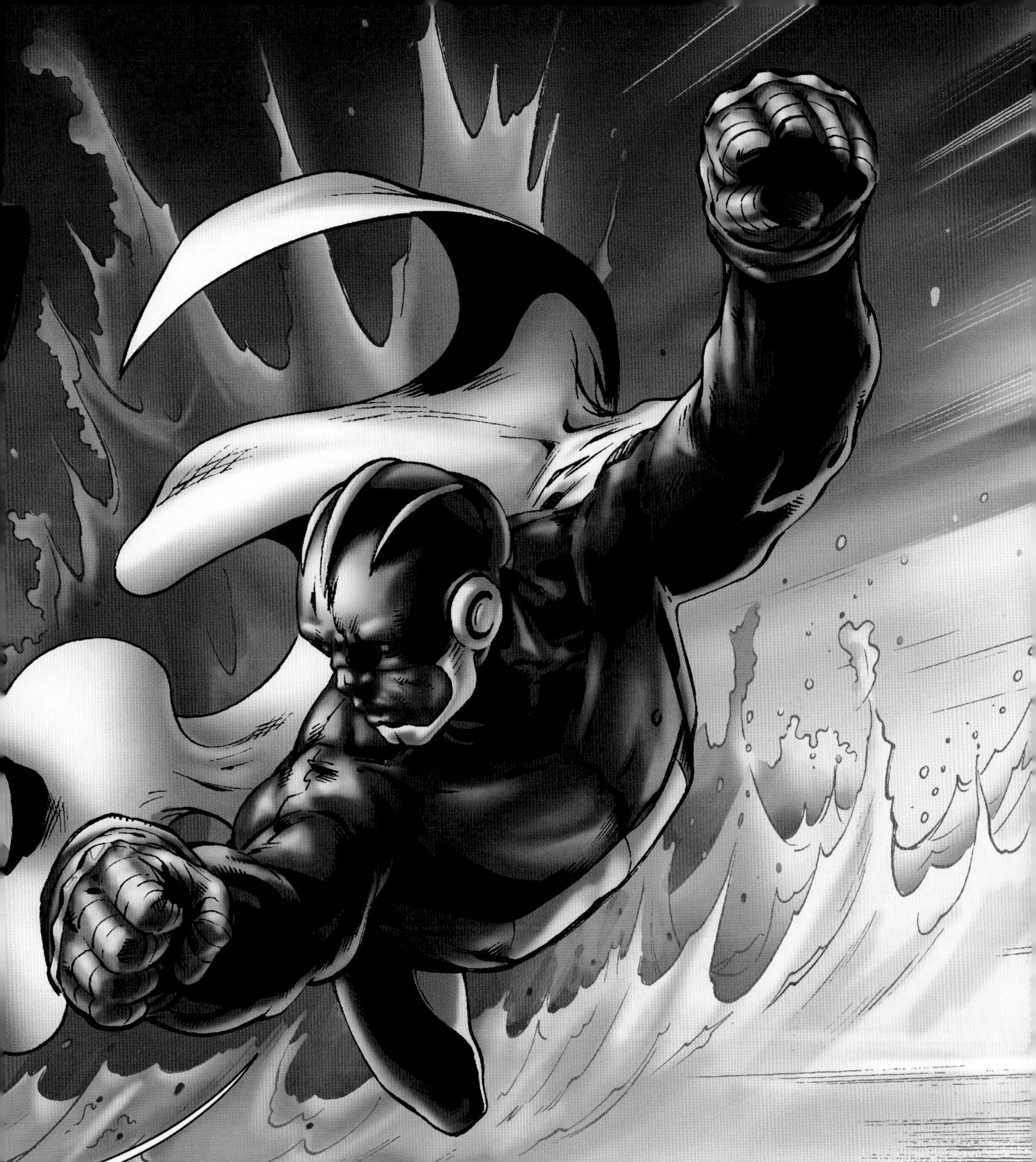

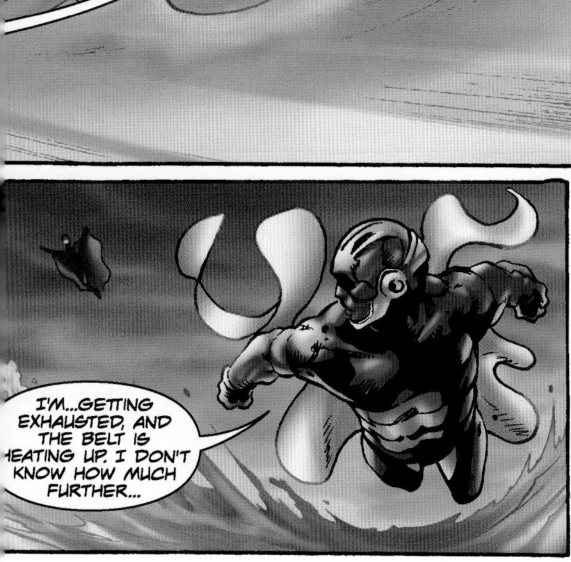
I'M...GETTING EXHAUSTED, AND THE BELT IS HEATING UP. I DON'T KNOW HOW MUCH FURTHER...

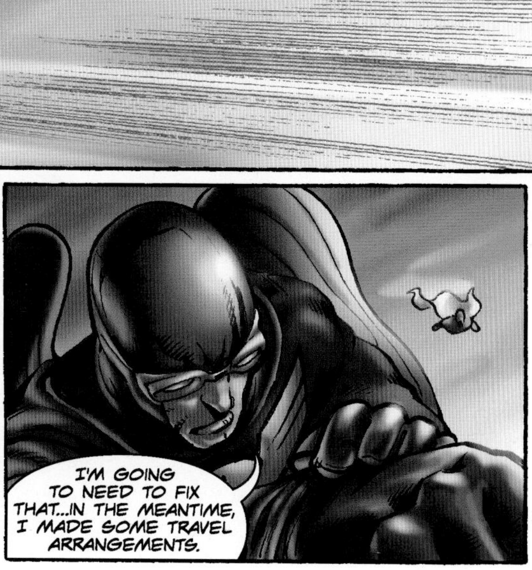
I'M GOING TO NEED TO FIX THAT...IN THE MEANTIME, I MADE SOME TRAVEL ARRANGEMENTS.

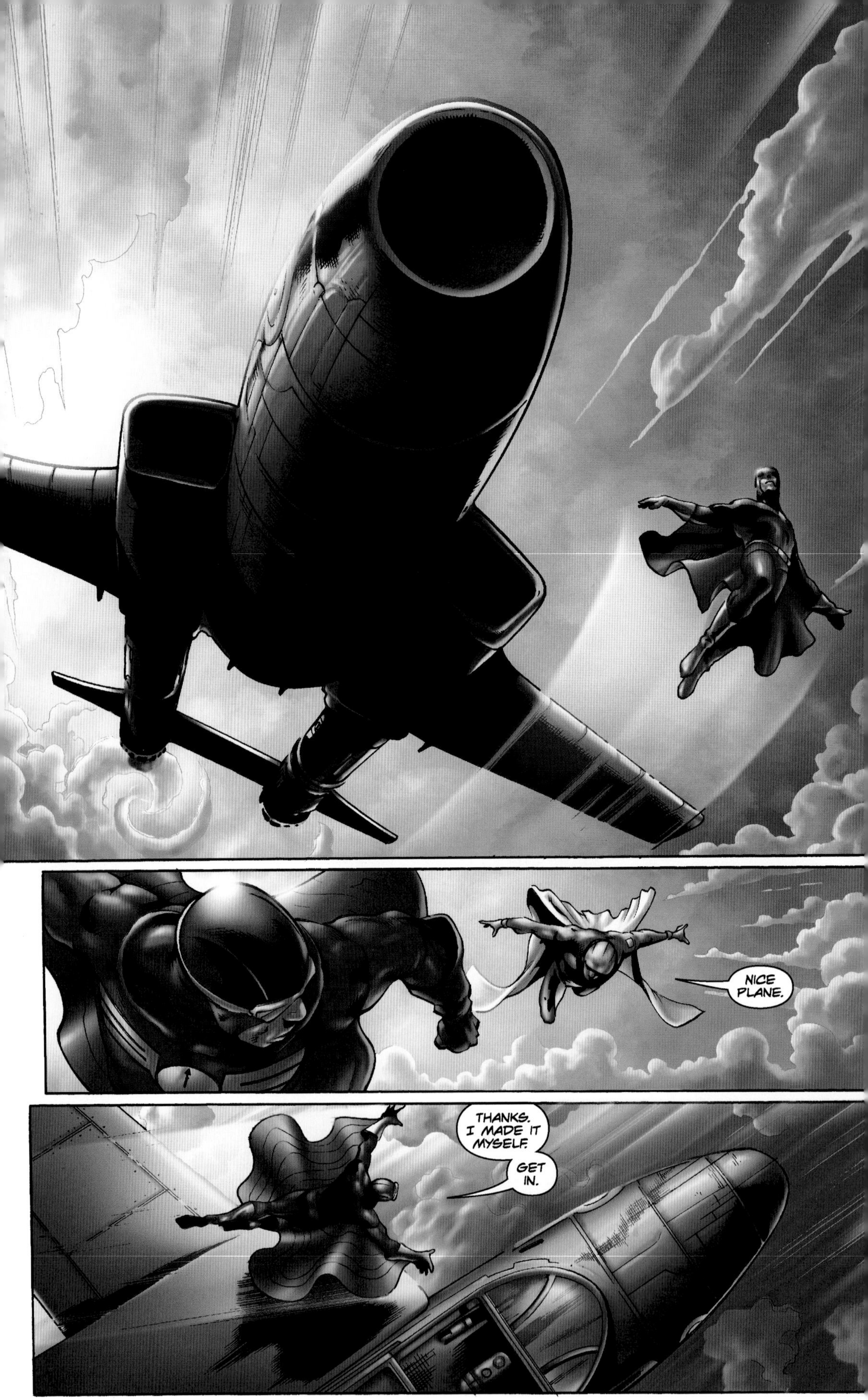
NICE PLANE.
THANKS. I MADE IT MYSELF.
GET IN.

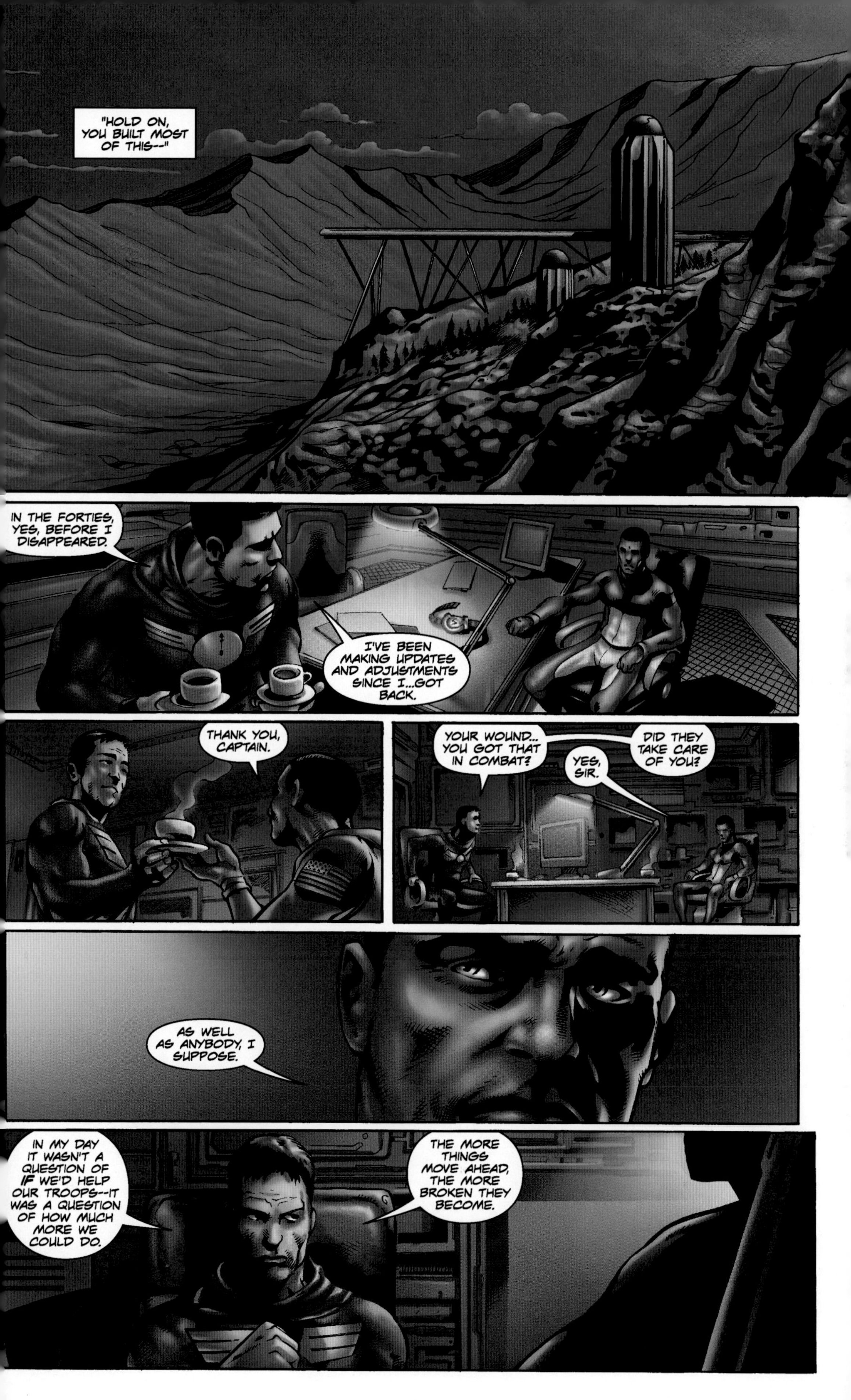
"HOLD ON, YOU BUILT MOST OF THIS--"
IN THE FORTIES, YES, BEFORE I DISAPPEARED.
I'VE BEEN MAKING UPDATES AND ADJUSTMENTS SINCE I...GOT BACK.
THANK YOU, CAPTAIN.
YOUR WOUND... YOU GOT THAT IN COMBAT?
YES, SIR.
DID THEY TAKE CARE OF YOU?
AS WELL AS ANYBODY, I SUPPOSE.
IN MY DAY IT WASN'T A QUESTION OF *IF* WE'D HELP OUR TROOPS--IT WAS A QUESTION OF HOW MUCH MORE WE COULD DO.
THE MORE THINGS MOVE AHEAD, THE MORE BROKEN THEY BECOME.

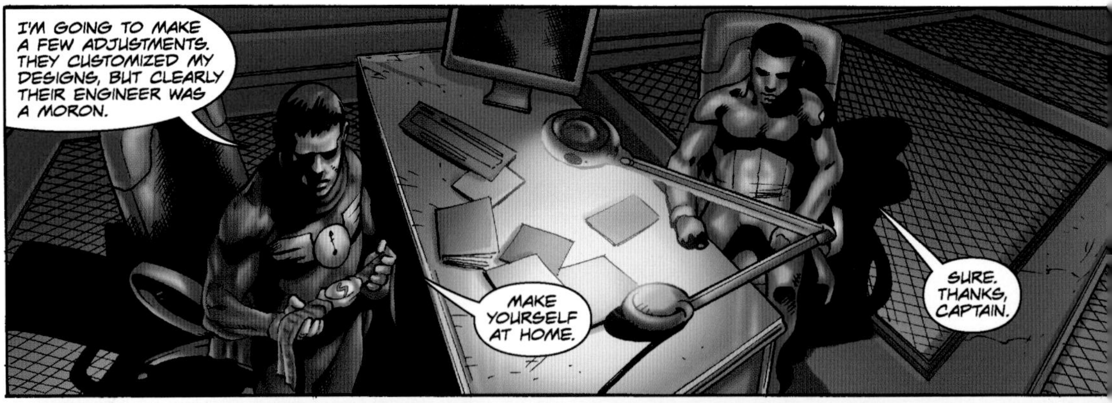
I'M GOING TO MAKE A FEW ADJUSTMENTS. THEY CUSTOMIZED MY DESIGNS, BUT CLEARLY THEIR ENGINEER WAS A MORON.
MAKE YOURSELF AT HOME.
SURE. THANKS, CAPTAIN.

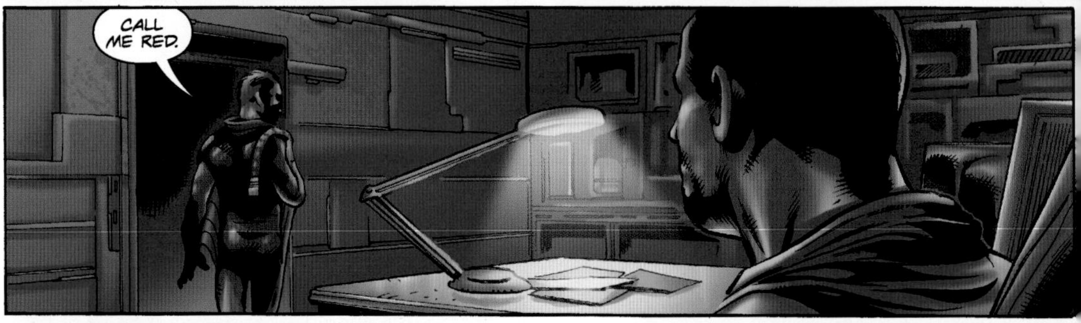
CALL ME RED.

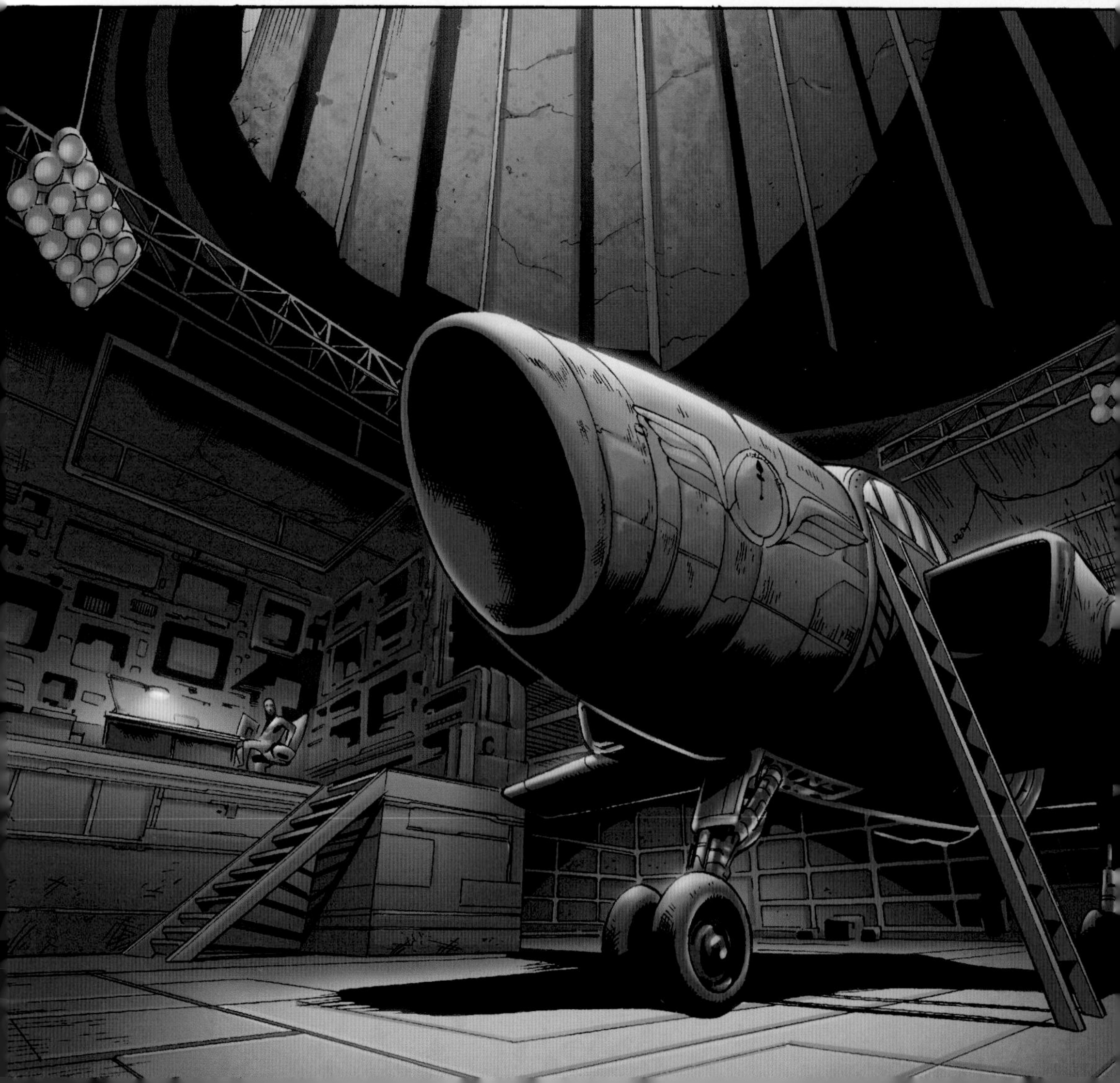

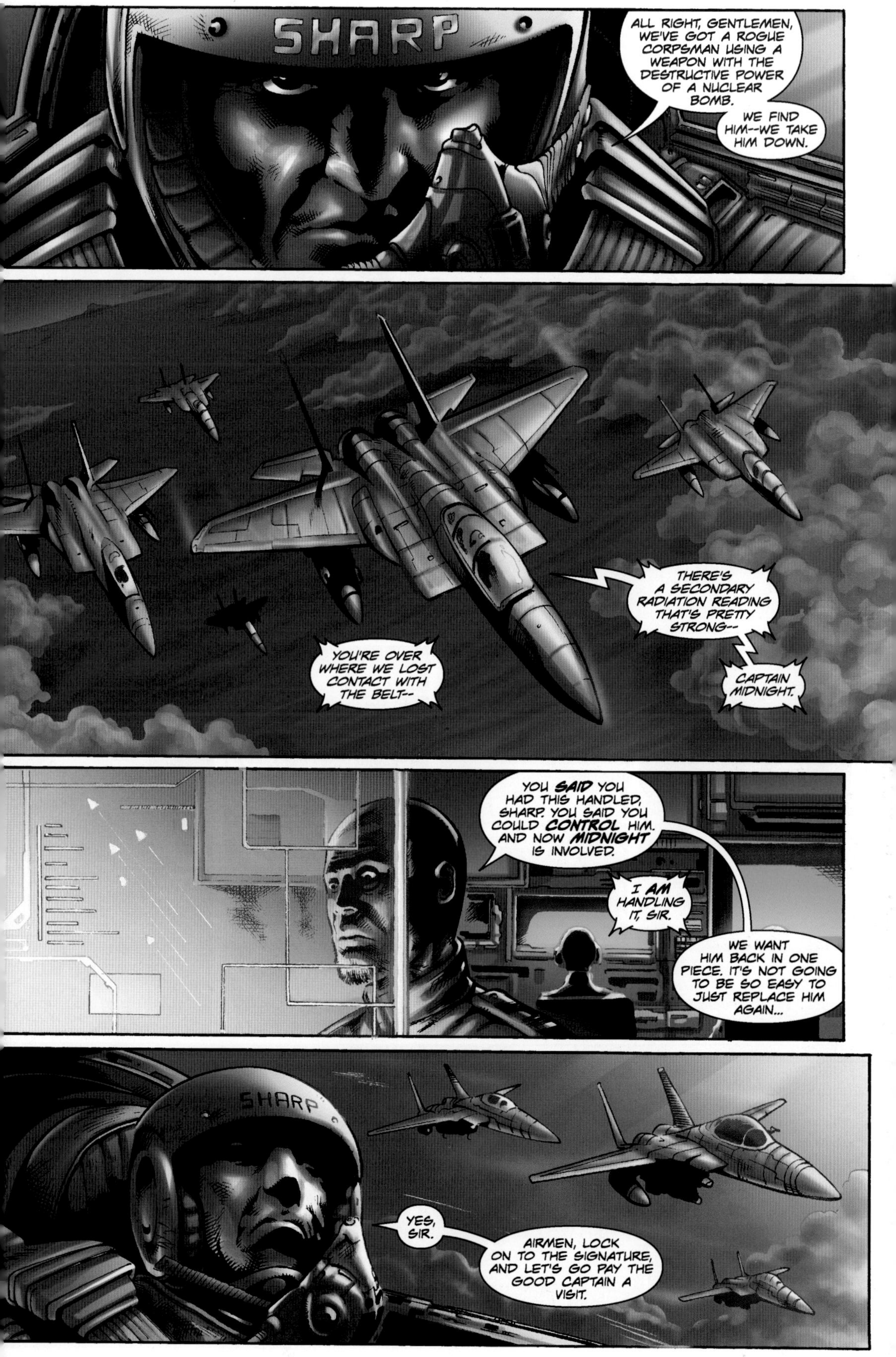
SHARP
ALL RIGHT, GENTLEMEN, WE'VE GOT A ROGUE CORPSMAN USING A WEAPON WITH THE DESTRUCTIVE POWER OF A NUCLEAR BOMB.
WE FIND HIM--WE TAKE HIM DOWN.
YOU'RE OVER WHERE WE LOST CONTACT WITH THE BELT--
THERE'S A SECONDARY RADIATION READING THAT'S PRETTY STRONG--
CAPTAIN MIDNIGHT.
YOU SAID YOU HAD THIS HANDLED, SHARP. YOU SAID YOU COULD CONTROL HIM. AND NOW MIDNIGHT IS INVOLVED.
I AM HANDLING IT, SIR.
WE WANT HIM BACK IN ONE PIECE. IT'S NOT GOING TO BE SO EASY TO JUST REPLACE HIM AGAIN...
SHARP
YES, SIR.
AIRMEN, LOCK ON TO THE SIGNATURE, AND LET'S GO PAY THE GOOD CAPTAIN A VISIT.

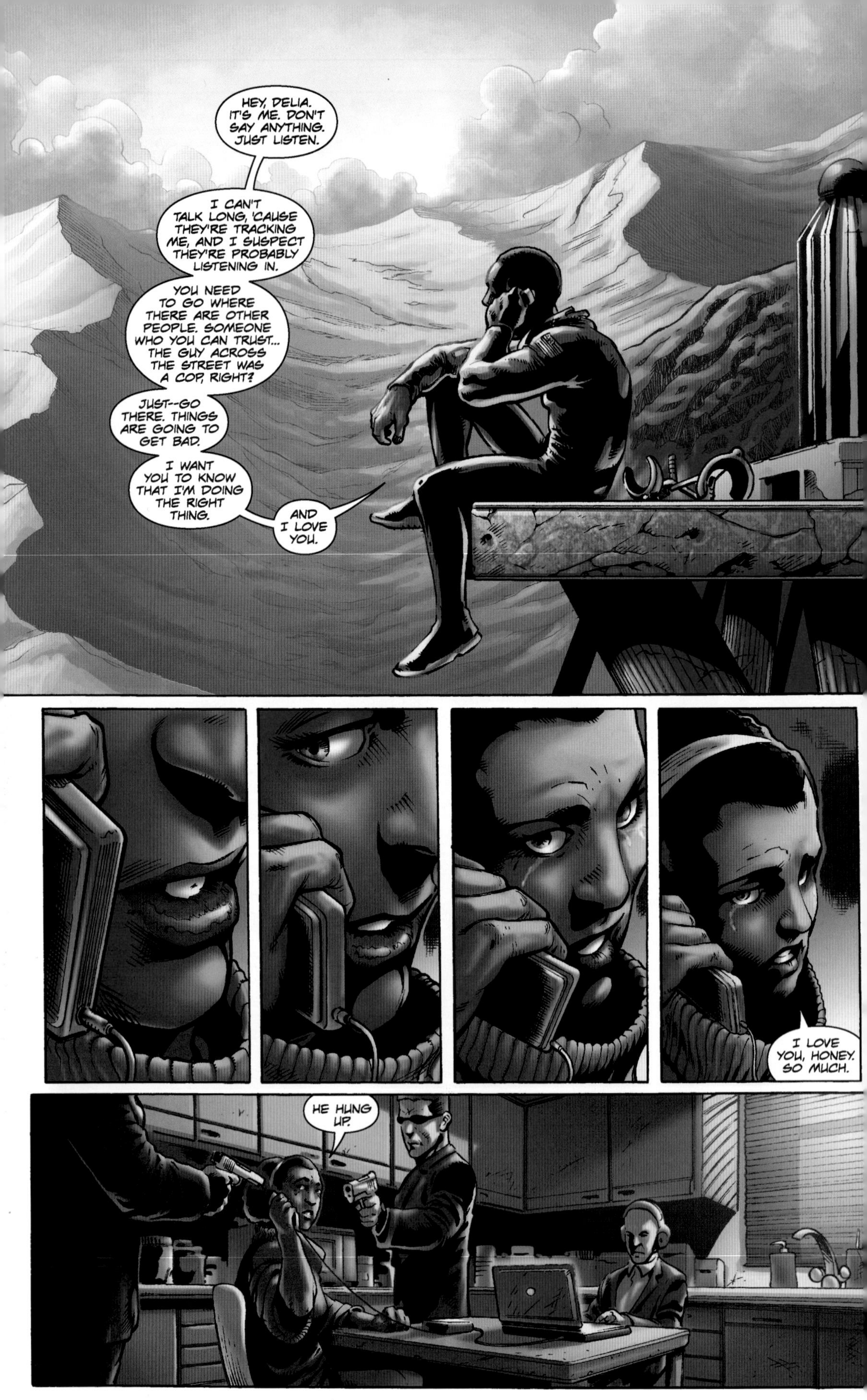
HEY, DELIA. IT'S ME. DON'T SAY ANYTHING. JUST LISTEN.
I CAN'T TALK LONG, 'CAUSE THEY'RE TRACKING ME, AND I SUSPECT THEY'RE PROBABLY LISTENING IN.
YOU NEED TO GO WHERE THERE ARE OTHER PEOPLE. SOMEONE WHO YOU CAN TRUST... THE GUY ACROSS THE STREET WAS A COP, RIGHT?
JUST--GO THERE. THINGS ARE GOING TO GET BAD.
I WANT YOU TO KNOW THAT I'M DOING THE RIGHT THING.
AND I LOVE YOU.
I LOVE YOU, HONEY. SO MUCH.
HE HUNG UP.

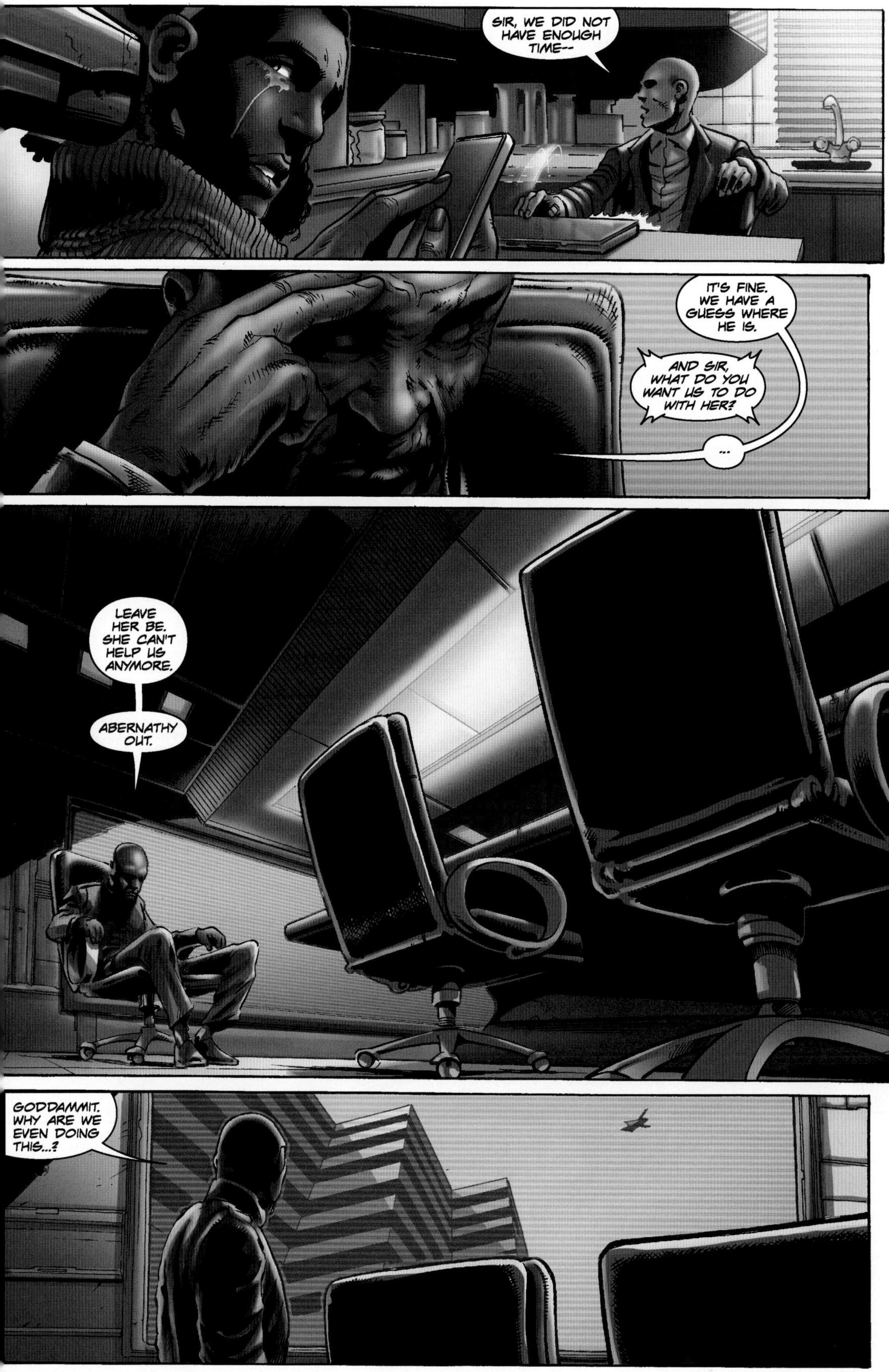
SIR, WE DID NOT HAVE ENOUGH TIME--
IT'S FINE. WE HAVE A GUESS WHERE HE IS.
AND SIR, WHAT DO YOU WANT US TO DO WITH HER?
...
LEAVE HER BE. SHE CAN'T HELP US ANYMORE.
ABERNATHY OUT.
GODDAMMIT. WHY ARE WE EVEN DOING THIS...?

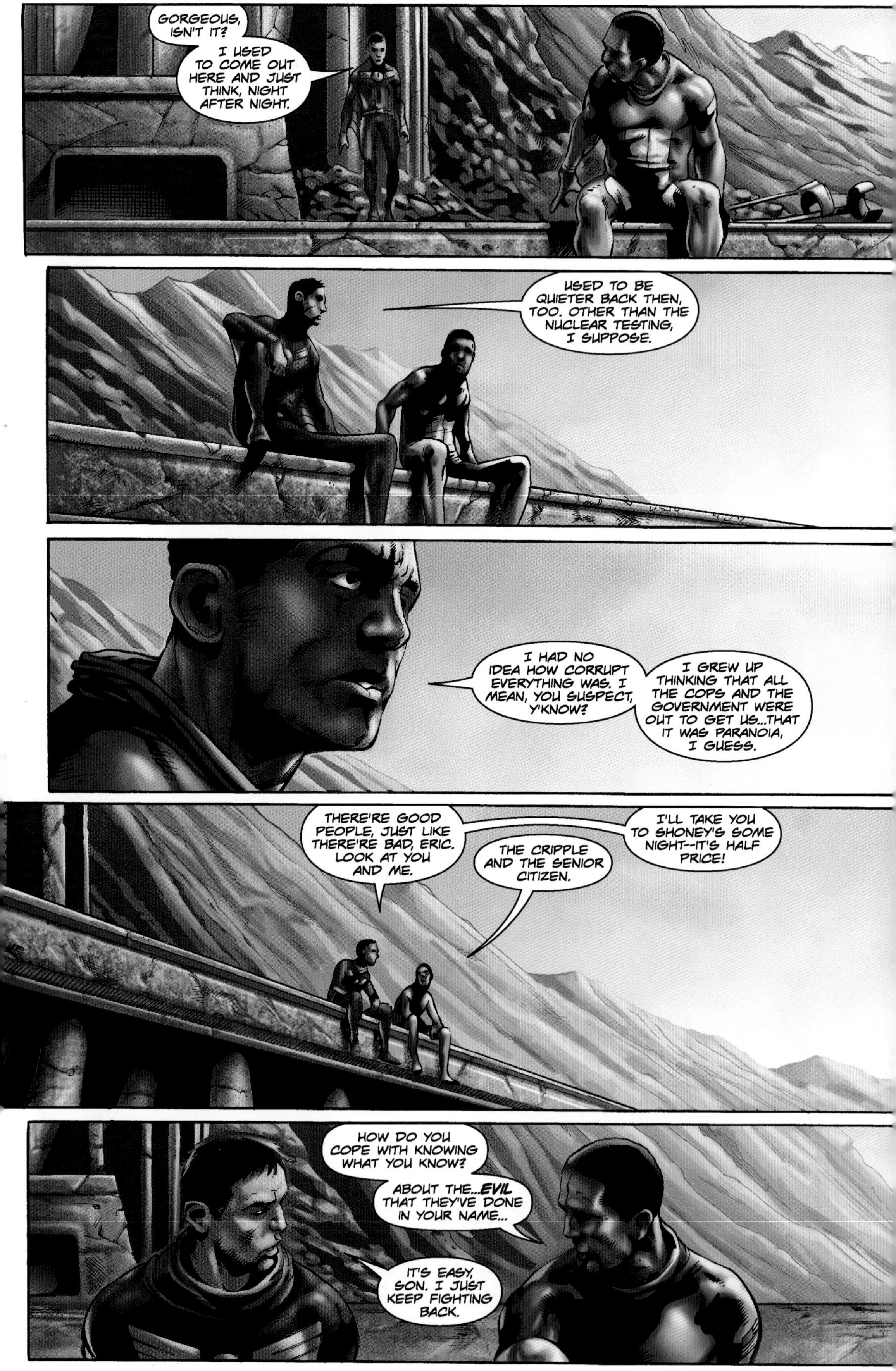
GORGEOUS, ISN'T IT?
I USED TO COME OUT HERE AND JUST THINK, NIGHT AFTER NIGHT.
USED TO BE QUIETER BACK THEN, TOO. OTHER THAN THE NUCLEAR TESTING, I SUPPOSE.
I HAD NO IDEA HOW CORRUPT EVERYTHING WAS. I MEAN, YOU SUSPECT, Y'KNOW?
I GREW UP THINKING THAT ALL THE COPS AND THE GOVERNMENT WERE OUT TO GET US...THAT IT WAS PARANOIA, I GUESS.
THERE'RE GOOD PEOPLE, JUST LIKE THERE'RE BAD, ERIC. LOOK AT YOU AND ME.
THE CRIPPLE AND THE SENIOR CITIZEN.
I'LL TAKE YOU TO SHONEY'S SOME NIGHT--IT'S HALF PRICE!
HOW DO YOU COPE WITH KNOWING WHAT YOU KNOW?
ABOUT THE...**EVIL** THAT THEY'VE DONE IN YOUR NAME...
IT'S EASY, SON. I JUST KEEP FIGHTING BACK.

YOU HEAR THAT?

YEAH. MY BELT?

INSIDE. IT'S DONE. MOSTLY.

URRRRR

MOSTLY?!

I DIDN'T HAVE TIME TO FINISH THE TWEAKS...

YOU CAN SURVIVE FALLING OUT OF THE SKY, RIGHT?

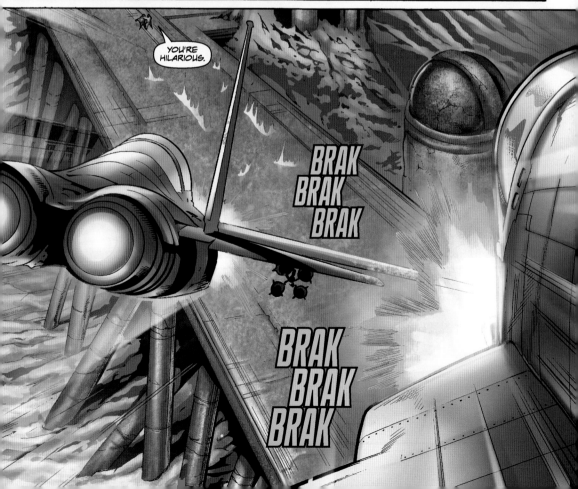

YOU'RE HILARIOUS.

BRAK
BRAK
BRAK

BRAK
BRAK
BRAK

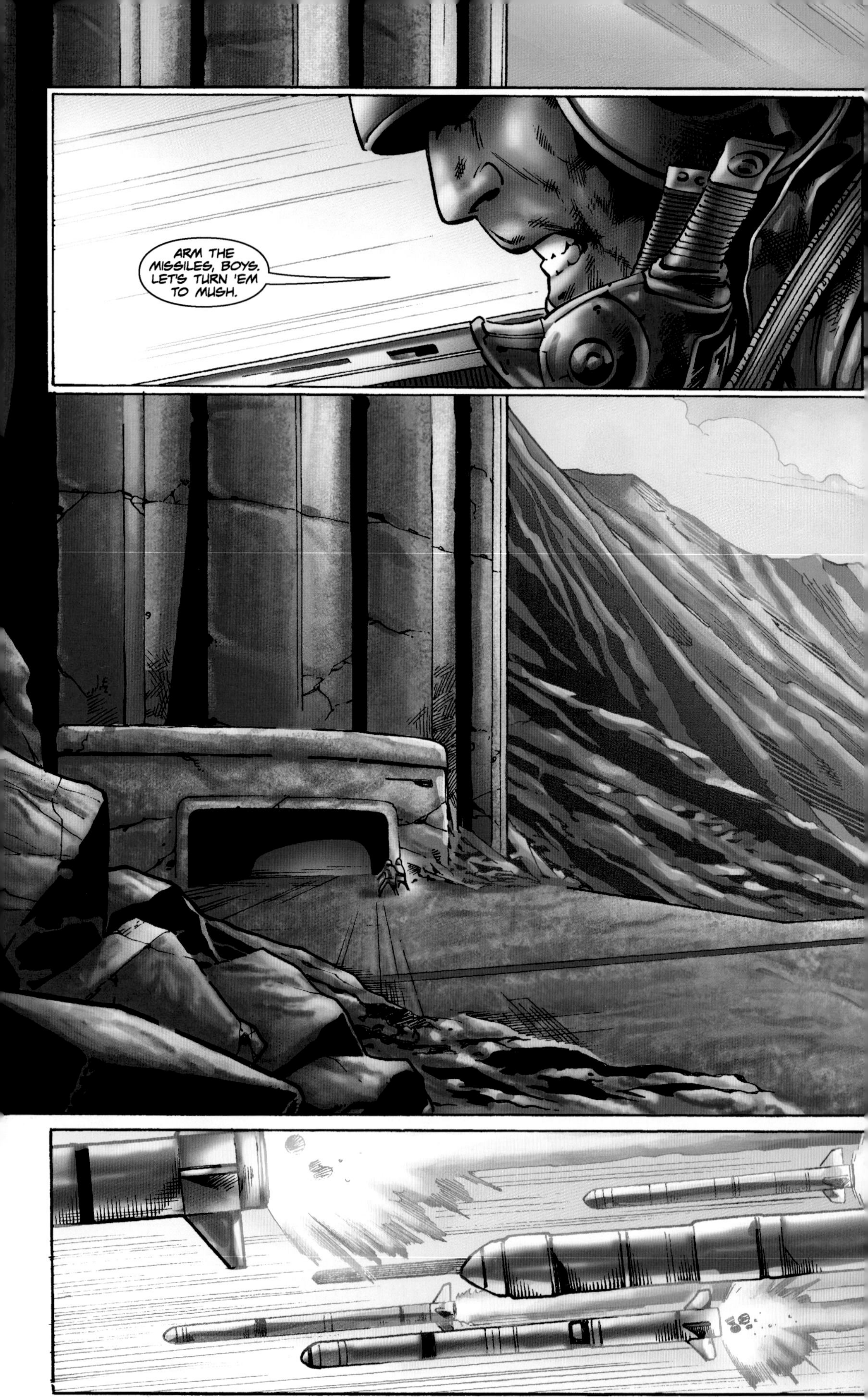
ARM THE MISSILES, BOYS. LET'S TURN 'EM TO MUSH.

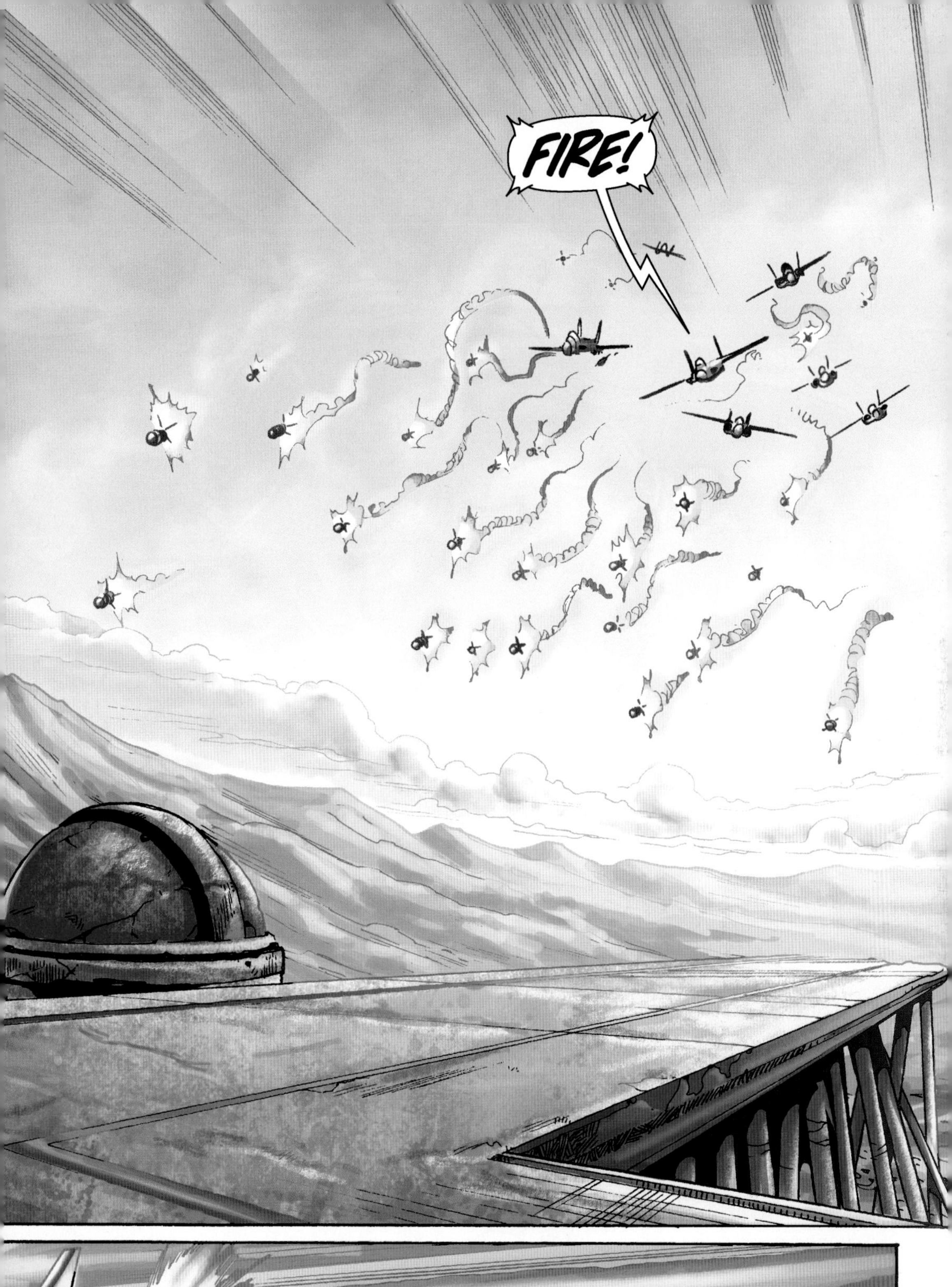
FIRE!

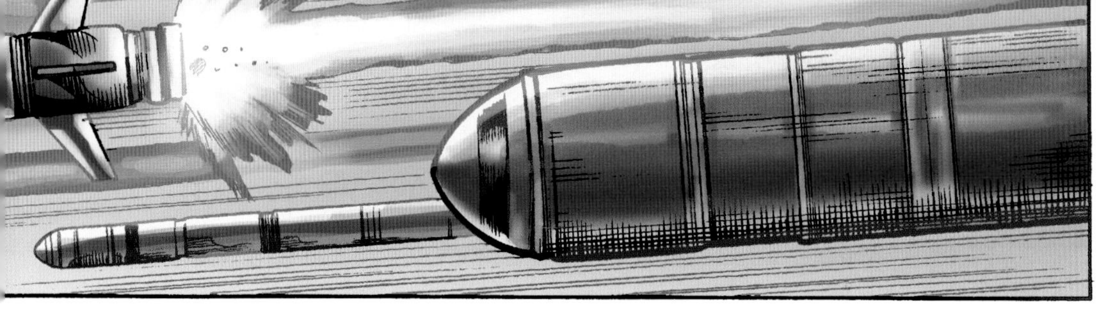

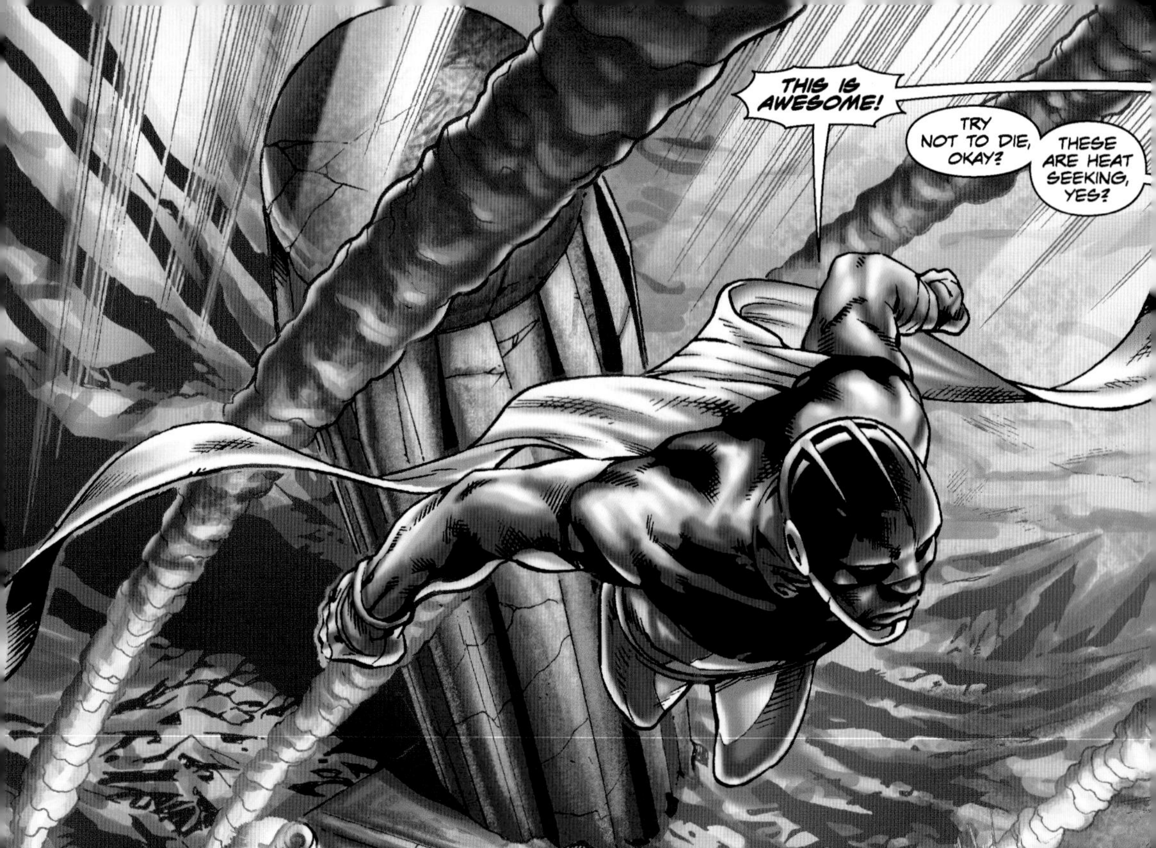
THIS IS AWESOME!
TRY NOT TO DIE, OKAY?
THESE ARE HEAT SEEKING, YES?

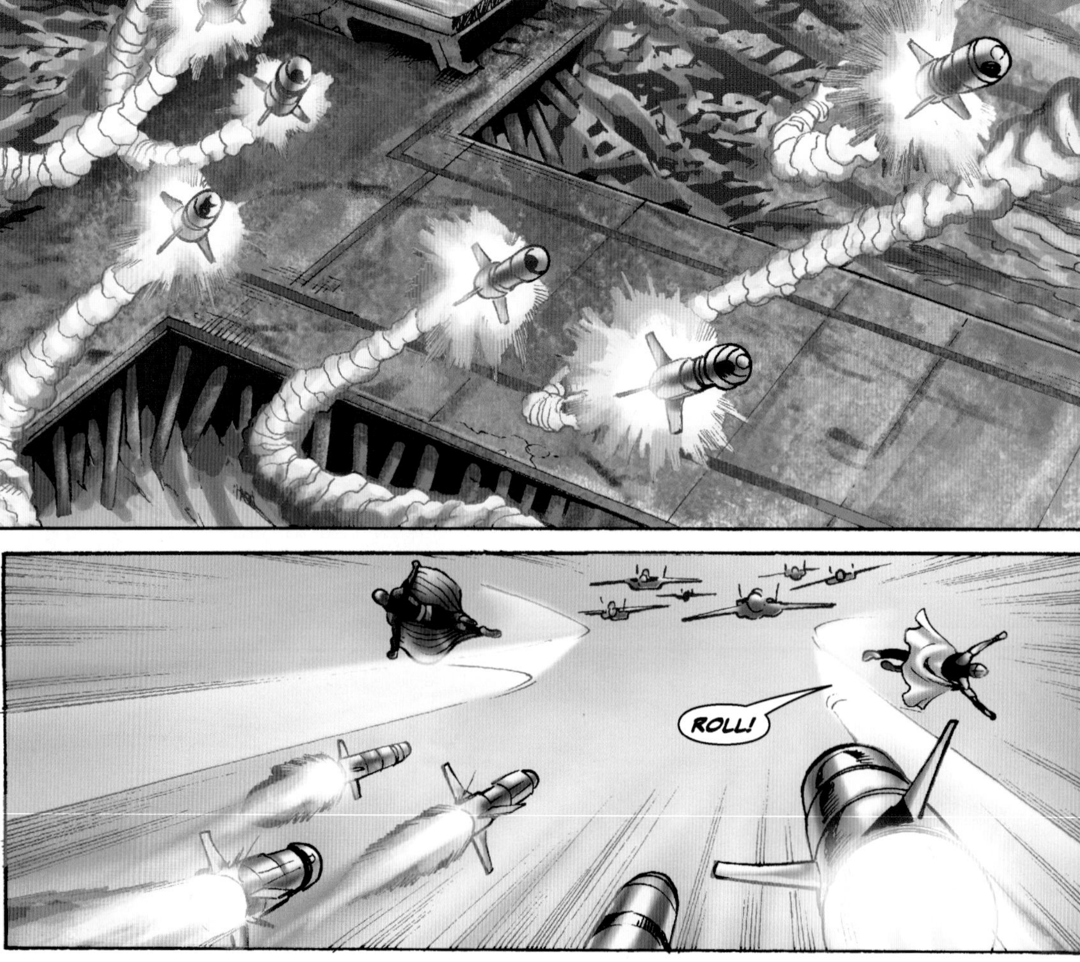
ROLL!

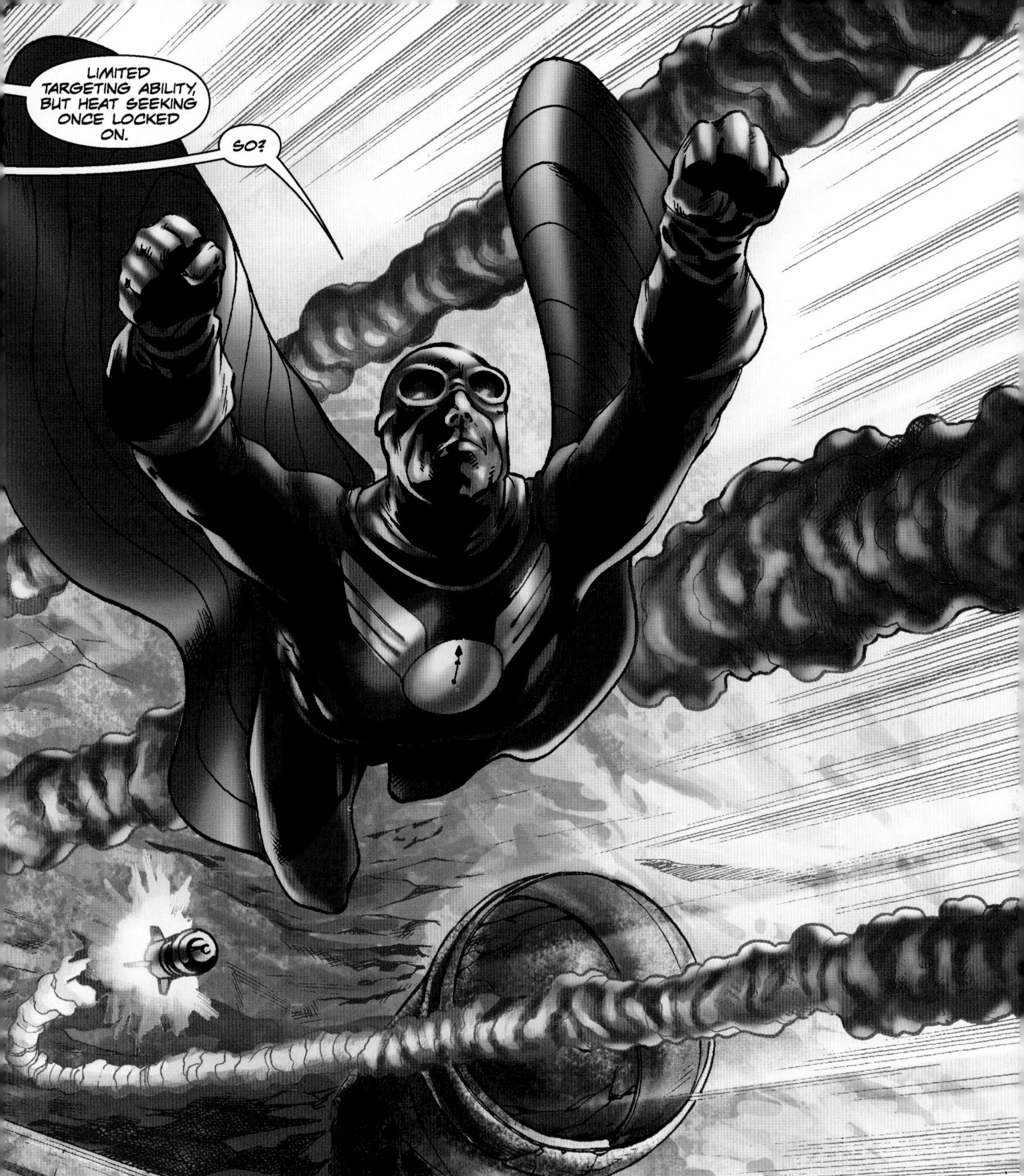
LIMITED TARGETING ABILITY, BUT HEAT SEEKING ONCE LOCKED ON.
SO?

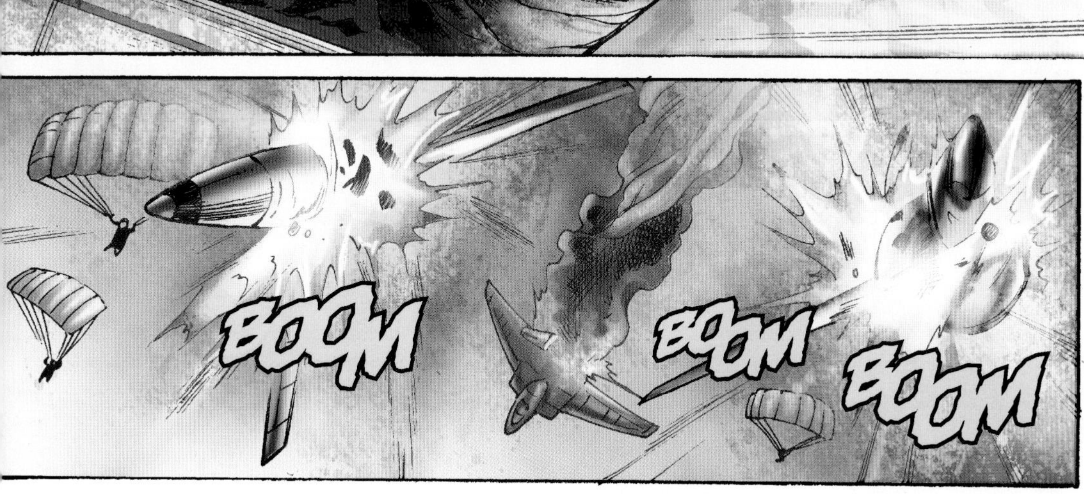
BOOM
BOOM
BOOM

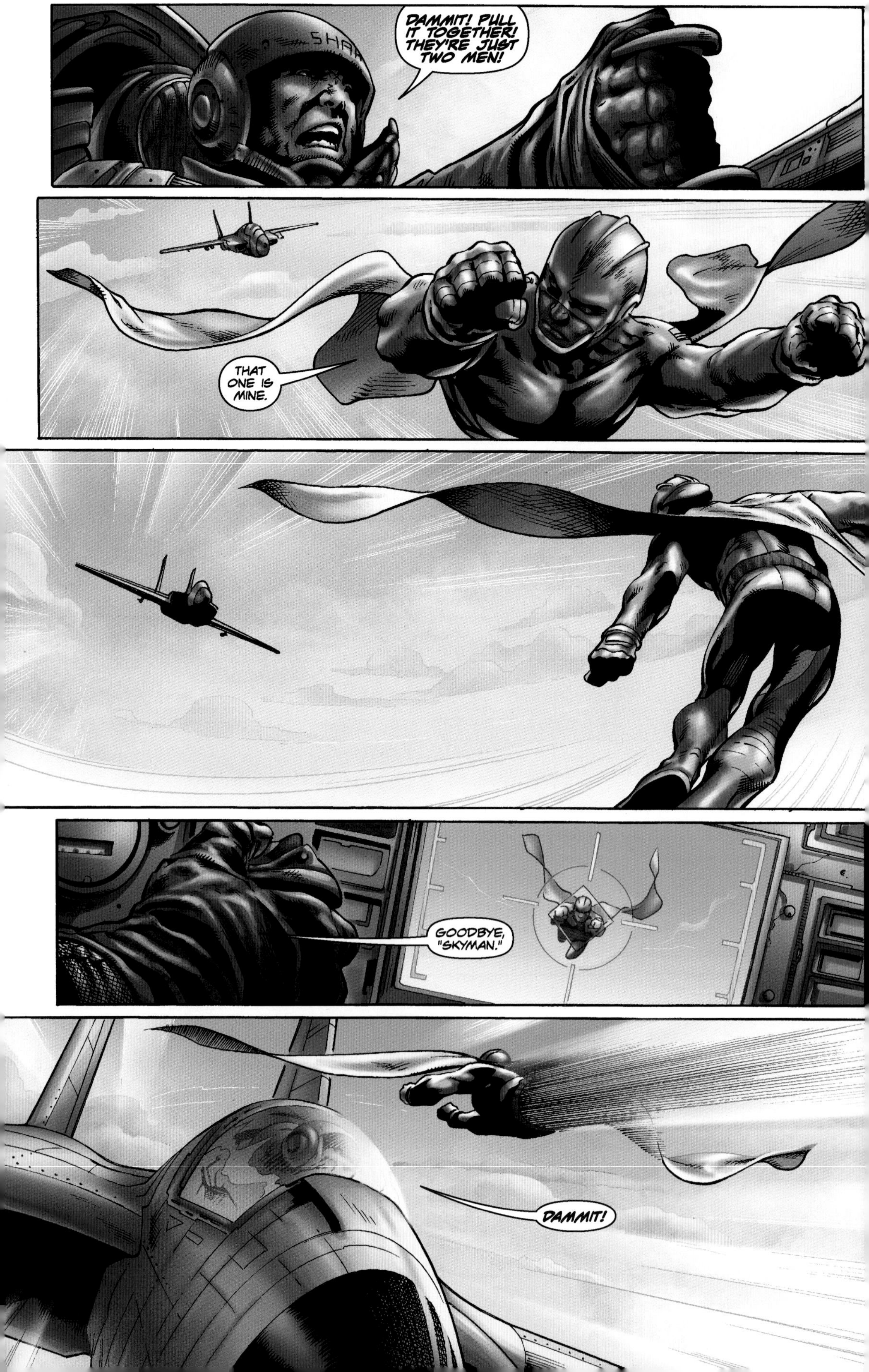
DAMMIT! PULL IT TOGETHER! THEY'RE JUST TWO MEN!
THAT ONE IS MINE.
GOODBYE, "SKYMAN."
DAMMIT!

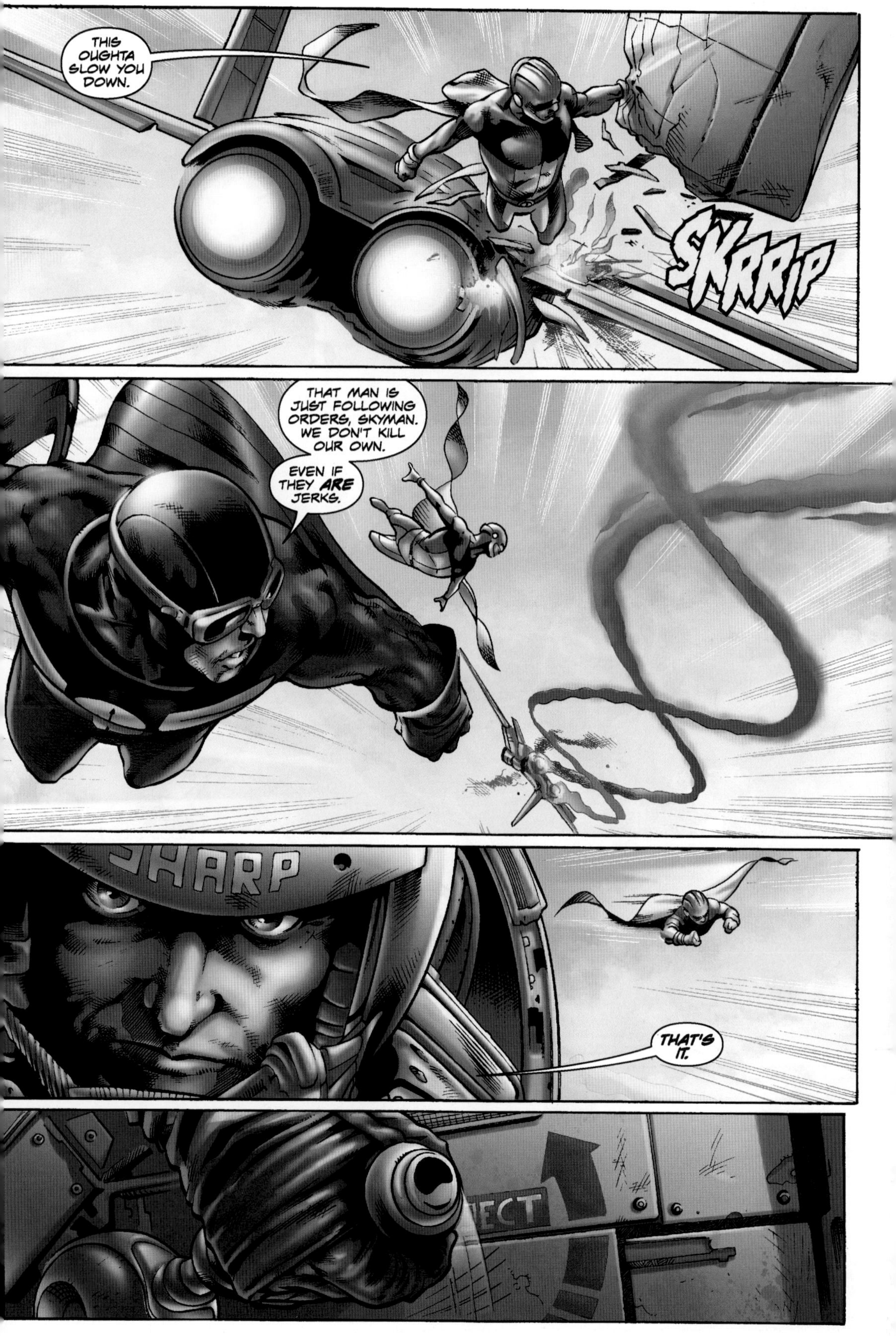
THIS OUGHTA SLOW YOU DOWN.
SKRRIP
THAT MAN IS JUST FOLLOWING ORDERS, SKYMAN. WE DON'T KILL OUR OWN.
EVEN IF THEY ARE JERKS.
SHARP
THAT'S IT.
EJECT

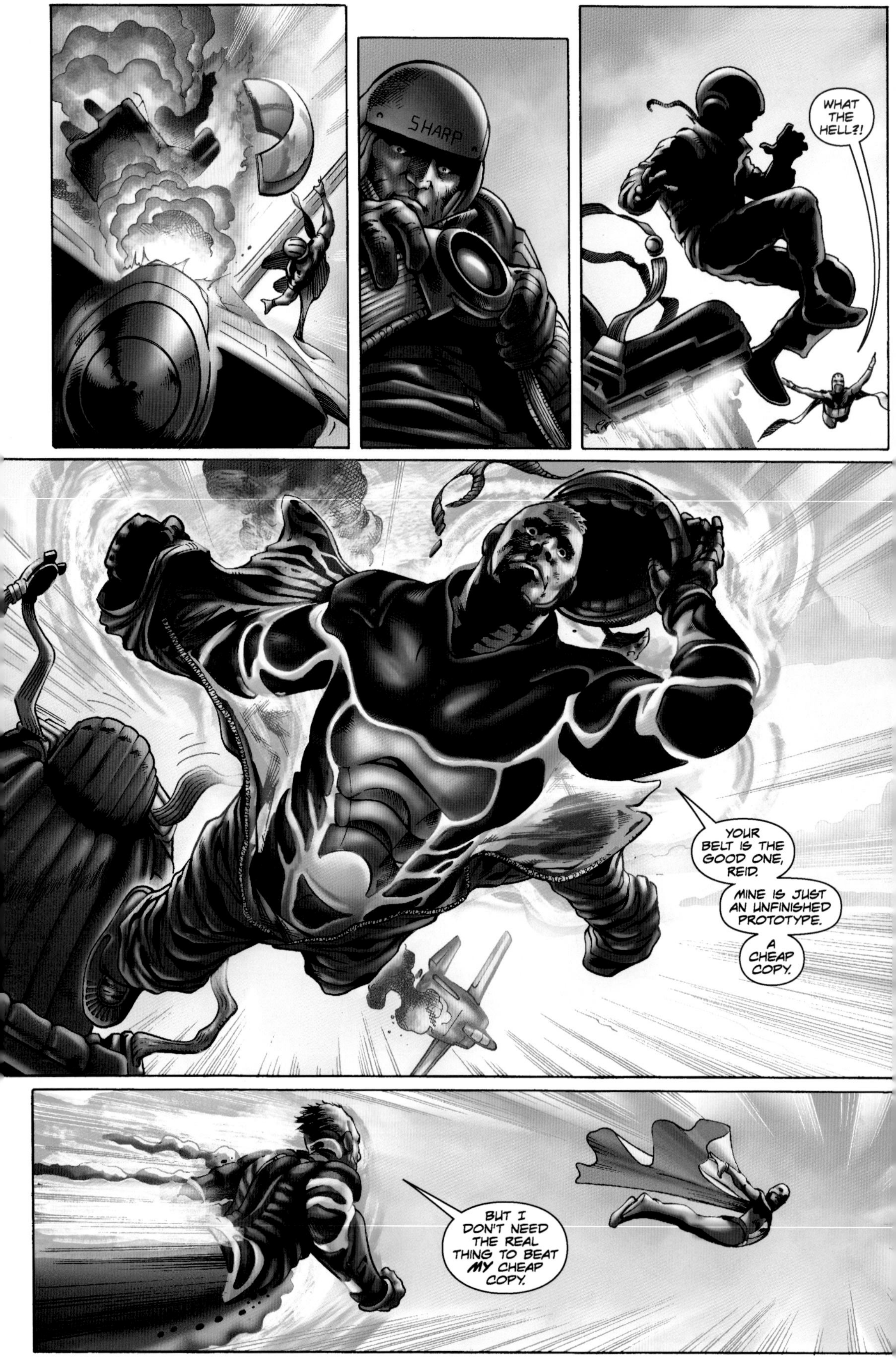
SHARP
WHAT THE HELL?!
YOUR BELT IS THE GOOD ONE, REID.
MINE IS JUST AN UNFINISHED PROTOTYPE.
A CHEAP COPY.
BUT I DON'T NEED THE REAL THING TO BEAT MY CHEAP COPY.

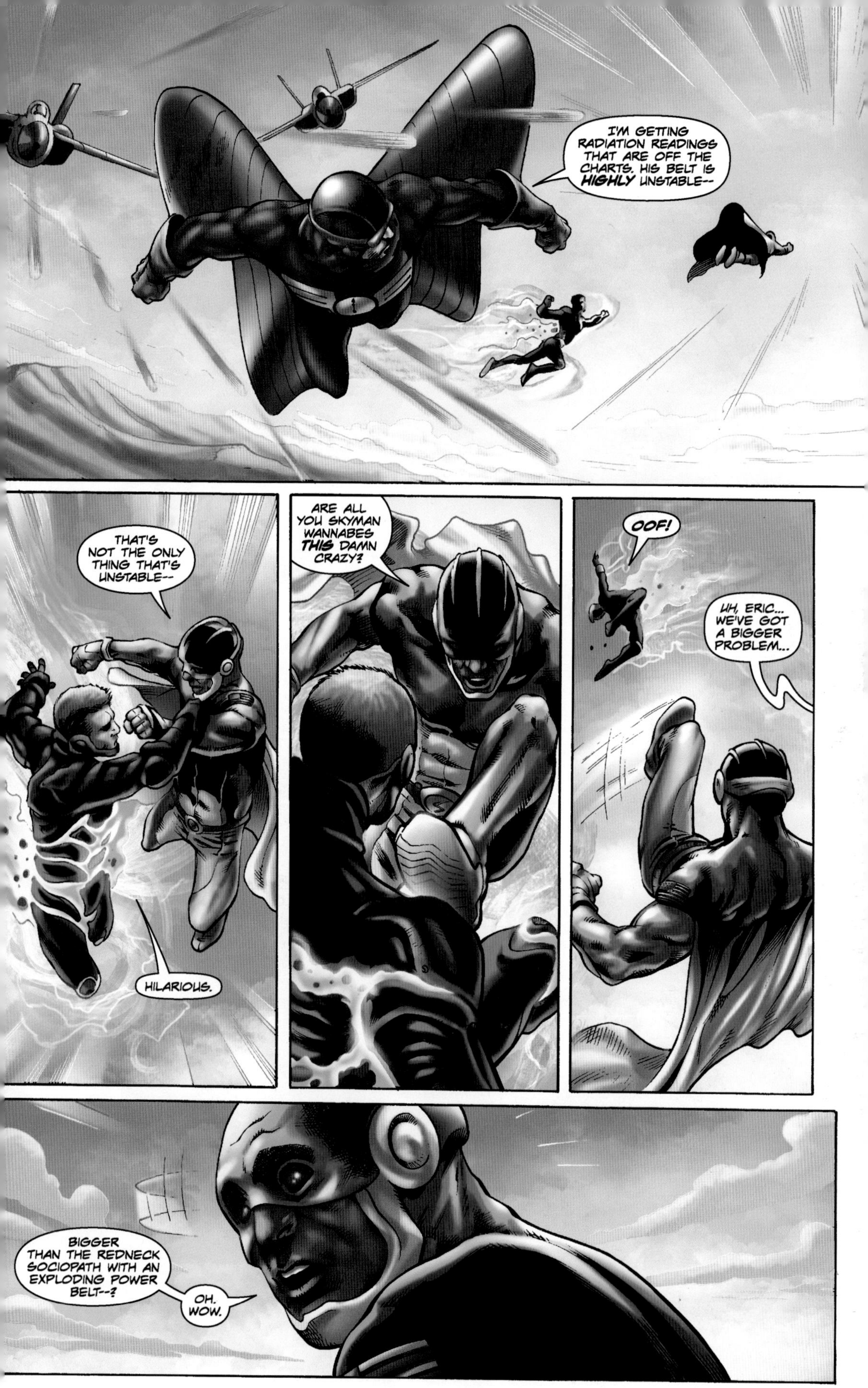
I'M GETTING RADIATION READINGS THAT ARE OFF THE CHARTS. HIS BELT IS *HIGHLY* UNSTABLE--
THAT'S NOT THE ONLY THING THAT'S UNSTABLE--
HILARIOUS.
ARE ALL YOU SKYMAN WANNABES *THIS* DAMN CRAZY?
OOF!
UH, ERIC... WE'VE GOT A BIGGER PROBLEM...
BIGGER THAN THE REDNECK SOCIOPATH WITH AN EXPLODING POWER BELT--?
OH. WOW.

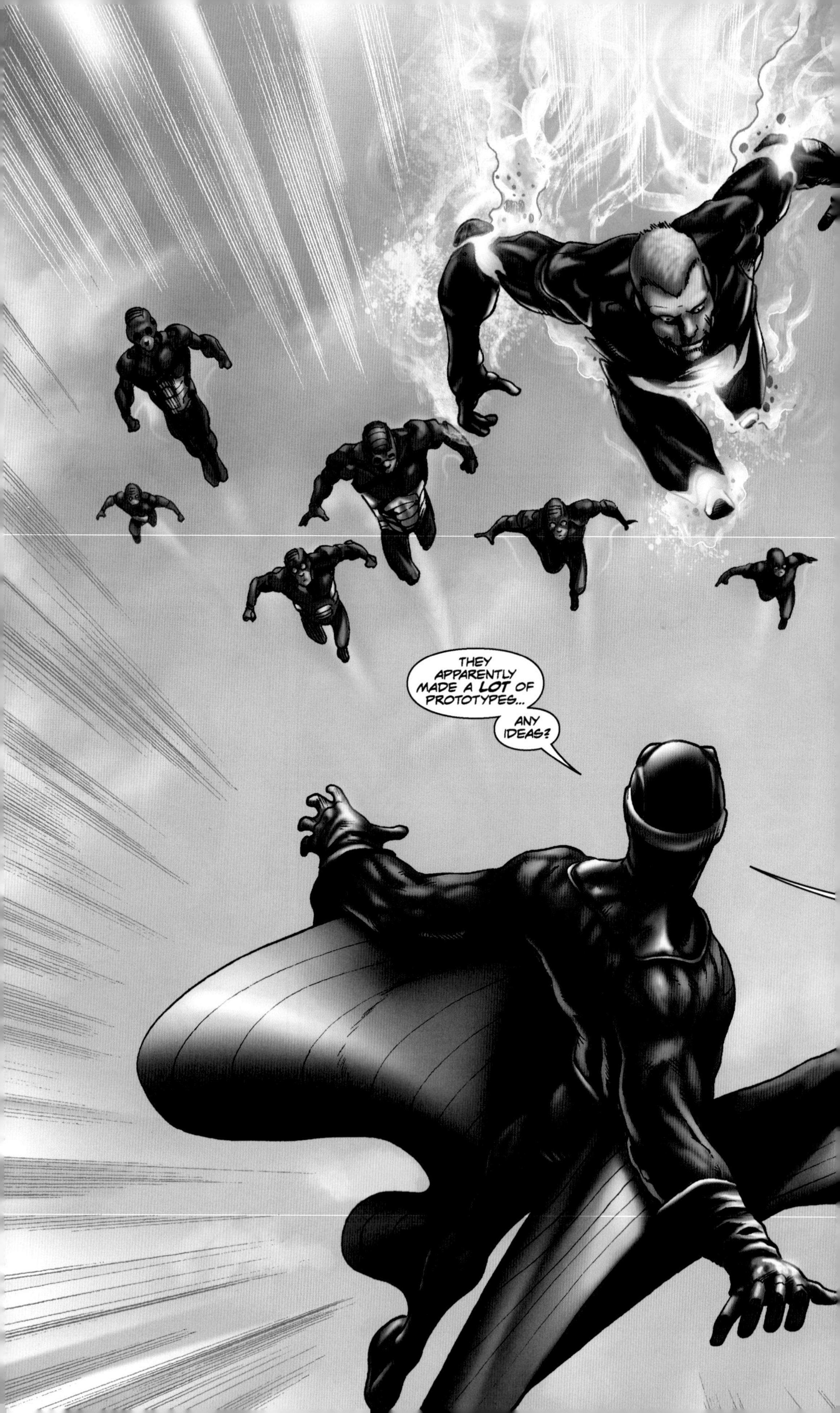
THEY APPARENTLY MADE A LOT OF PROTOTYPES...
ANY IDEAS?

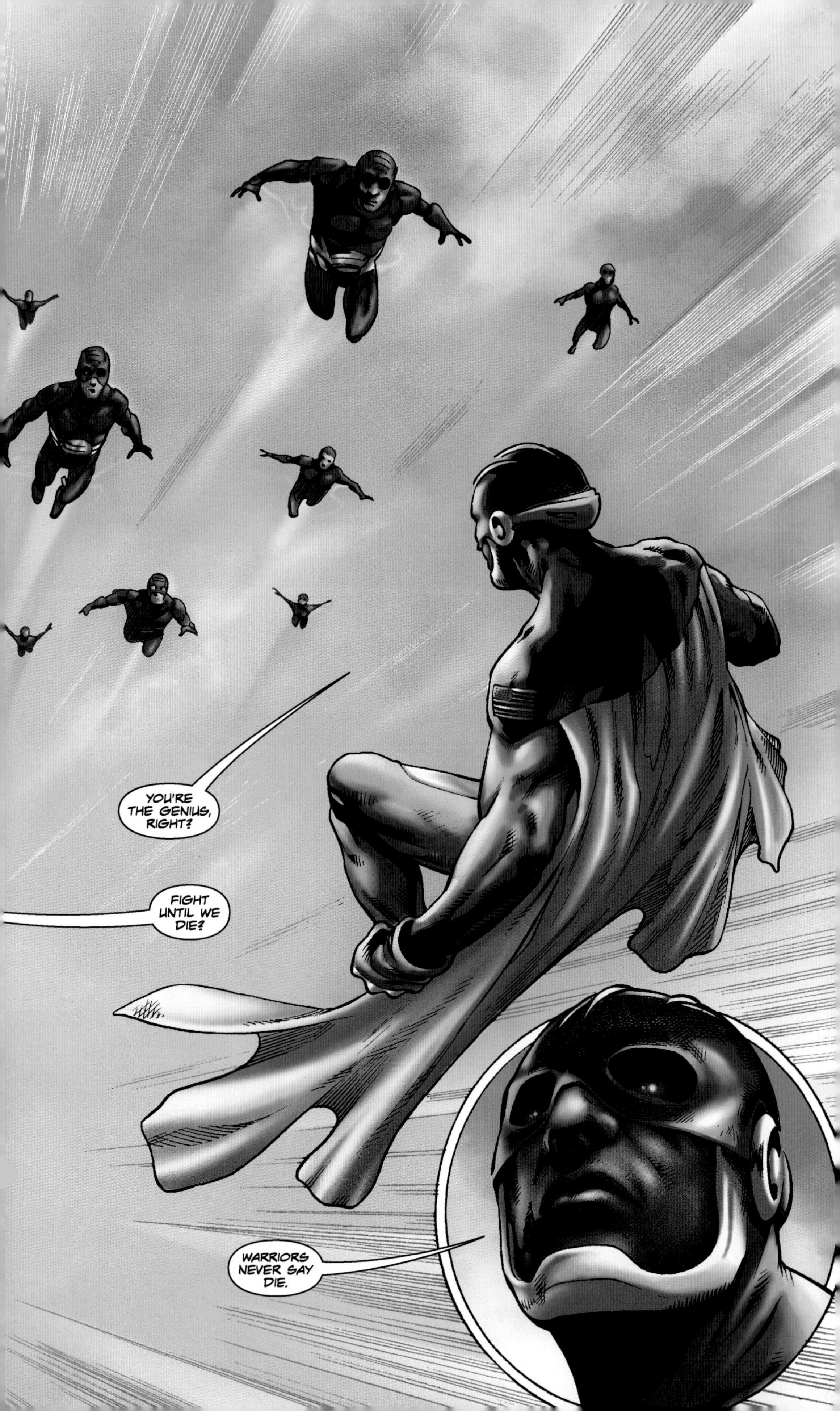

YOU'RE THE GENIUS, RIGHT?
FIGHT UNTIL WE DIE?
WARRIORS NEVER SAY DIE.

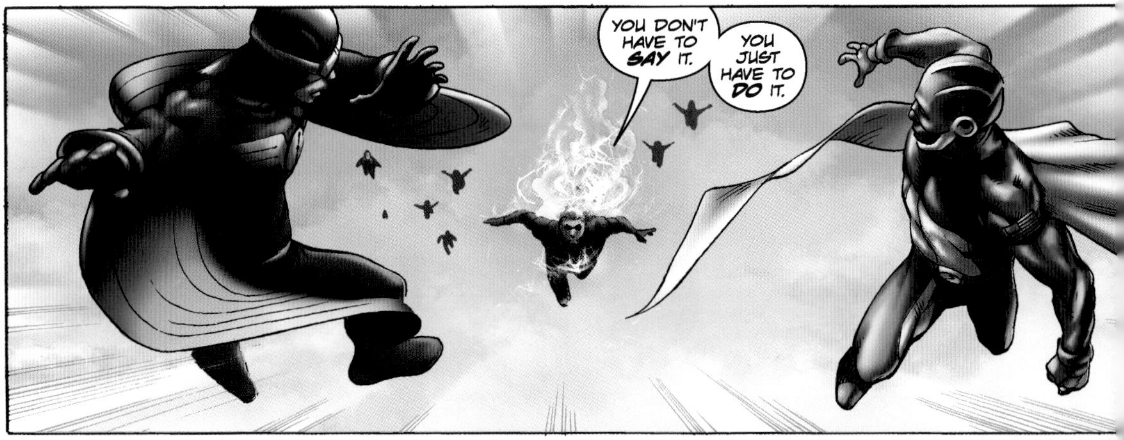
YOU DON'T HAVE TO SAY IT.
YOU JUST HAVE TO DO IT.

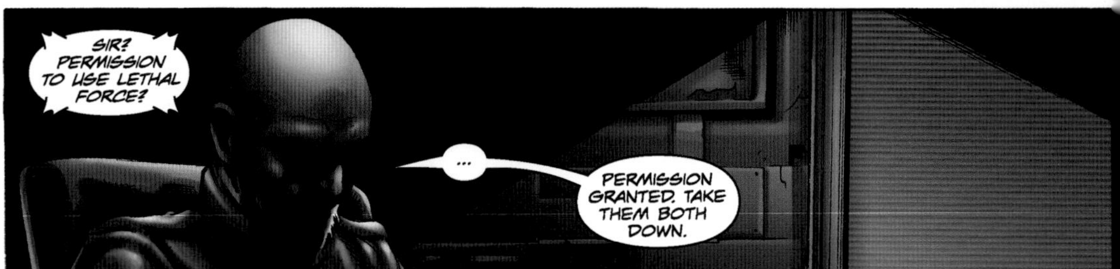
SIR? PERMISSION TO USE LETHAL FORCE?
...
PERMISSION GRANTED. TAKE THEM BOTH DOWN.

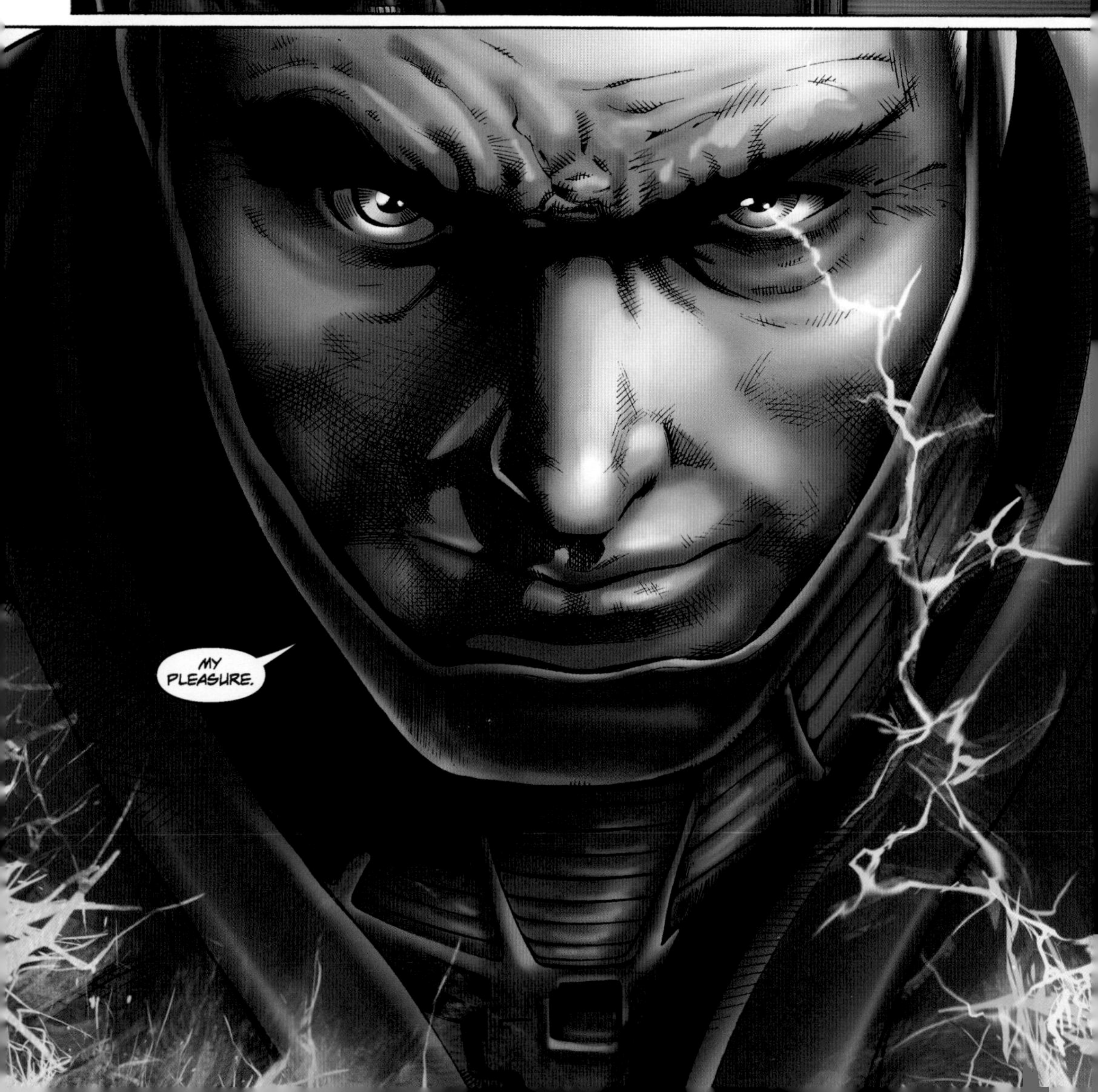
MY PLEASURE.

# CHAPTER 4

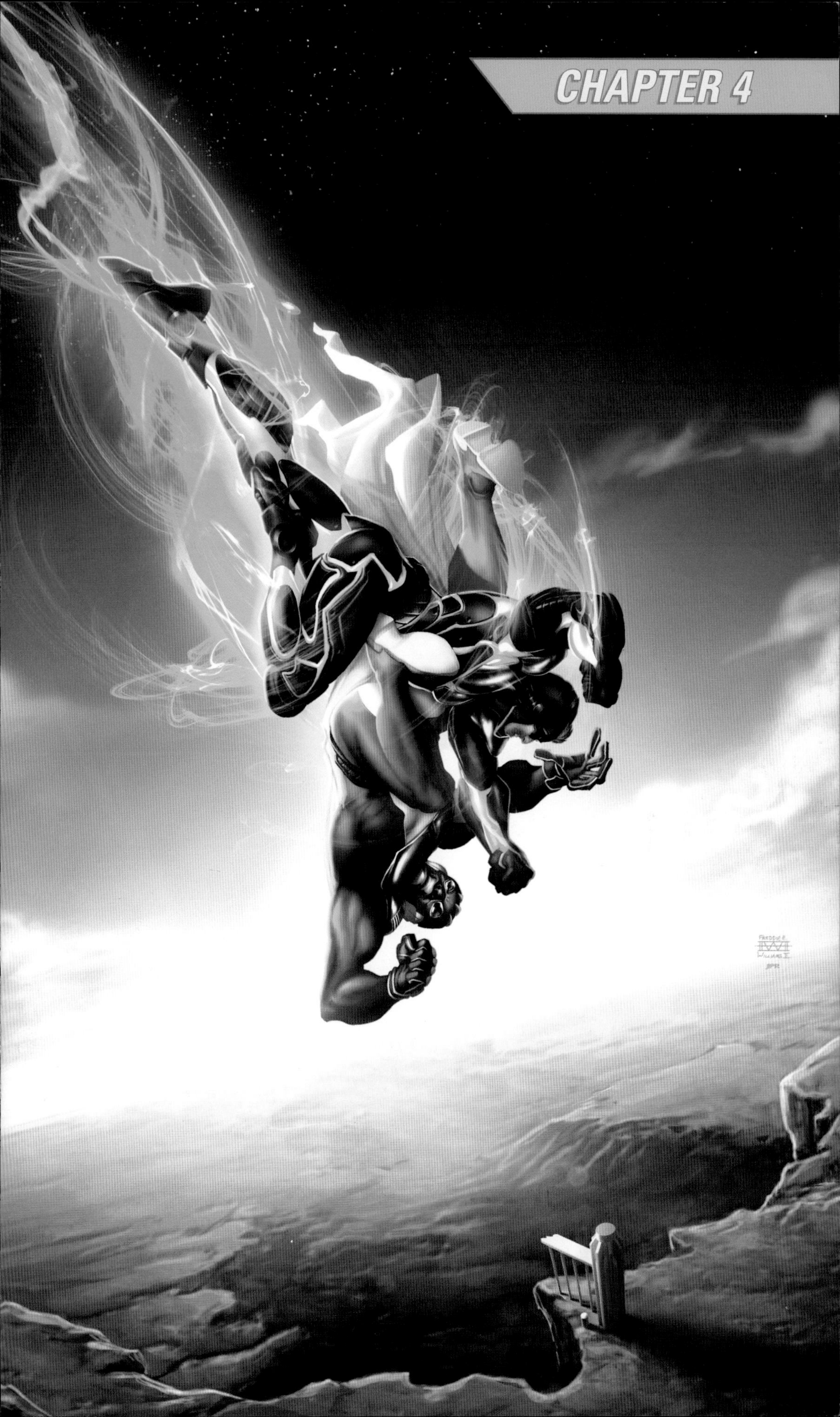

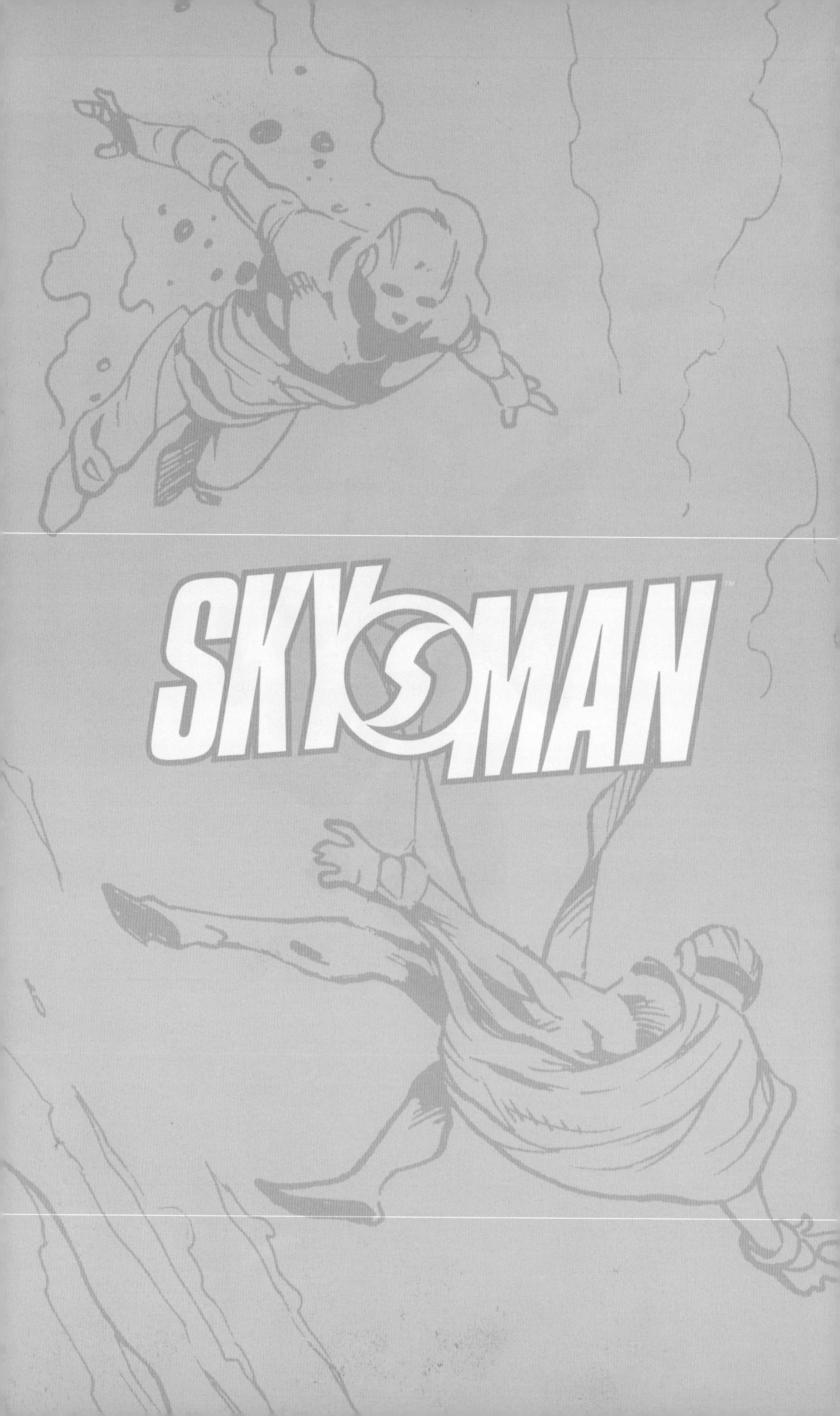
SKYMAN™

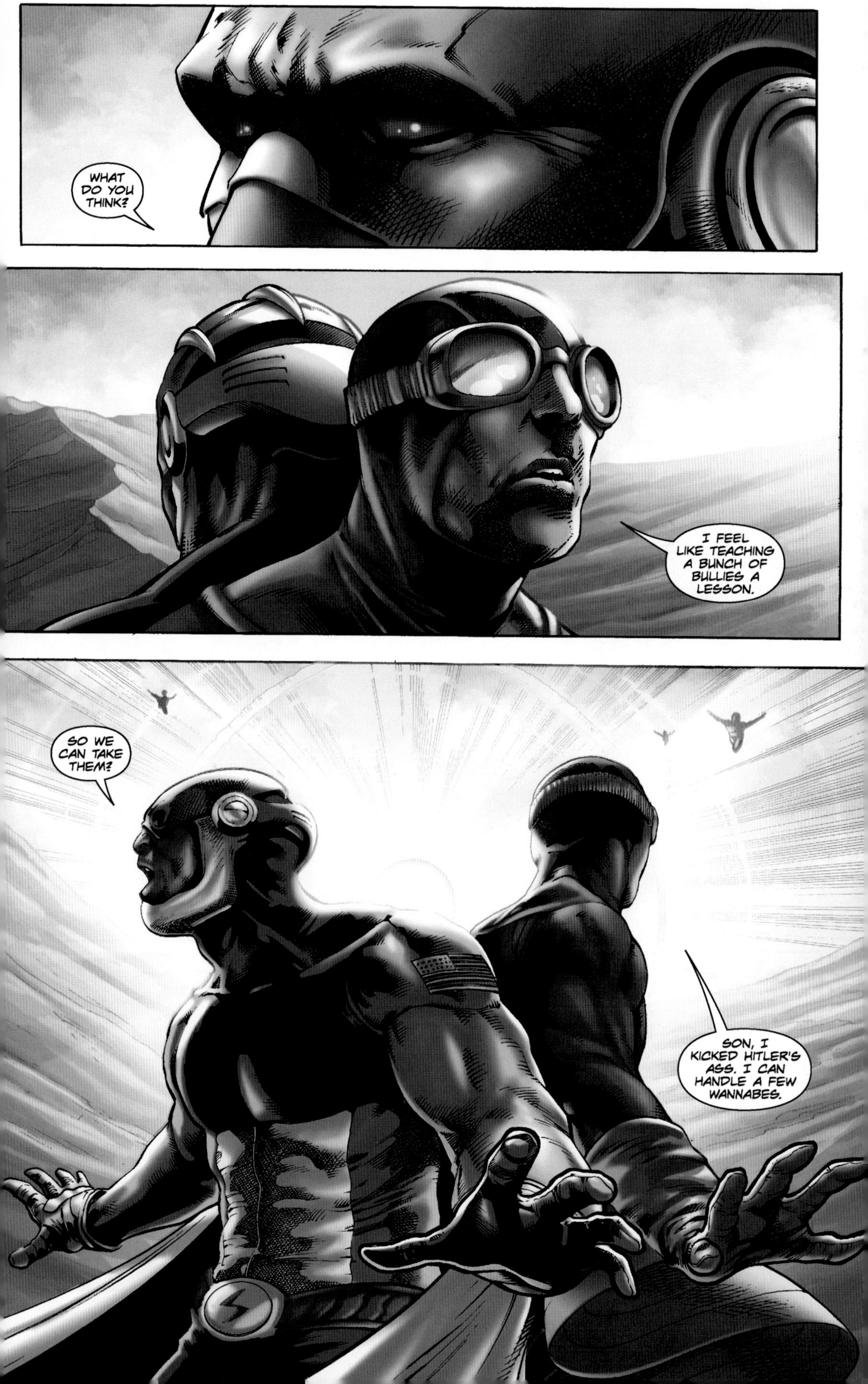
WHAT DO YOU THINK?
I FEEL LIKE TEACHING A BUNCH OF BULLIES A LESSON.
SO WE CAN TAKE THEM?
SON, I KICKED HITLER'S ASS. I CAN HANDLE A FEW WANNABES.

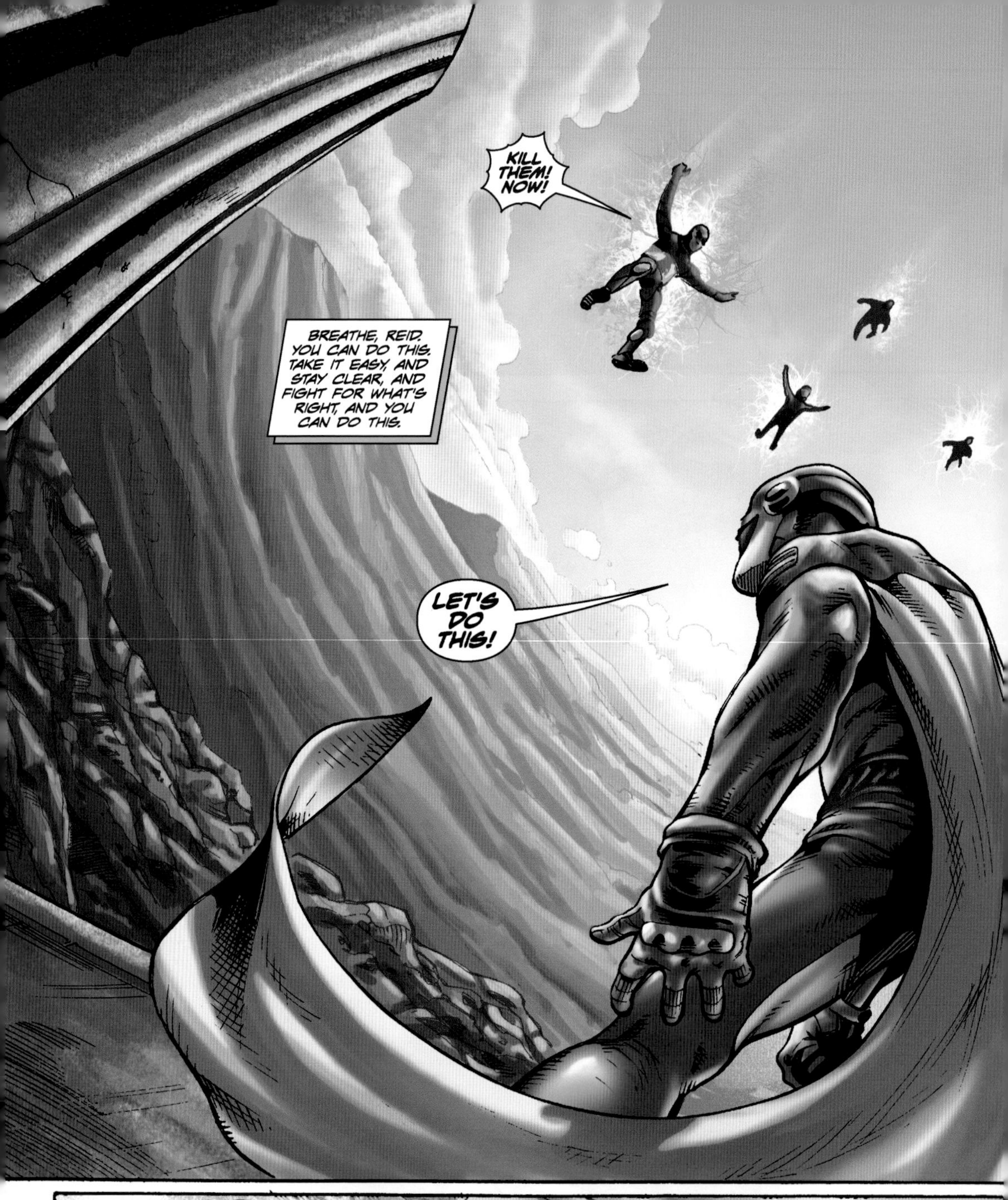
KILL THEM! NOW!
BREATHE, REID. YOU CAN DO THIS. TAKE IT EASY, AND STAY CLEAR, AND FIGHT FOR WHAT'S RIGHT, AND YOU CAN DO THIS.
LET'S DO THIS!

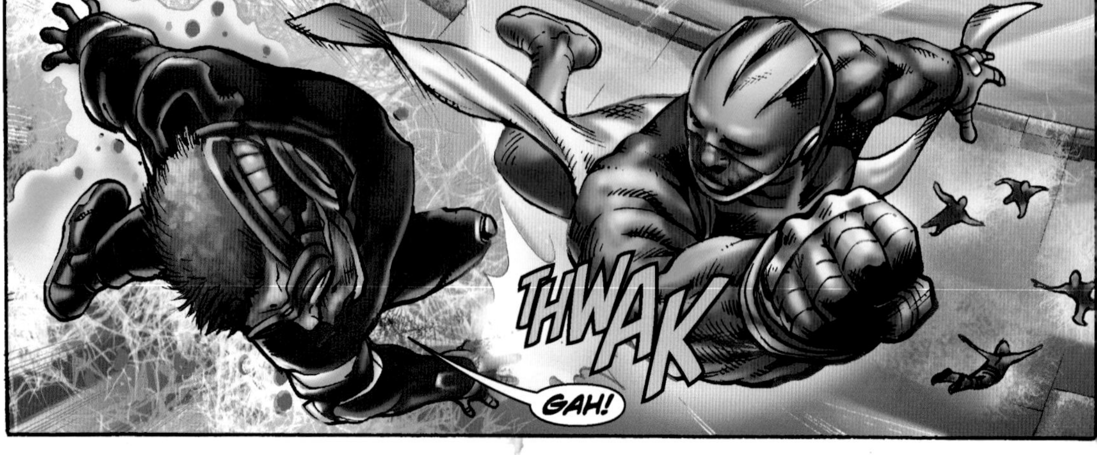
THWAK
GAH!

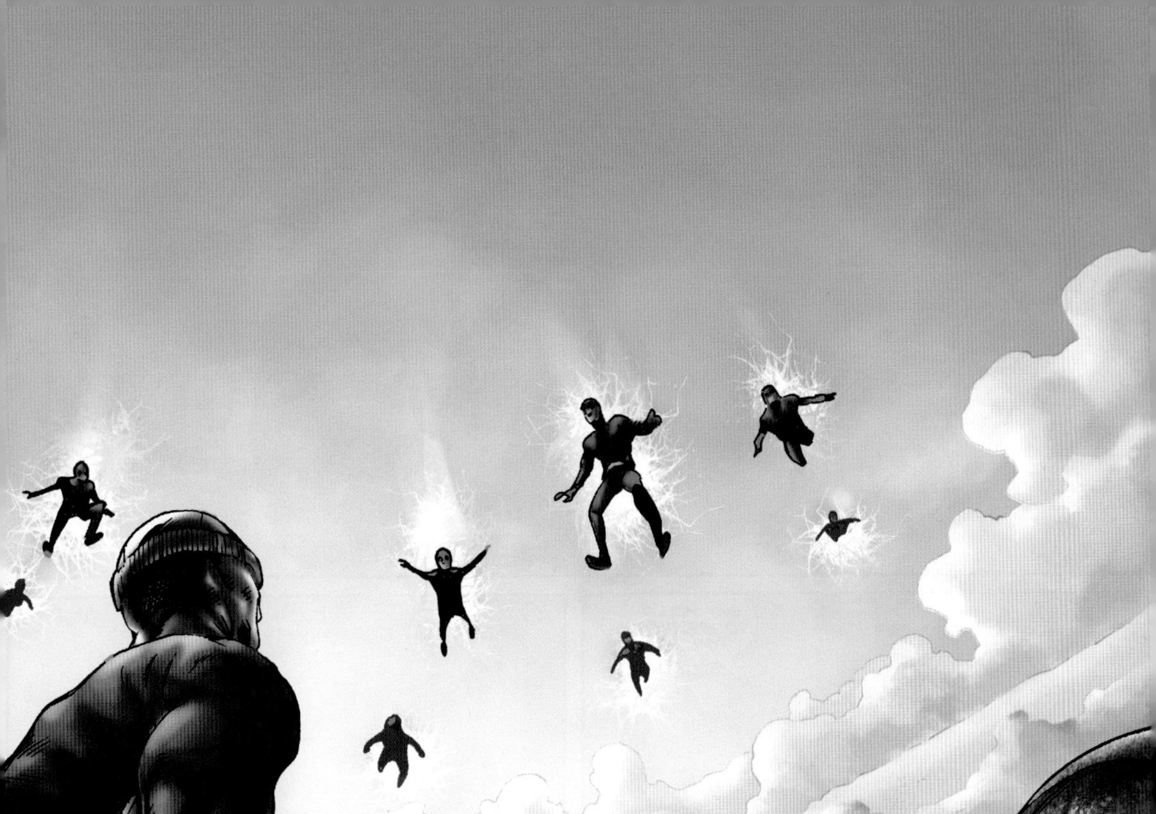

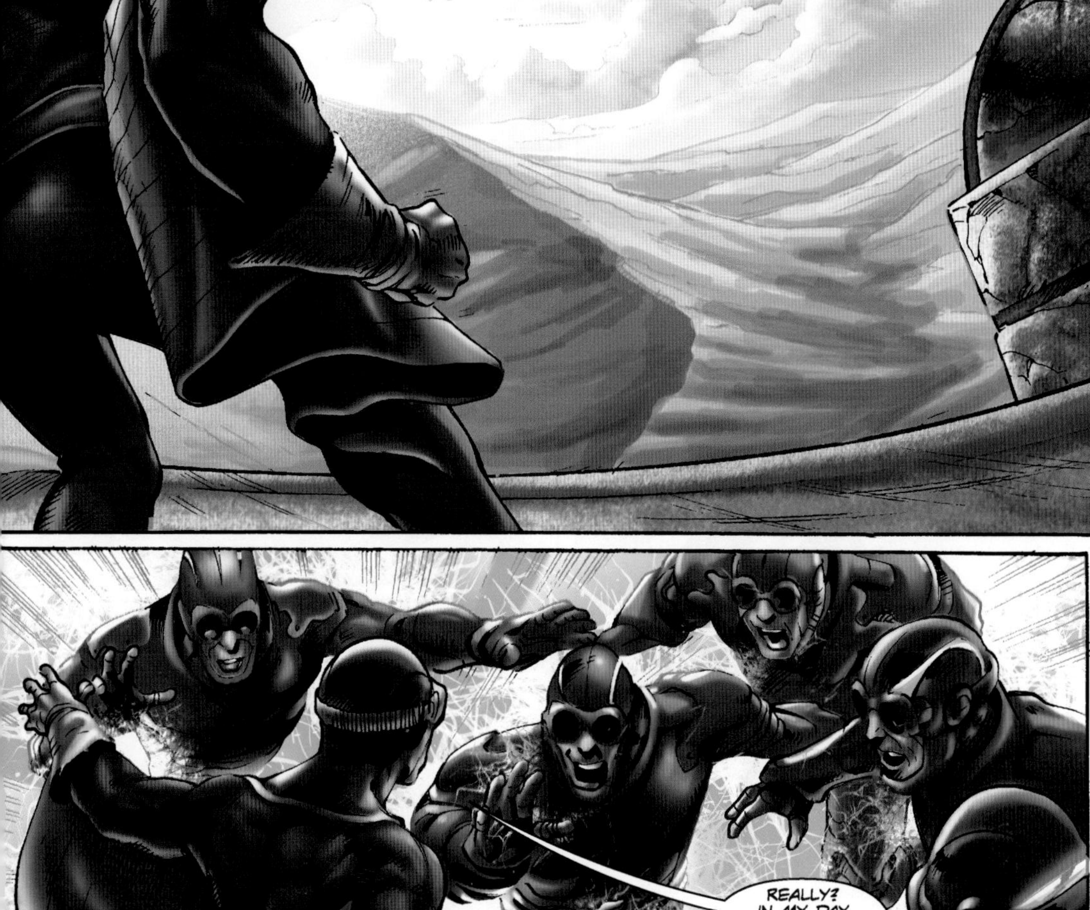
REALLY? IN MY DAY, AIRMEN ACTUALLY KNEW HOW TO FIGHT.

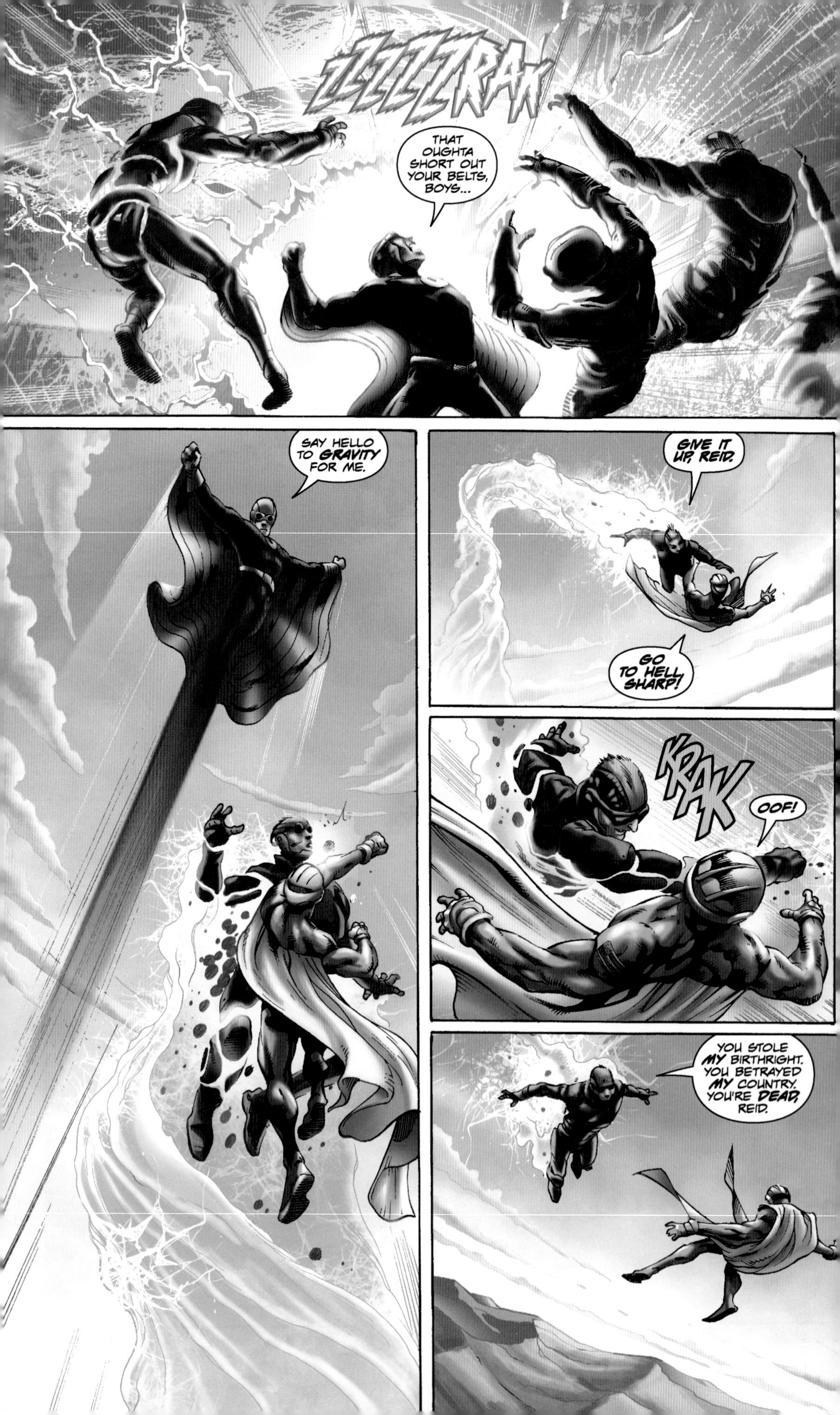
ZZZZZRAK
THAT OUGHTA SHORT OUT YOUR BELTS, BOYS...
SAY HELLO TO GRAVITY FOR ME.
GIVE IT UP, REID.
GO TO HELL, SHARP!
KRAK
OOF!
YOU STOLE MY BIRTHRIGHT. YOU BETRAYED MY COUNTRY. YOU'RE DEAD, REID.

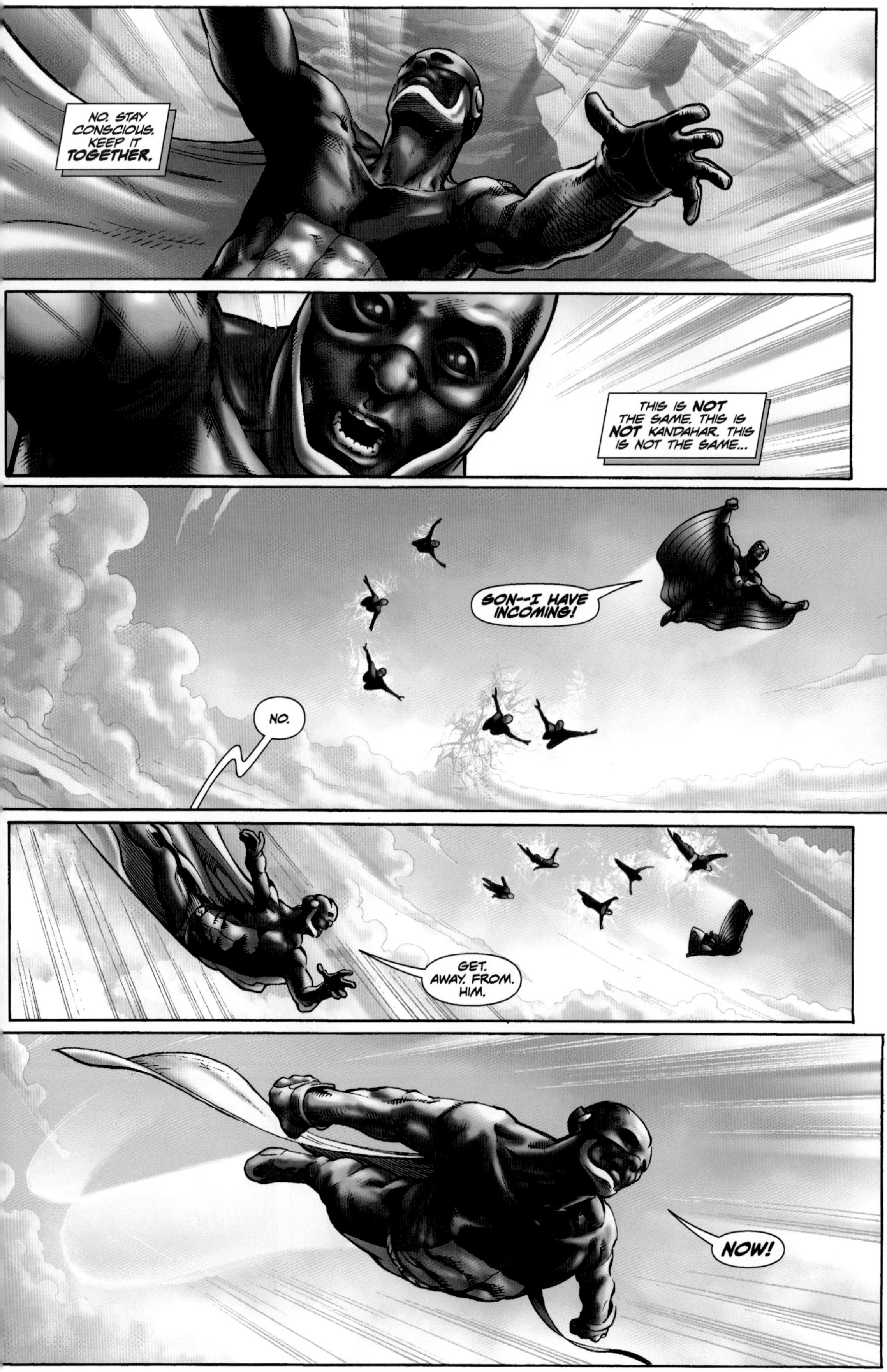
NO. STAY CONSCIOUS. KEEP IT TOGETHER.
THIS IS NOT THE SAME. THIS IS NOT KANDAHAR. THIS IS NOT THE SAME...
SON--I HAVE INCOMING!
NO.
GET. AWAY. FROM. HIM.
NOW!

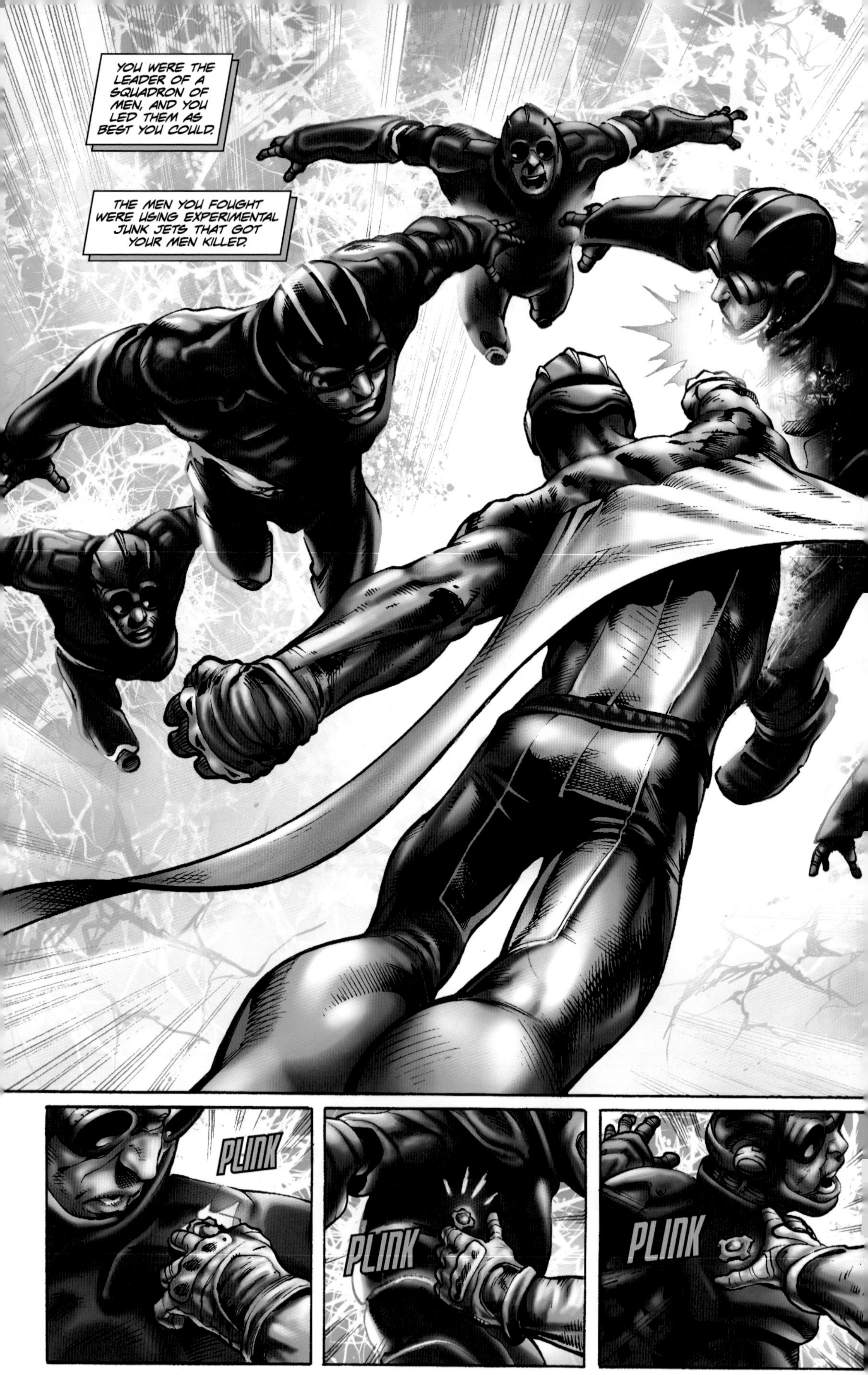
YOU WERE THE LEADER OF A SQUADRON OF MEN, AND YOU LED THEM AS BEST YOU COULD.
THE MEN YOU FOUGHT WERE USING EXPERIMENTAL JUNK JETS THAT GOT YOUR MEN KILLED.
PLINK
PLINK
PLINK

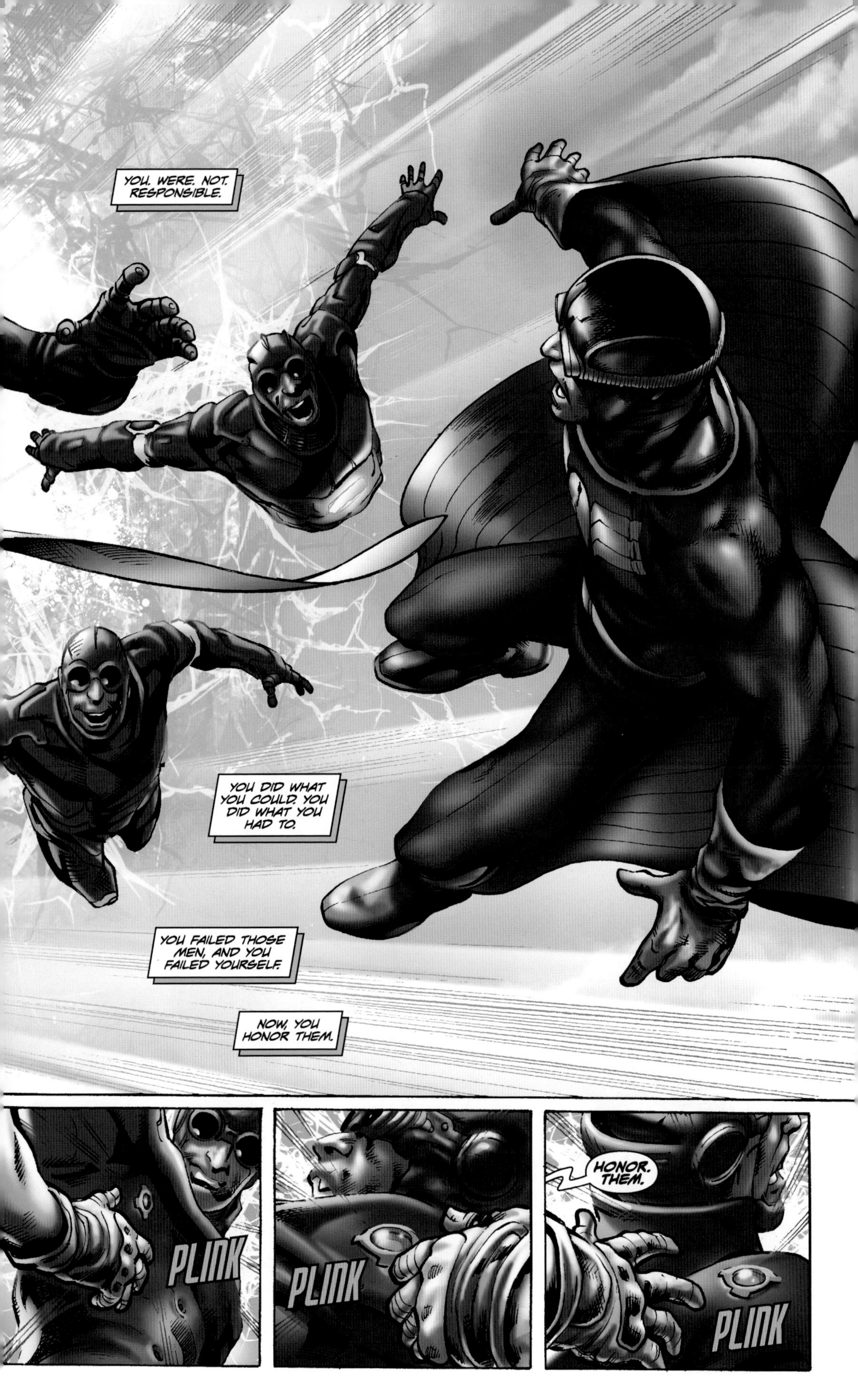

YOU. WERE. NOT. RESPONSIBLE.
YOU DID WHAT YOU COULD. YOU DID WHAT YOU HAD TO.
YOU FAILED THOSE MEN, AND YOU FAILED YOURSELF.
NOW, YOU HONOR THEM.
PLINK
PLINK
HONOR. THEM.
PLINK

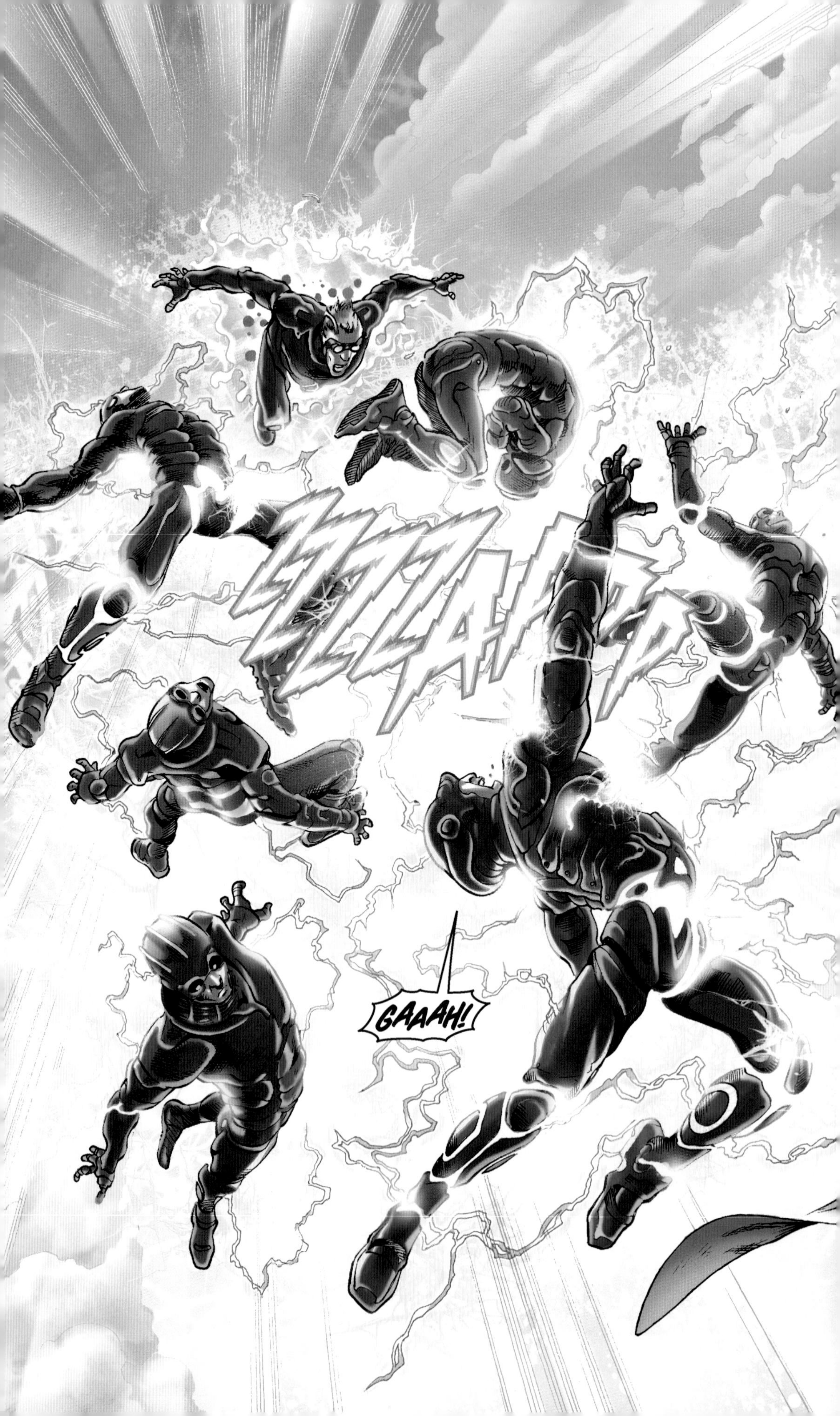
GAAAH!

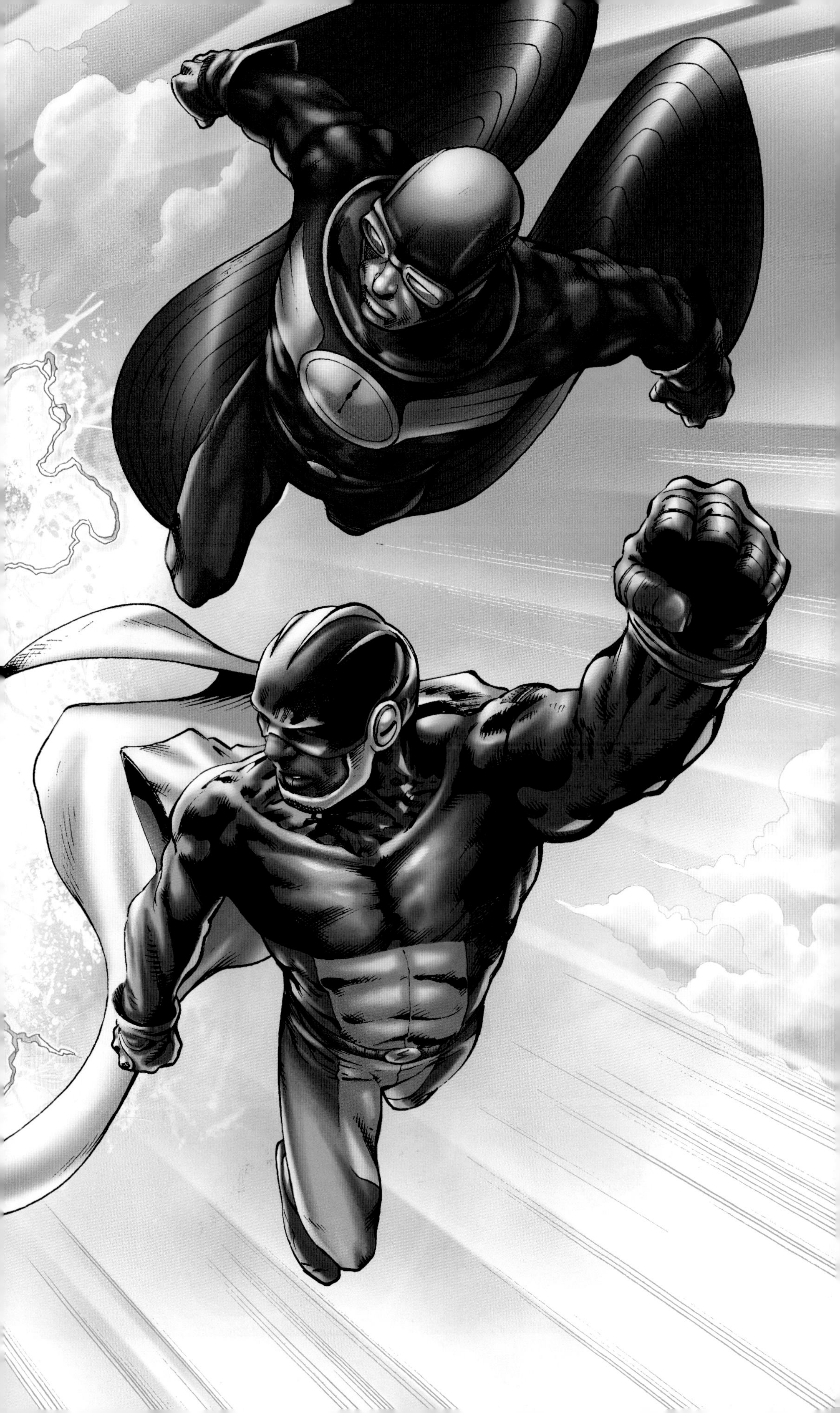

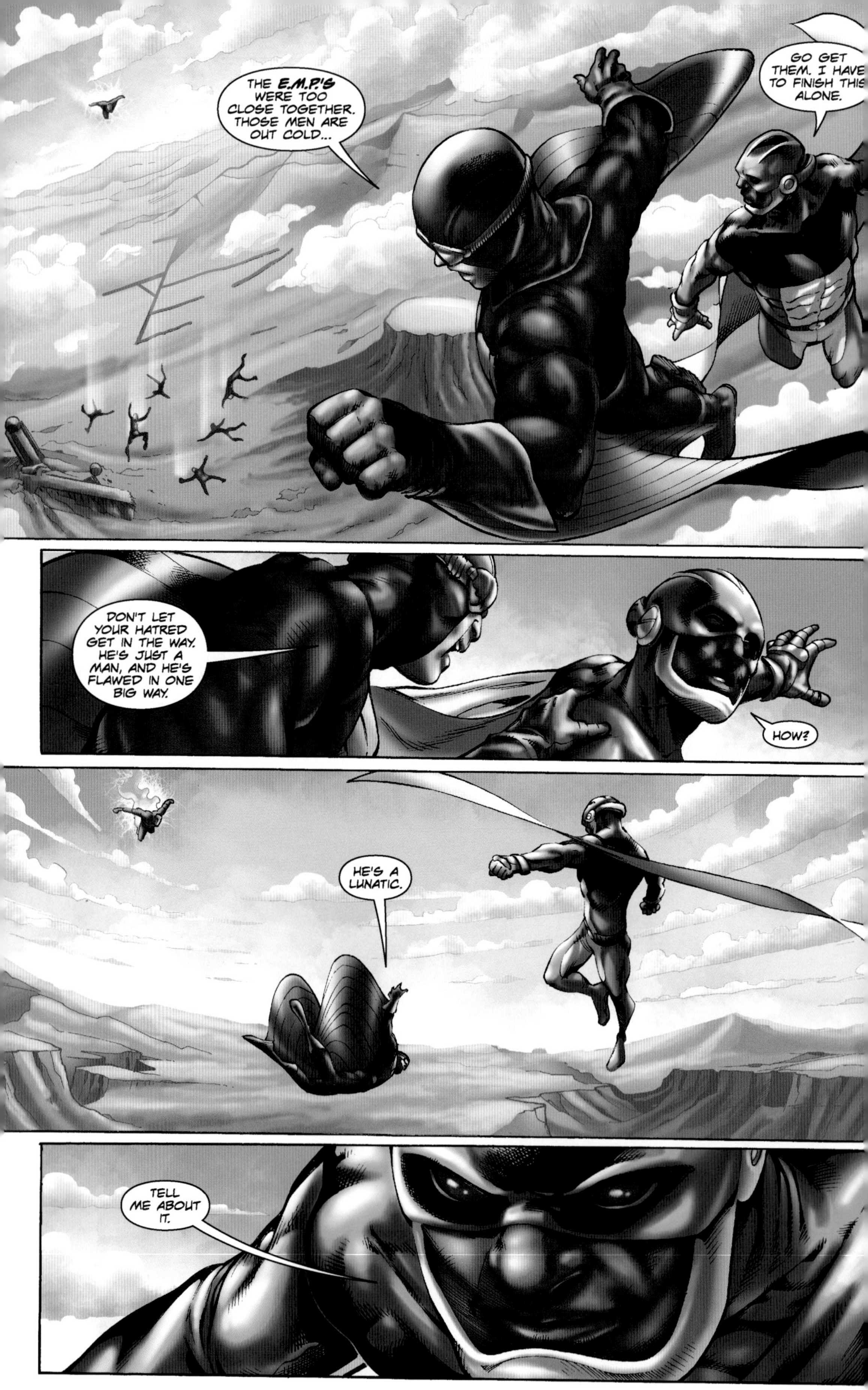
THE E.M.P.'S WERE TOO CLOSE TOGETHER. THOSE MEN ARE OUT COLD...
GO GET THEM. I HAVE TO FINISH THIS ALONE.
DON'T LET YOUR HATRED GET IN THE WAY. HE'S JUST A MAN, AND HE'S FLAWED IN ONE BIG WAY.
HOW?
HE'S A LUNATIC.
TELL ME ABOUT IT.

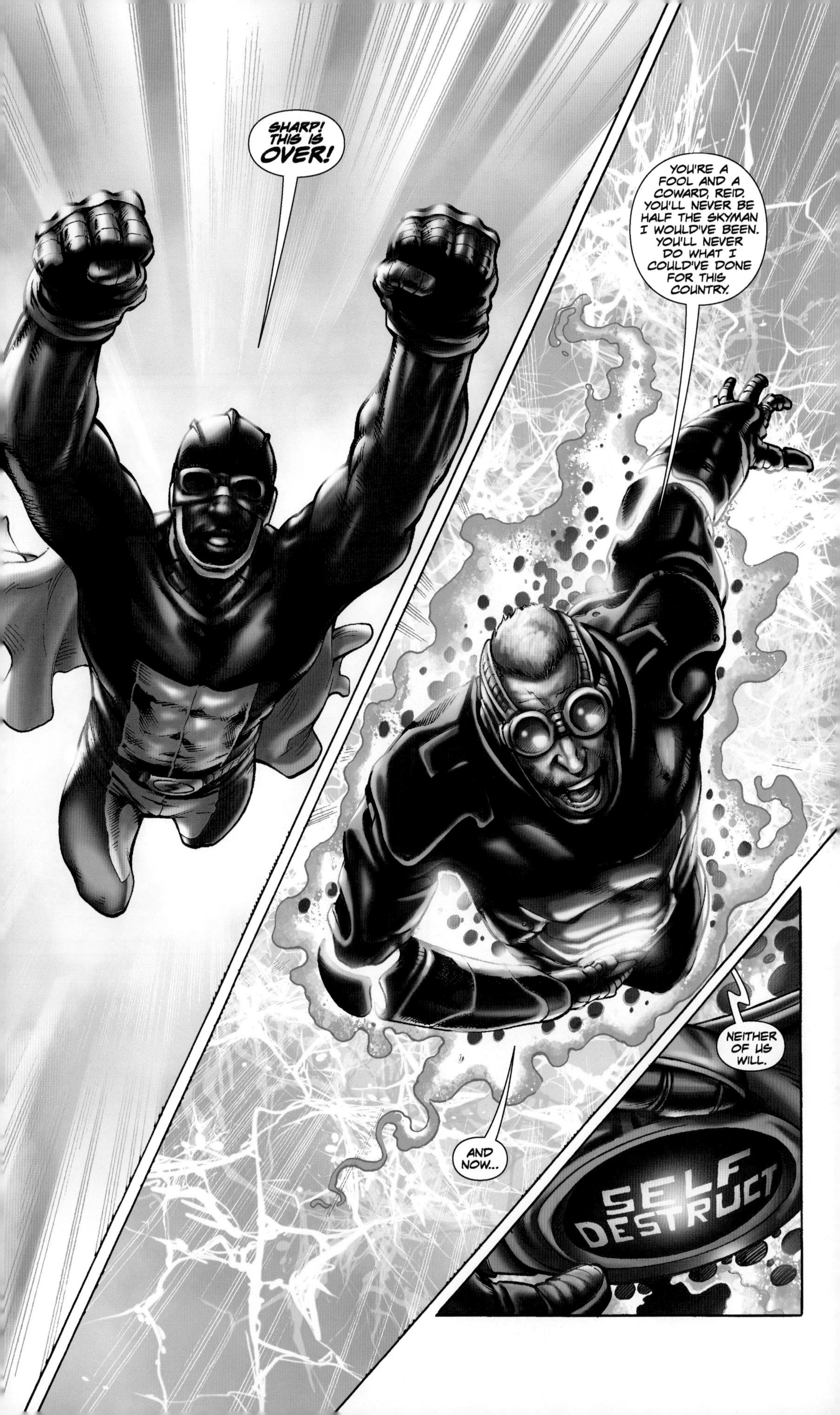
SHARP! THIS IS OVER!
YOU'RE A FOOL AND A COWARD, REID. YOU'LL NEVER BE HALF THE SKYMAN I WOULD'VE BEEN. YOU'LL NEVER DO WHAT I COULD'VE DONE FOR THIS COUNTRY.
AND NOW...
NEITHER OF US WILL.
SELF DESTRUCT

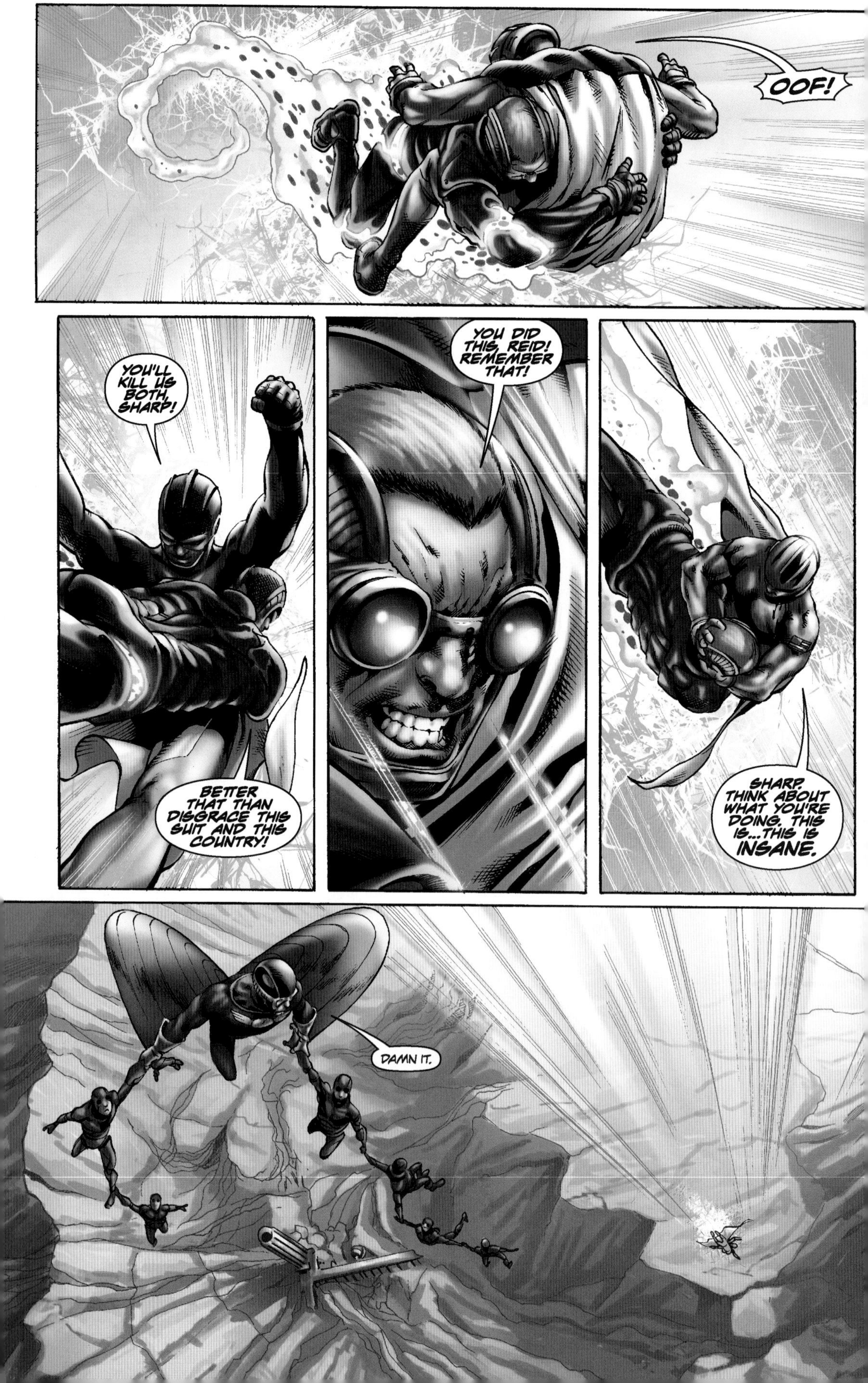
OOF!
YOU'LL KILL US BOTH, SHARP!
BETTER THAT THAN DISGRACE THIS SUIT AND THIS COUNTRY!
YOU DID THIS, REID! REMEMBER THAT!
SHARP. THINK ABOUT WHAT YOU'RE DOING. THIS IS...THIS IS INSANE.
DAMN IT.

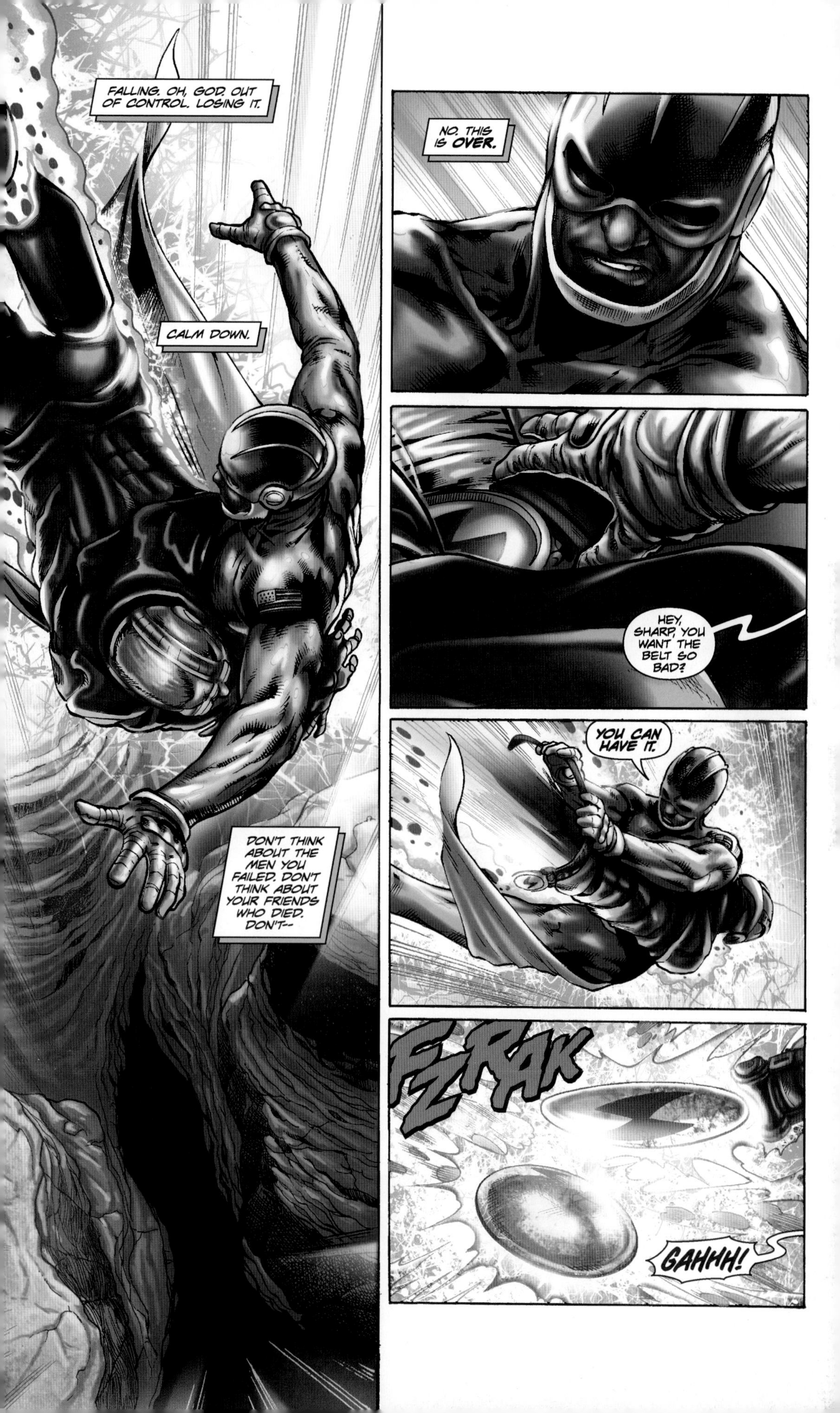
FALLING. OH, GOD. OUT OF CONTROL. LOSING IT.
CALM DOWN.
DON'T THINK ABOUT THE MEN YOU FAILED. DON'T THINK ABOUT YOUR FRIENDS WHO DIED. DON'T--
NO. THIS IS OVER.
HEY, SHARP, YOU WANT THE BELT SO BAD?
YOU CAN HAVE IT.
FZRAK
GAHHH!

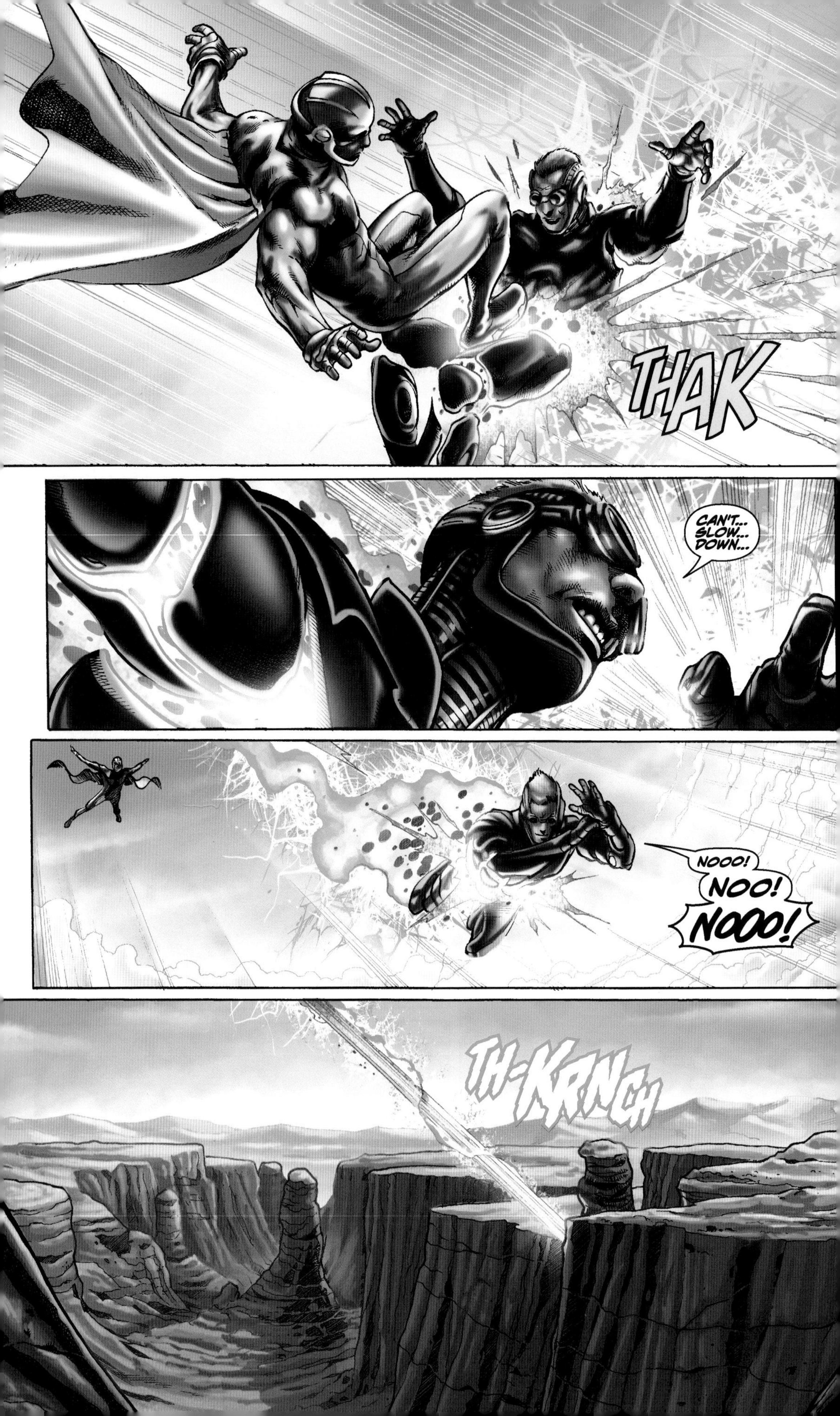
THAK
CAN'T... SLOW... DOWN...
NOOO!
NOO!
NOOO!
TH-KRNCH

SORRY, SHARP.

AT LEAST HE WENT FIRST.

I'M COMING TO JOIN YOU GUYS. MY SQUADRON. BACK TOGETHER.

I DID WHAT I COULD. I'M...

...NOT SCARED TO DIE--

NEED A LIFT?

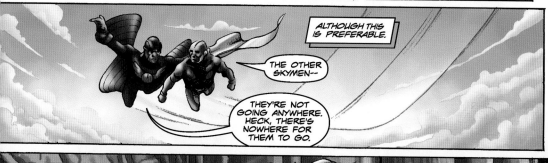

ALTHOUGH THIS IS PREFERABLE.

THE OTHER SKYMEN--

THEY'RE NOT GOING ANYWHERE. HECK, THERE'S NOWHERE FOR THEM TO GO.

AND SHARP...?

THAT WAS QUICK THINKING. THE TWO BELTS AMPLIFIED EACH OTHER--GAVE HIM MORE THRUST THAN HE COULD CONTROL.

HOW'D YOU KNOW THAT'D WORK?

I WAS ON A MISSION OVER KANDAHAR. WE WERE BEING CHASED BY THESE SOUPED-UP MIGS.

WE GOT INTO A TIGHT CORNER, AND THEY COULDN'T MANEUVER.

THEY WEREN'T DESIGNED FOR THE THRUST THEY WERE PACKING.

WHEN WE HIT THEM, THEY DIDN'T GO DOWN--THEY WENT OUT.

THE SHRAPNEL COMPROMISED OUR PLANES. MY WHOLE TEAM WENT DOWN.

I'VE BEEN BEATING MYSELF UP ABOUT IT EVER SINCE.

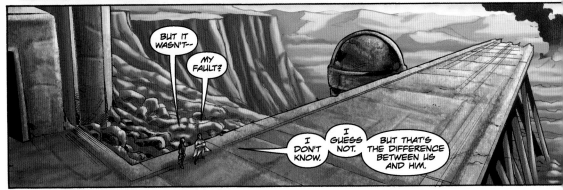

BUT IT WASN'T--

MY FAULT?

I DON'T KNOW.

I GUESS NOT.

BUT THAT'S THE DIFFERENCE BETWEEN US AND HIM.

WE CARE ABOUT WHAT HAPPENS TO OTHER PEOPLE.

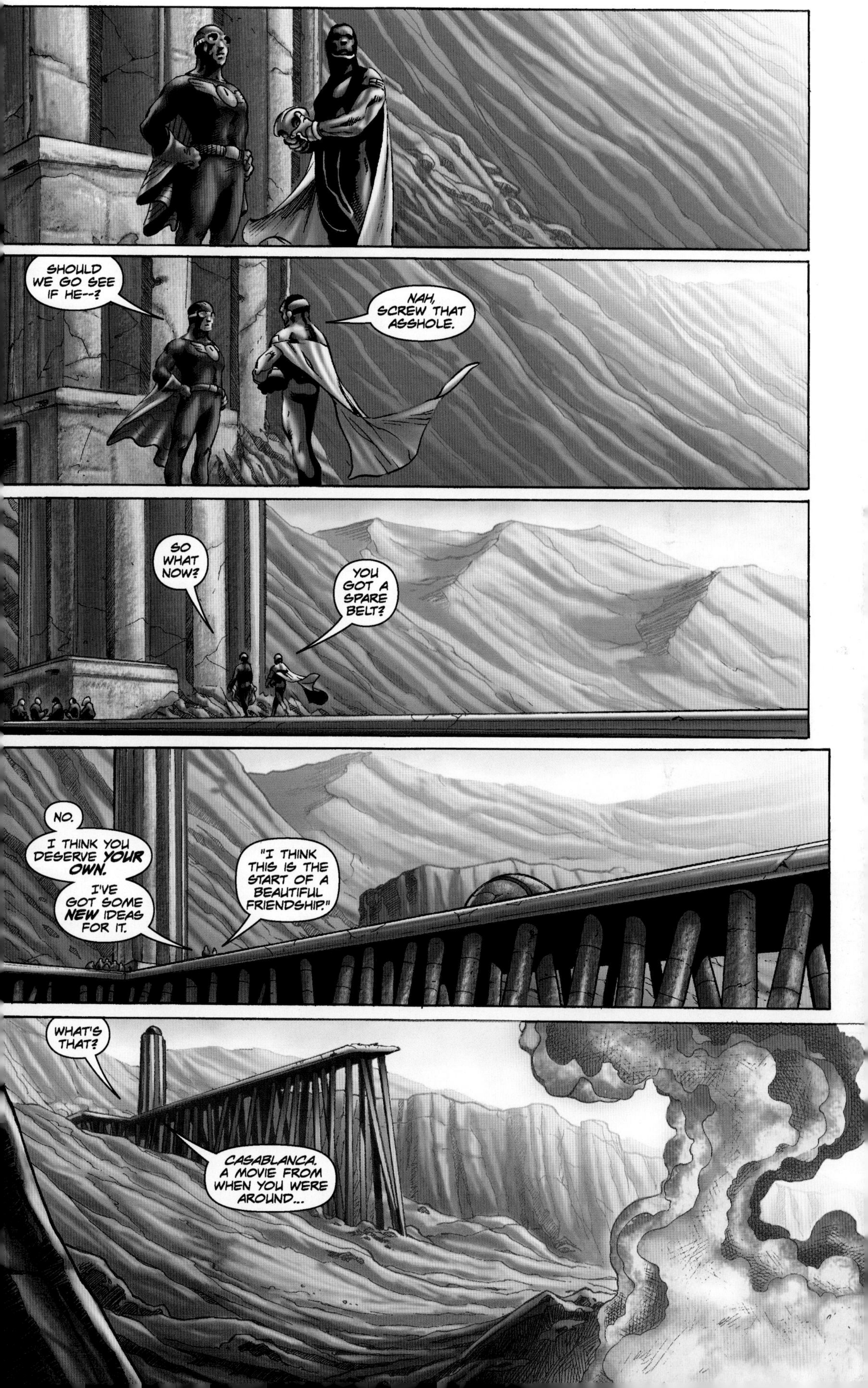
SHOULD WE GO SEE IF HE--?
NAH, SCREW THAT ASSHOLE.
SO WHAT NOW?
YOU GOT A SPARE BELT?
NO.
I THINK YOU DESERVE YOUR OWN.
I'VE GOT SOME NEW IDEAS FOR IT.
"I THINK THIS IS THE START OF A BEAUTIFUL FRIENDSHIP."
WHAT'S THAT?
CASABLANCA. A MOVIE FROM WHEN YOU WERE AROUND...

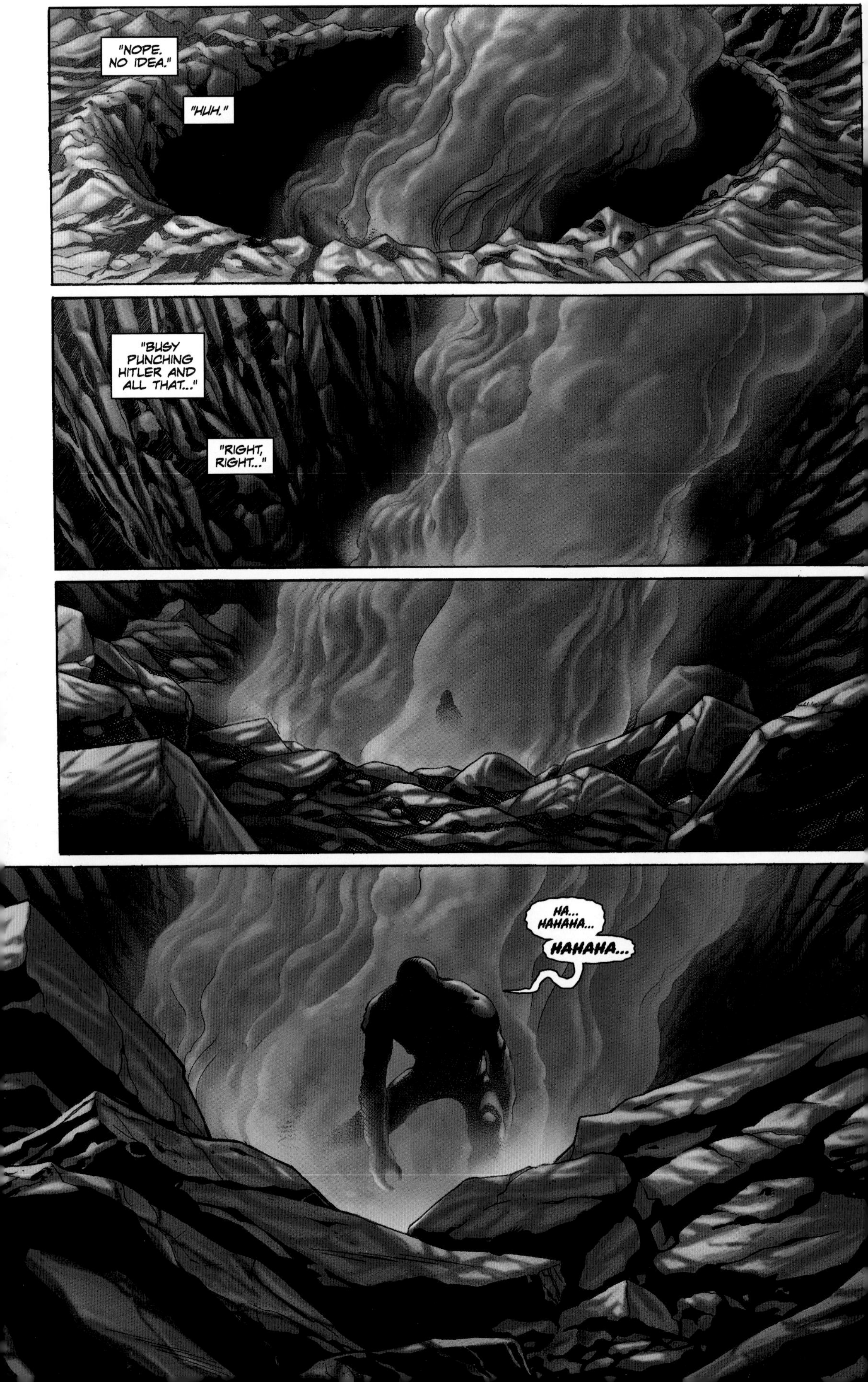
"NOPE. NO IDEA."
"HUH."
"BUSY PUNCHING HITLER AND ALL THAT..."
"RIGHT, RIGHT..."
HA... HAHAHA... HAHAHA...

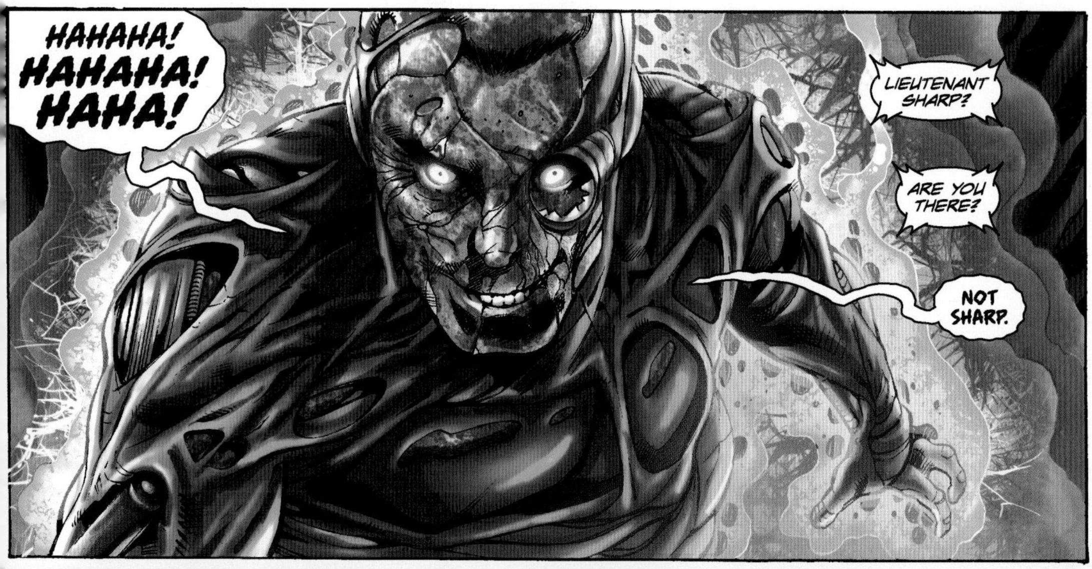
HAHAHA! HAHAHA! HAHA!
LIEUTENANT SHARP?
ARE YOU THERE?
NOT SHARP.

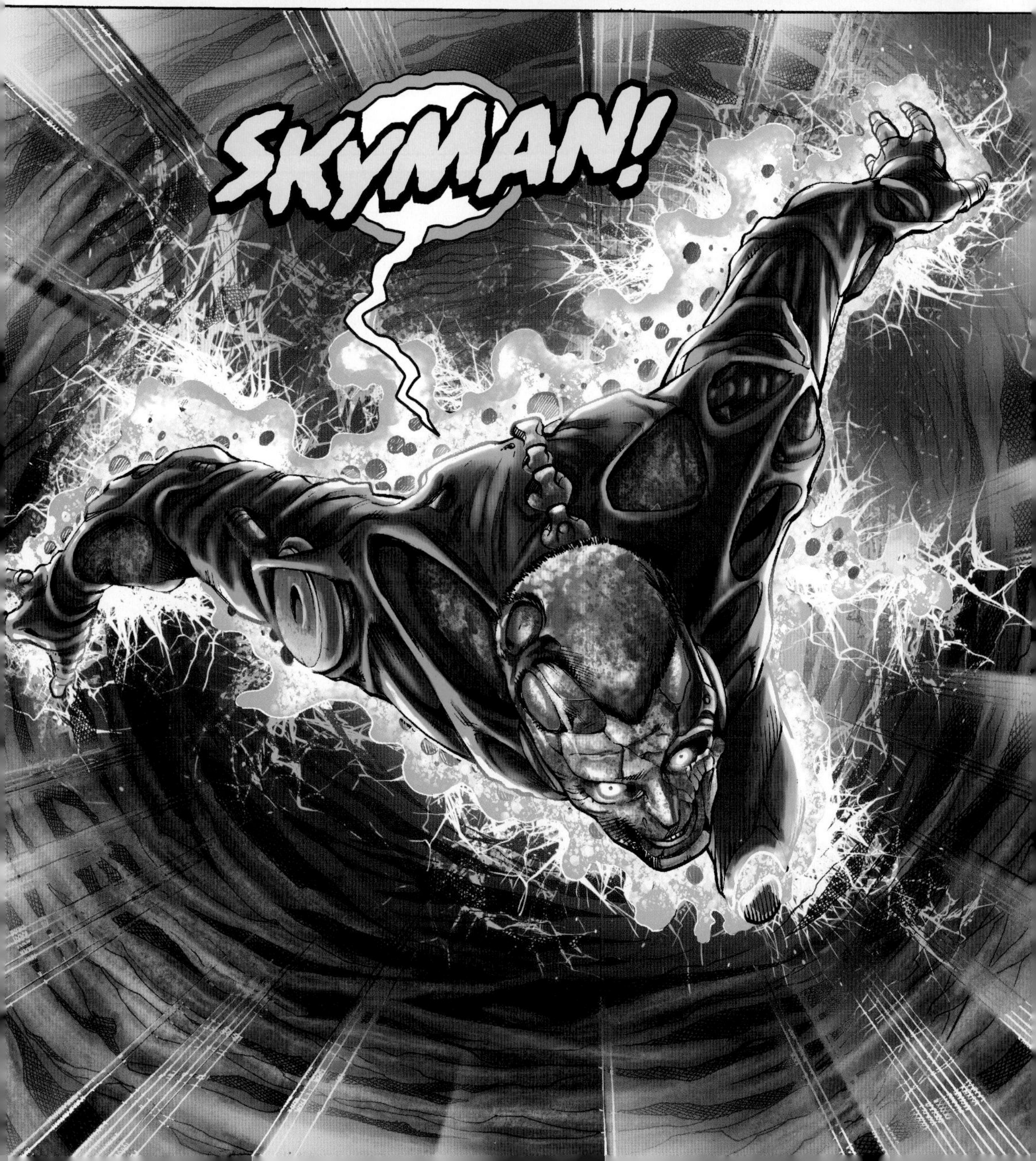
SKYMAN!

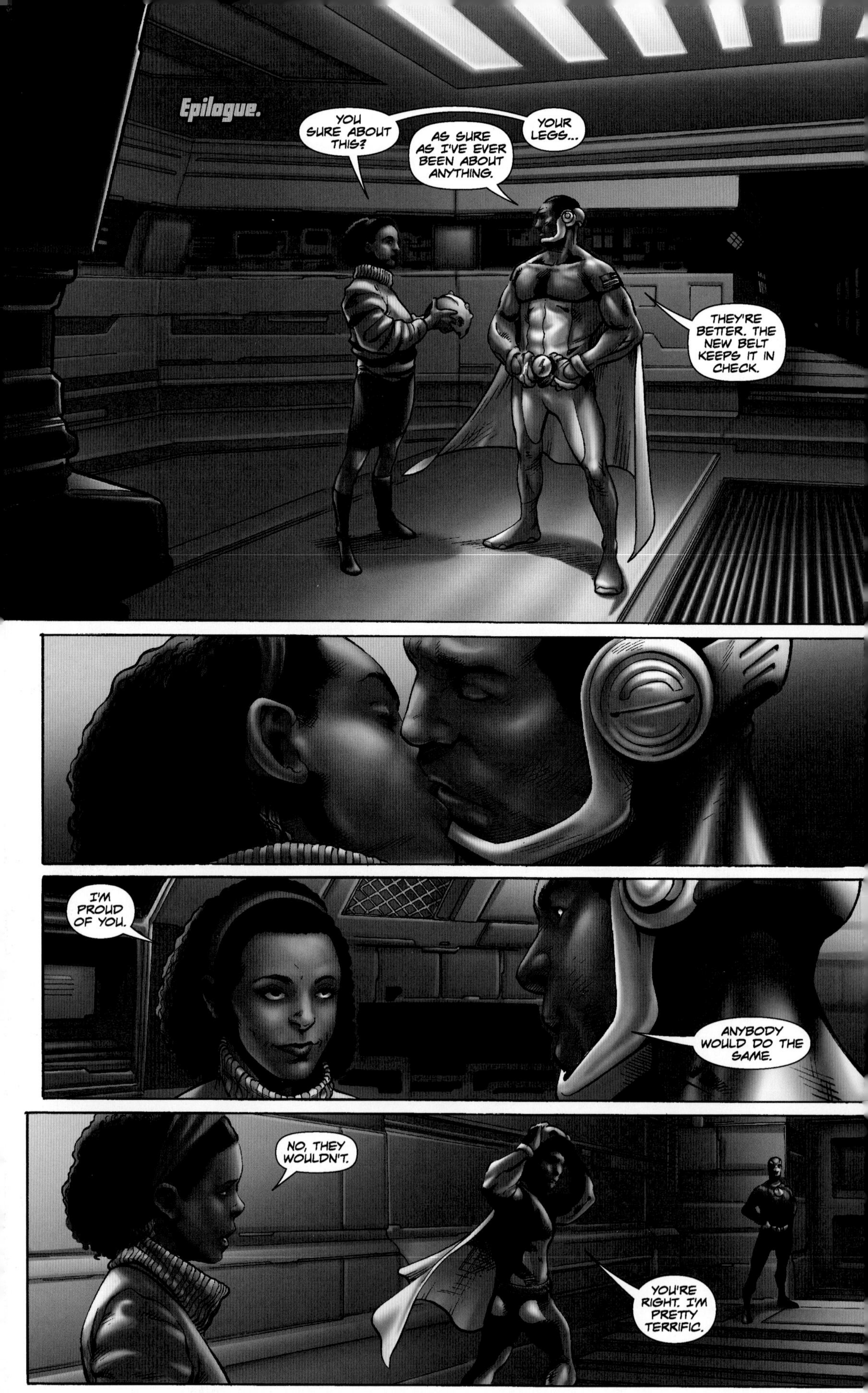
Epilogue.
YOU SURE ABOUT THIS?
AS SURE AS I'VE EVER BEEN ABOUT ANYTHING.
YOUR LEGS...
THEY'RE BETTER. THE NEW BELT KEEPS IT IN CHECK.
I'M PROUD OF YOU.
ANYBODY WOULD DO THE SAME.
NO, THEY WOULDN'T.
YOU'RE RIGHT. I'M PRETTY TERRIFIC.

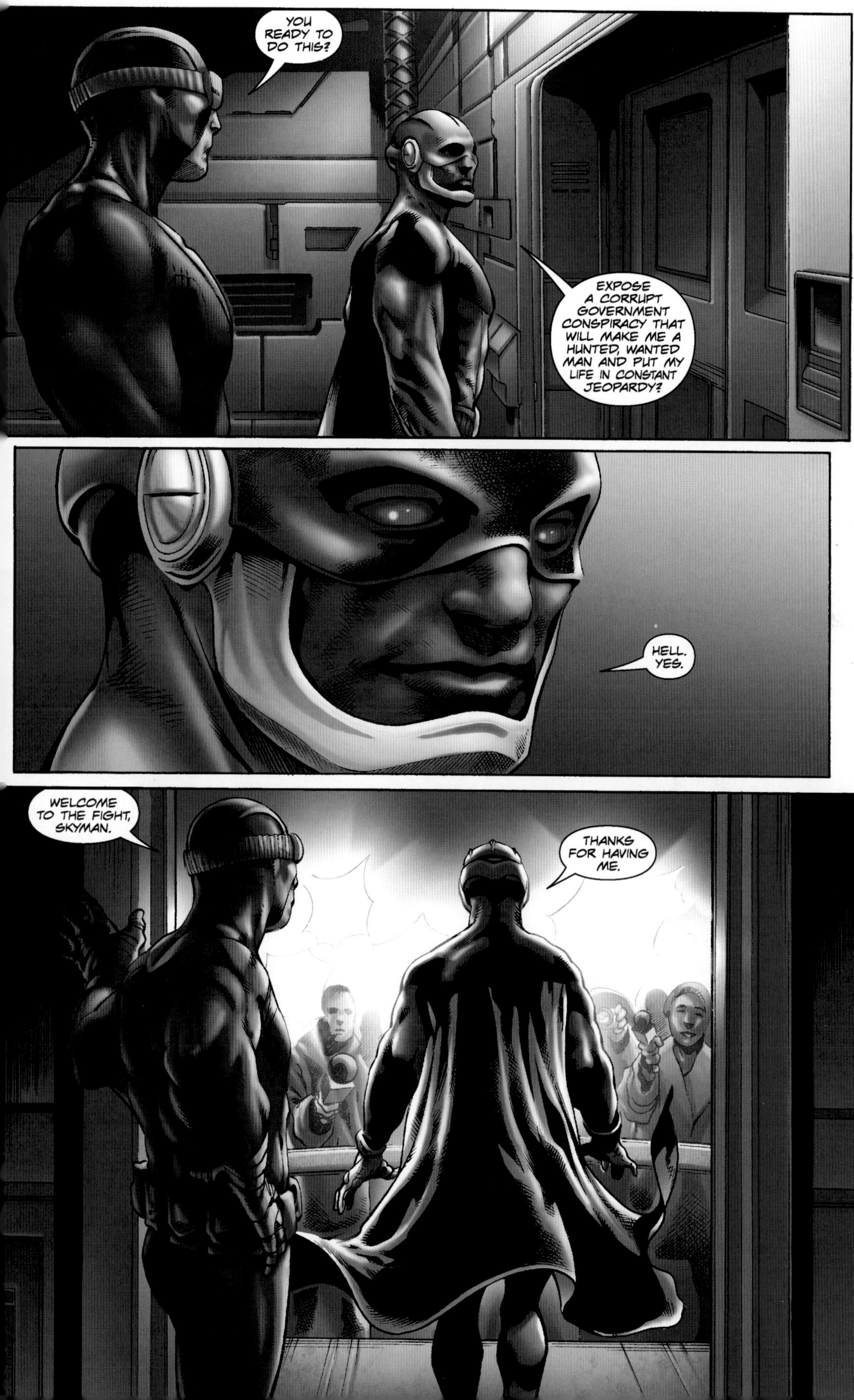
YOU READY TO DO THIS?
EXPOSE A CORRUPT GOVERNMENT CONSPIRACY THAT WILL MAKE ME A HUNTED, WANTED MAN AND PUT MY LIFE IN CONSTANT JEOPARDY?
HELL. YES.
WELCOME TO THE FIGHT, SKYMAN.
THANKS FOR HAVING ME.

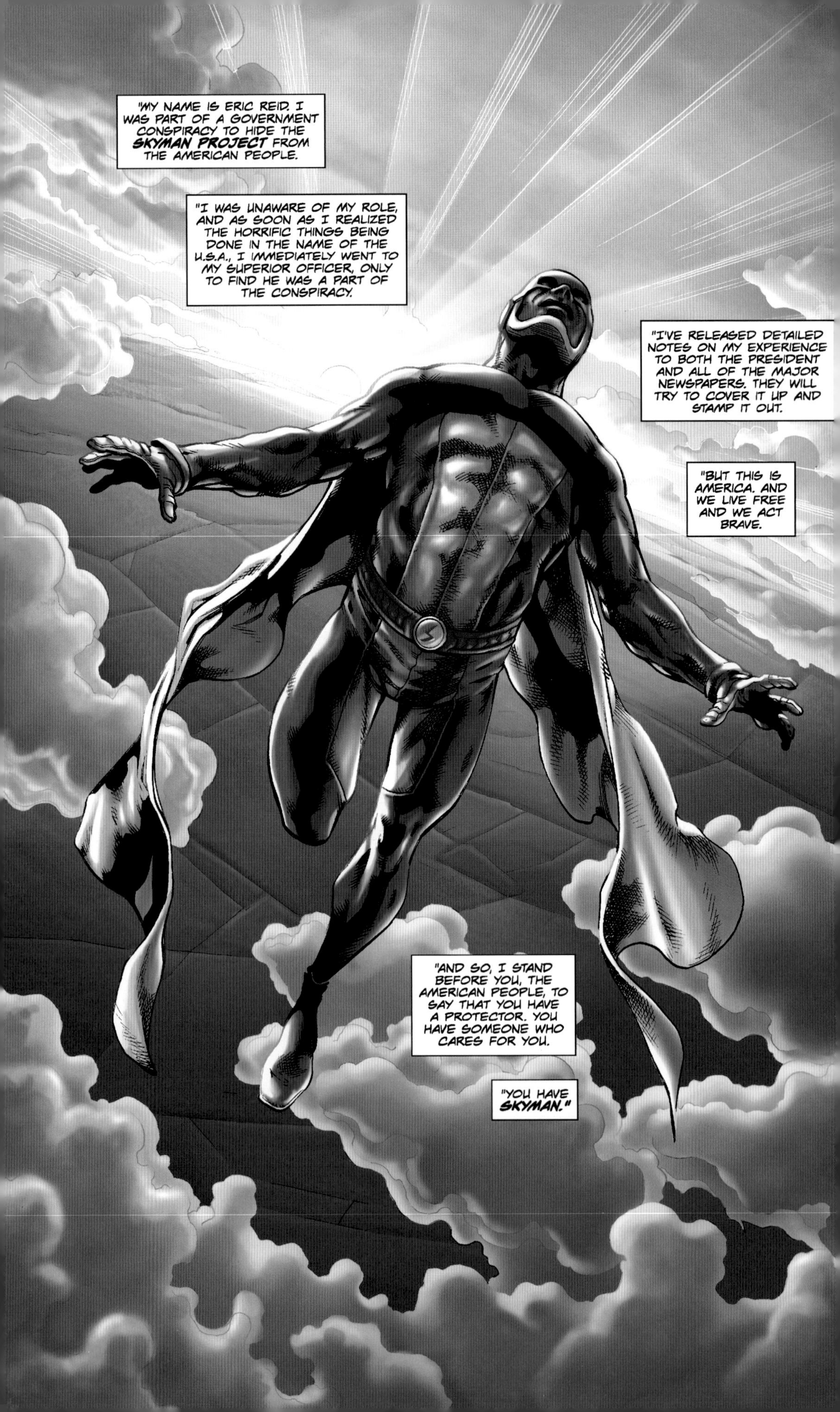
"MY NAME IS ERIC REID. I WAS PART OF A GOVERNMENT CONSPIRACY TO HIDE THE **SKYMAN PROJECT** FROM THE AMERICAN PEOPLE.
"I WAS UNAWARE OF MY ROLE, AND AS SOON AS I REALIZED THE HORRIFIC THINGS BEING DONE IN THE NAME OF THE U.S.A., I IMMEDIATELY WENT TO MY SUPERIOR OFFICER, ONLY TO FIND HE WAS A PART OF THE CONSPIRACY.
"I'VE RELEASED DETAILED NOTES ON MY EXPERIENCE TO BOTH THE PRESIDENT AND ALL OF THE MAJOR NEWSPAPERS. THEY WILL TRY TO COVER IT UP AND STAMP IT OUT.
"BUT THIS IS AMERICA. AND WE LIVE FREE AND WE ACT BRAVE.
"AND SO, I STAND BEFORE YOU, THE AMERICAN PEOPLE, TO SAY THAT YOU HAVE A PROTECTOR. YOU HAVE SOMEONE WHO CARES FOR YOU.
"YOU HAVE **SKYMAN.**"

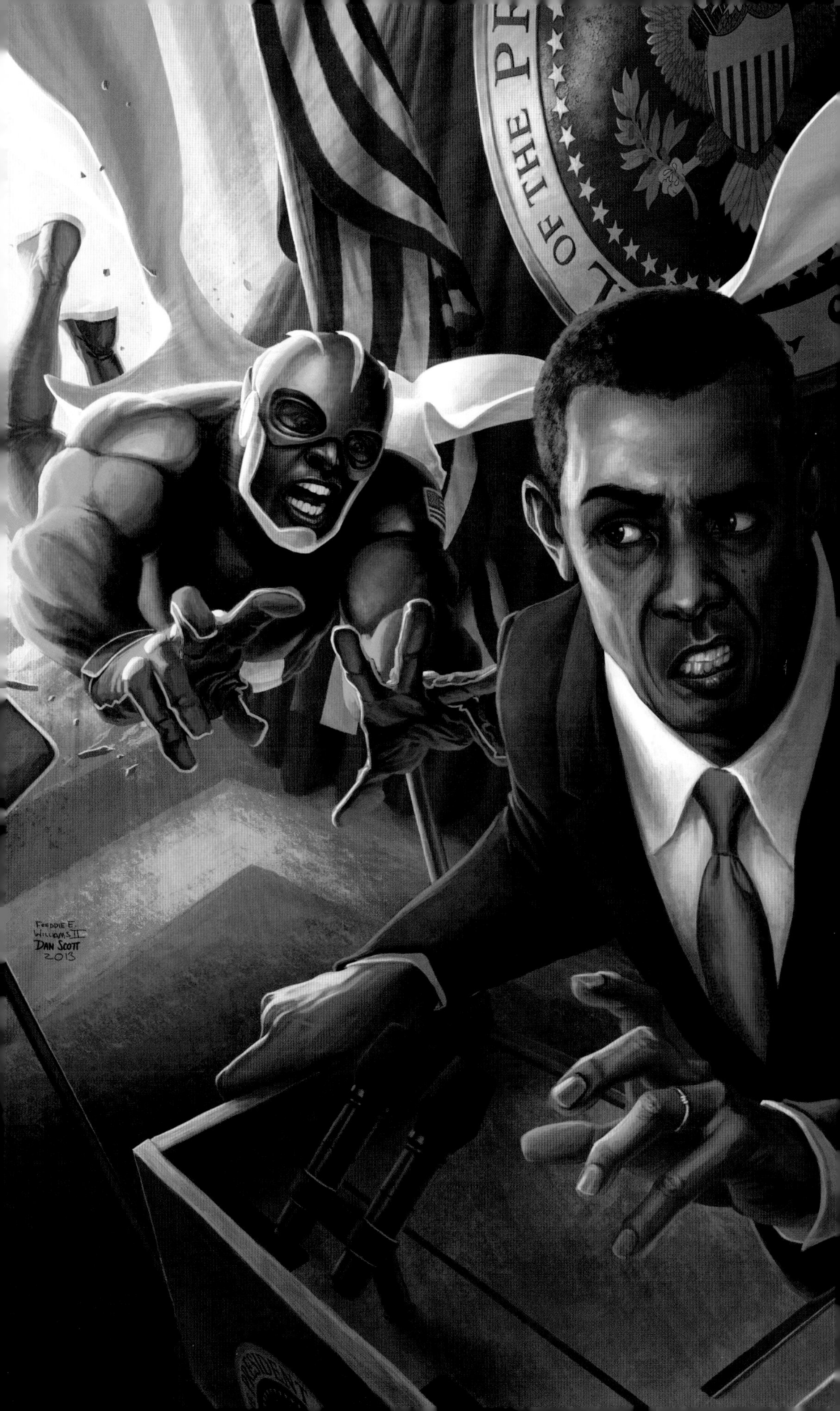
FREDDIE E. WILLIAMS II
DAN SCOTT
2013

# SKYMAN™

## SKETCHBOOK

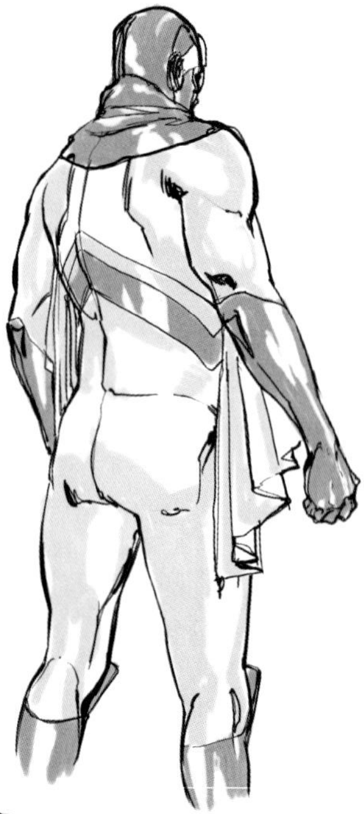

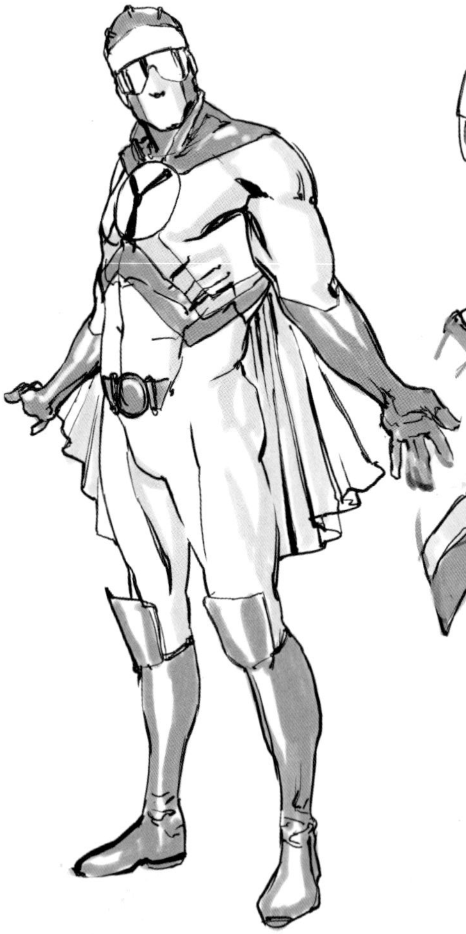

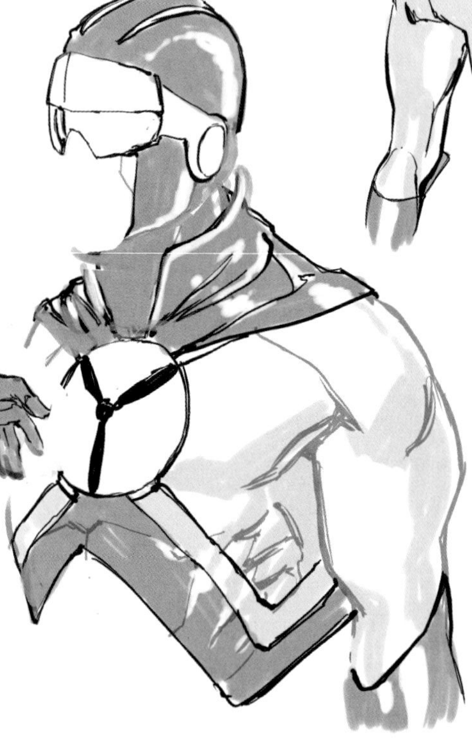

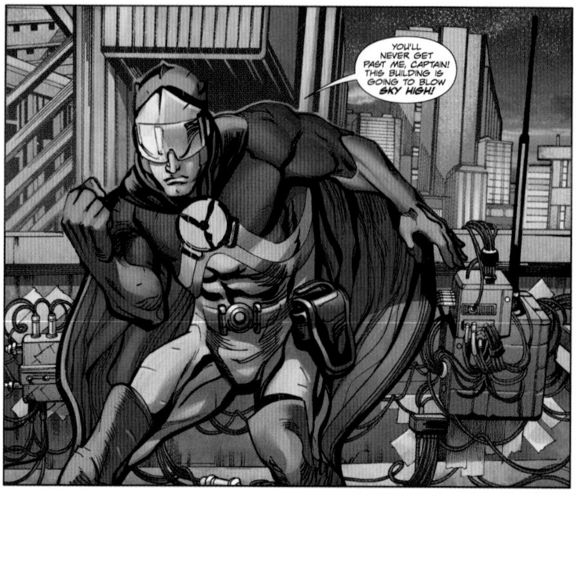
YOU'LL NEVER GET PAST ME, CAPTAIN! THIS BUILDING IS GOING TO BLOW *SKY HIGH!*

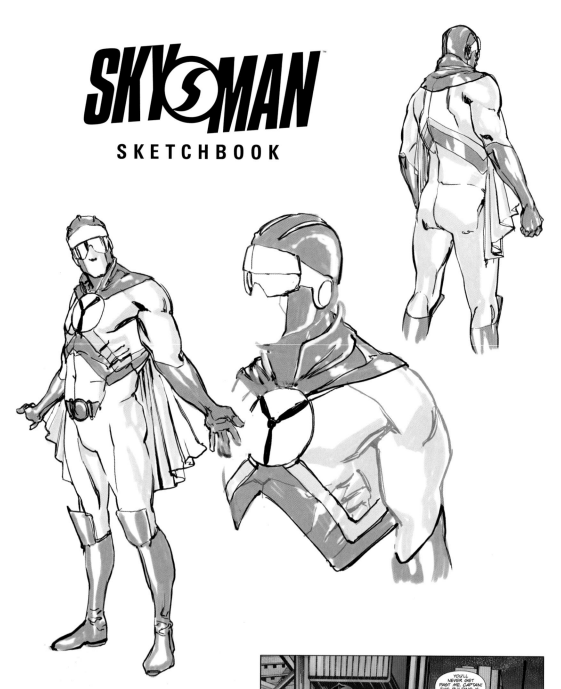

Originally appearing as an antagonist in *Captain Midnight* #4 and #5, the disgraced Skyman who appears in the first pages of this volume wore the original Golden Age Skyman costume, updated by artist Eduardo Francisco (above). And when Eric Reid became a new face for the Skyman Program in this series, a new look was needed to showcase the change in direction for this character. Artist Manuel Garcia worked with writer Joshua Hale Fialkov and the Dark Horse editorial team to find this new look. That process, as you can see on the next page, began with many takes on the flying hero.

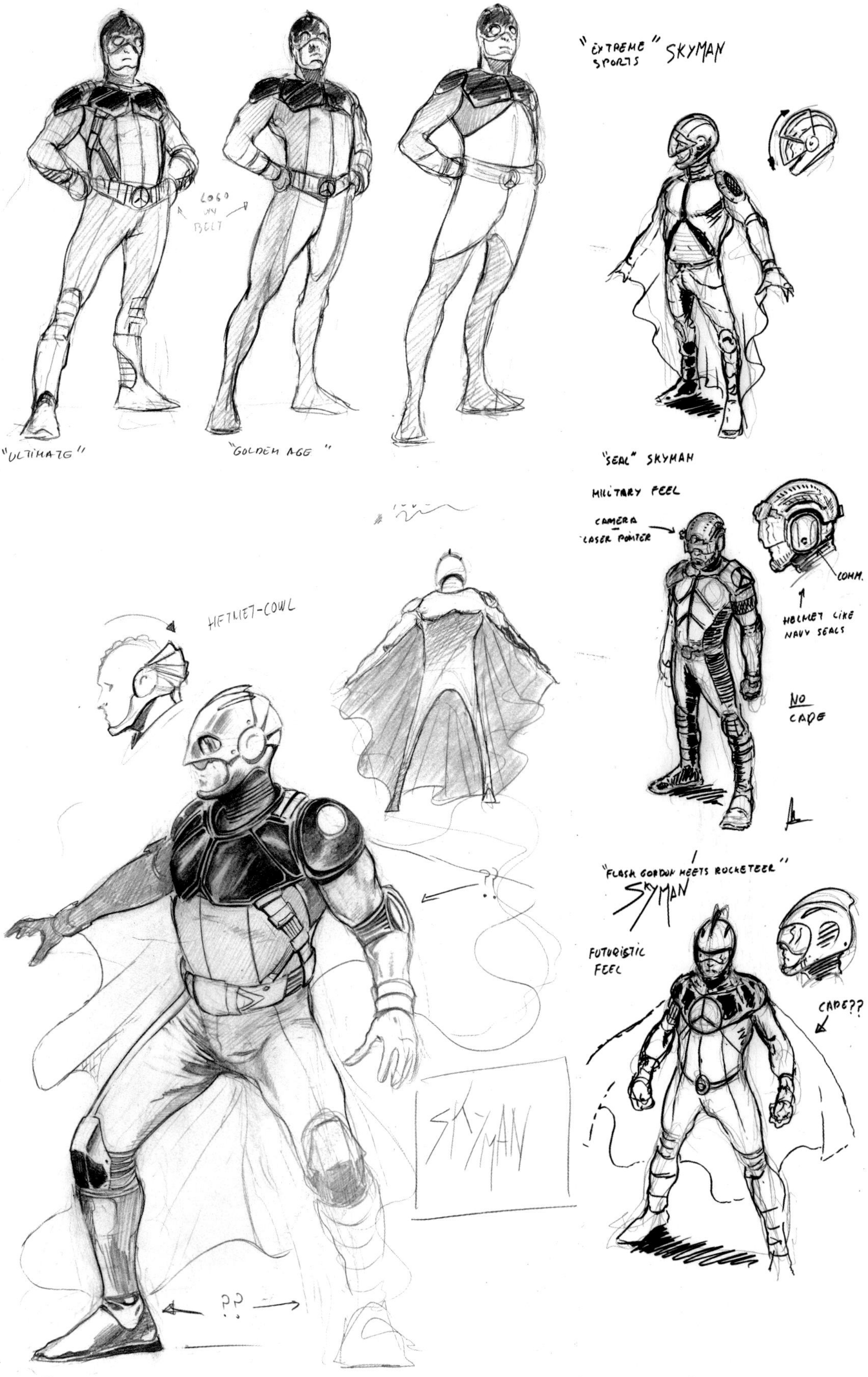
"ULTIMATE"
LOGO ON BELT
"GOLDEN AGE"
"EXTREME SPORTS" SKYMAN
"SEAL" SKYMAN
MILITARY FEEL
CAMERA LASER POINTER
COMM.
HELMET LIKE NAVY SEALS
NO CAPE
HELMET-COWL
??
"FLASH GORDON MEETS ROCKETEER"
SKYMAN
FUTURISTIC FEEL
CAPE??
SKYMAN
??

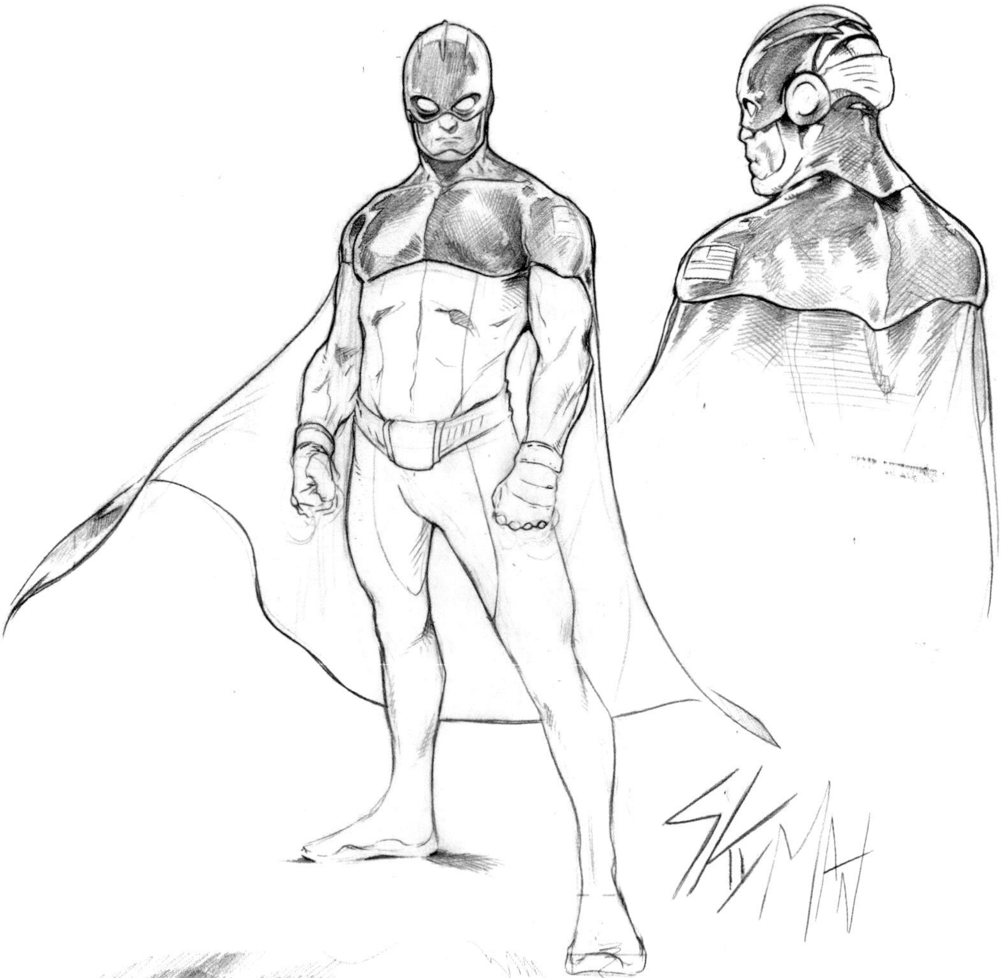
SKYMAN

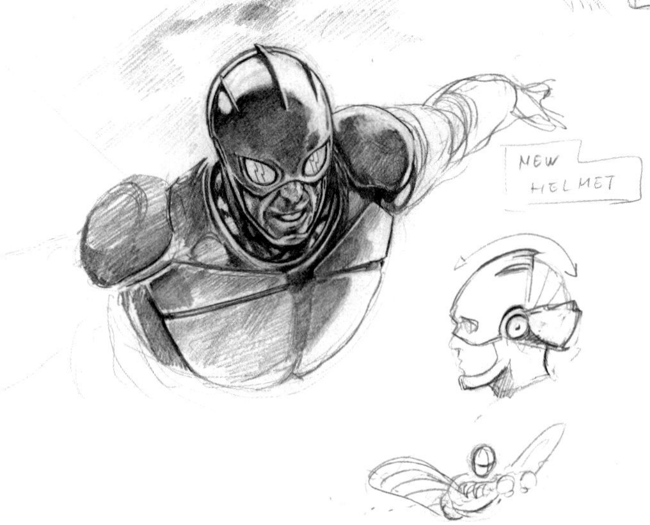
NEW HELMET

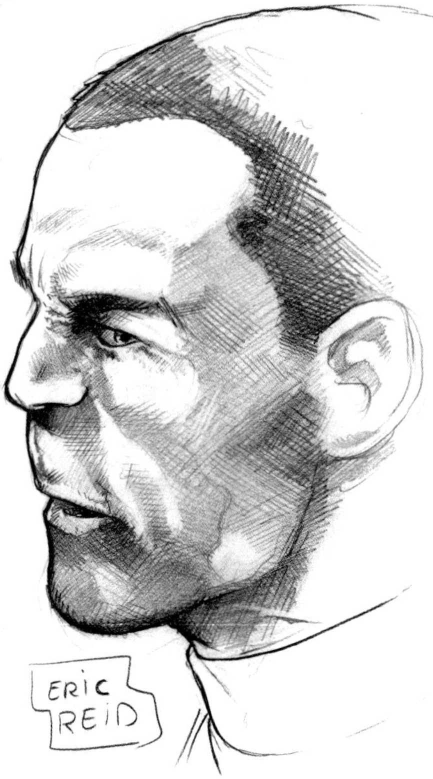
ERIC REID

To set the public's mind at ease after the fall of the last Skyman, the new Skyman needed to look one part military weapon and one part superhero. Garcia combined some of his ideas into a modern, but very classic, patriotic super man. This was his first sketch of Eric Reid's face, showcasing the tough but very human character this story would focus on.

Manuel Garcia also designed the alternate, and very volatile, Skyman suit worn by Lieutenant Sharp, as well as the twisted and shrapnel-covered "Skyman" Sharp became at the end of the series.

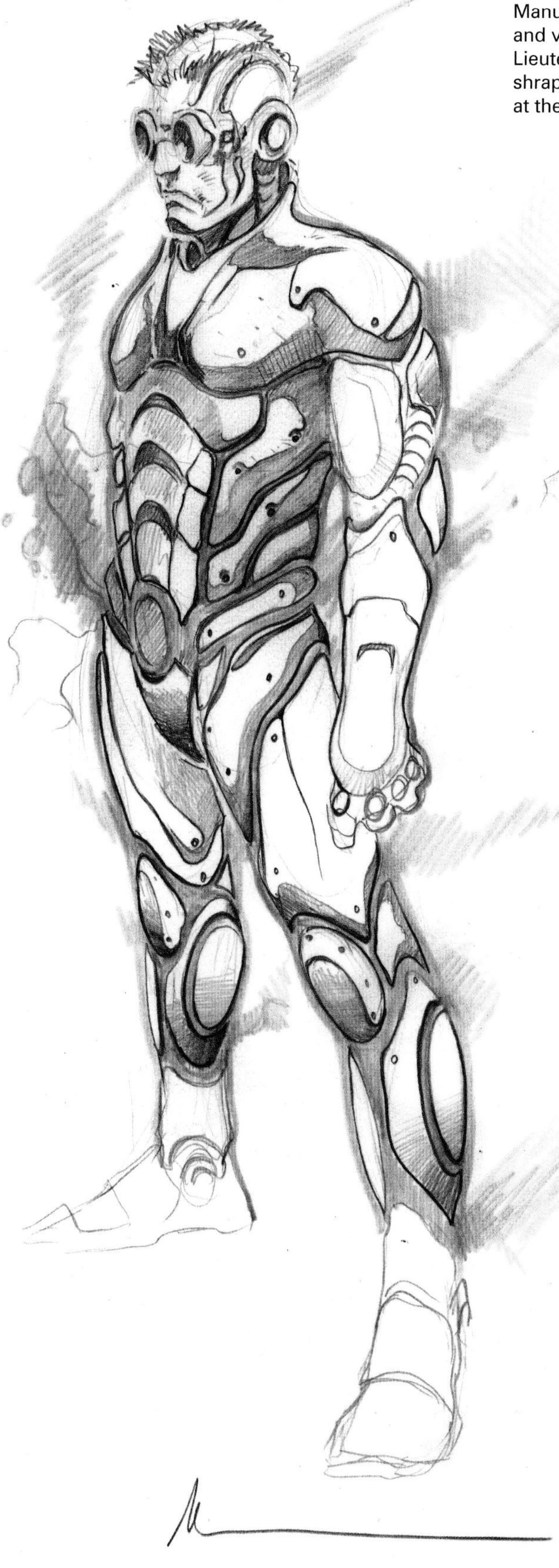

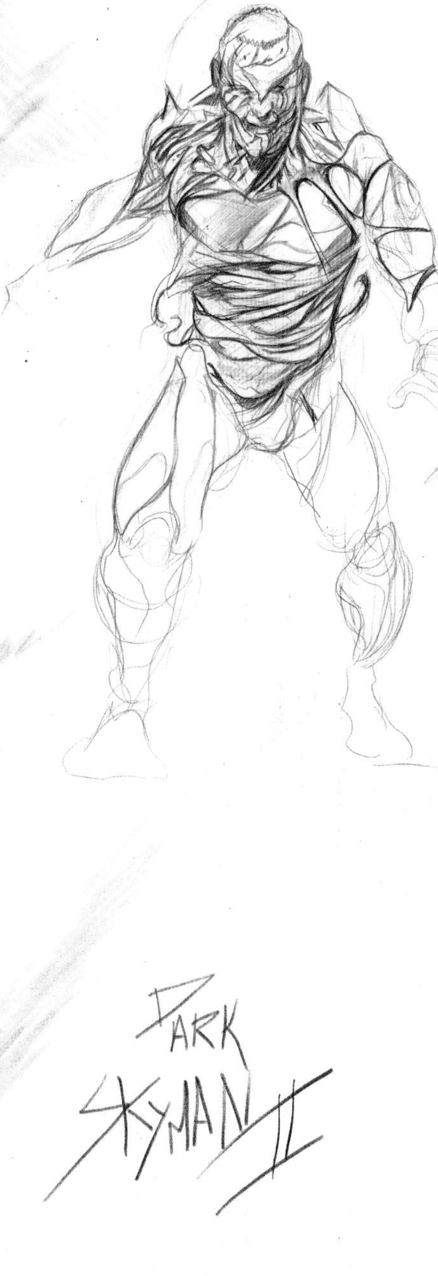
DARK
SKYMAN II

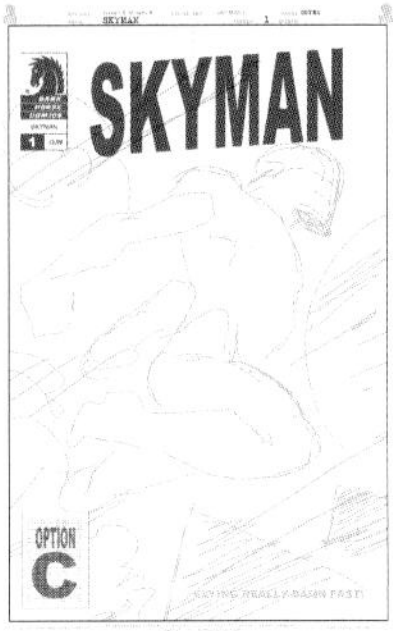
SKYMAN
OPTION C
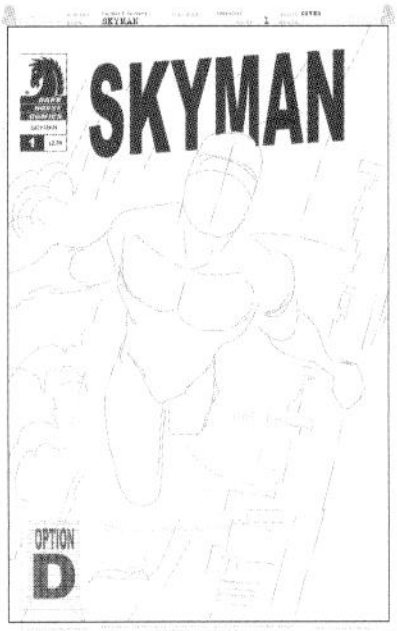
SKYMAN
OPTION D
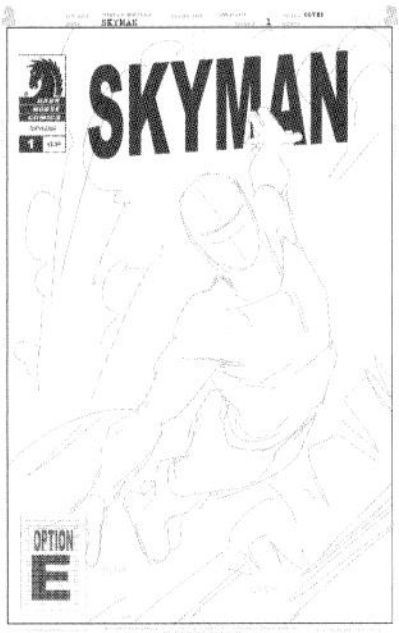
SKYMAN
OPTION E
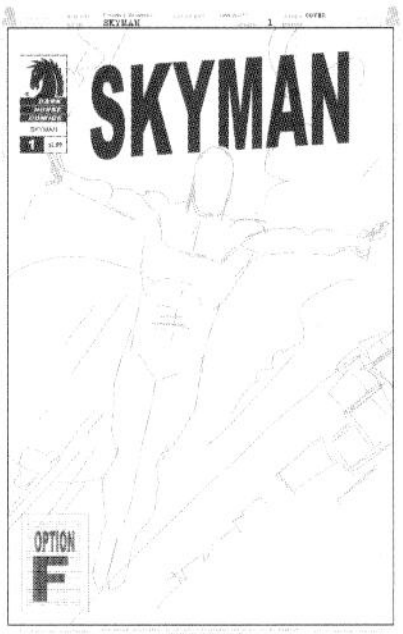
SKYMAN
OPTION F
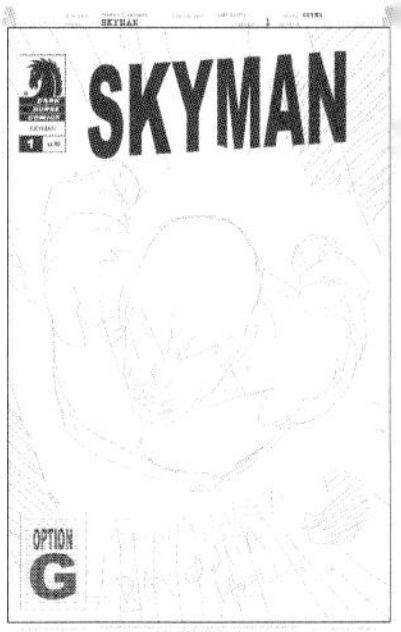
SKYMAN
OPTION G
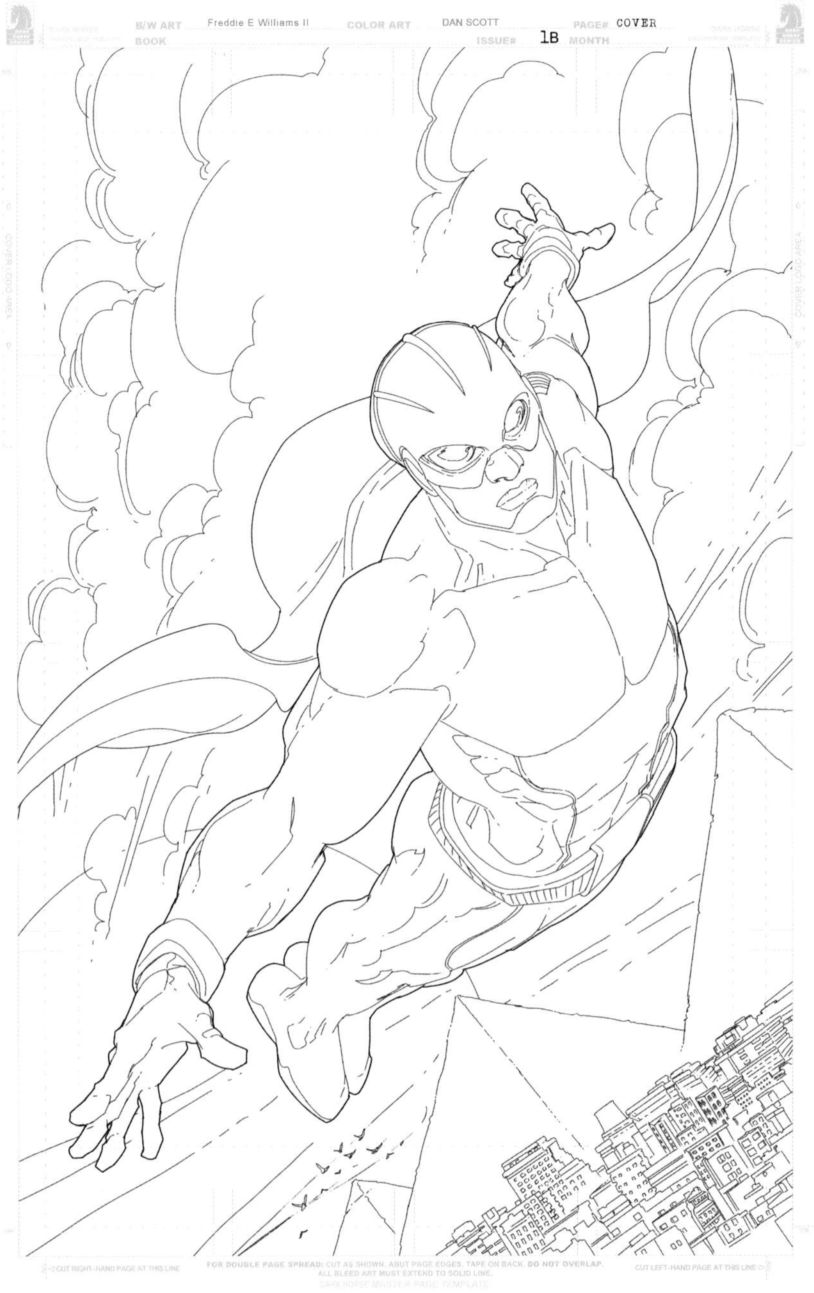
B/W ART Freddie E Williams II
COLOR ART DAN SCOTT
PAGE# COVER
BOOK
ISSUE# 1B
MONTH

After delivering two epic and action-packed covers for *Captain Midnight* #6 and #7, Freddie Williams II seemed like a natural choice for covers on *Skyman*, accompanied by painter Dan Scott on issues #1 and #2, as well as the issue #1 variant cover, and Jeremy Roberts on #3 and #4. For his covers, Williams II would first provide a number of quick sketch concepts, then finalize his digital wireframes (the equivalent of penciled art), before the cover went to Scott and Roberts for painted colors.

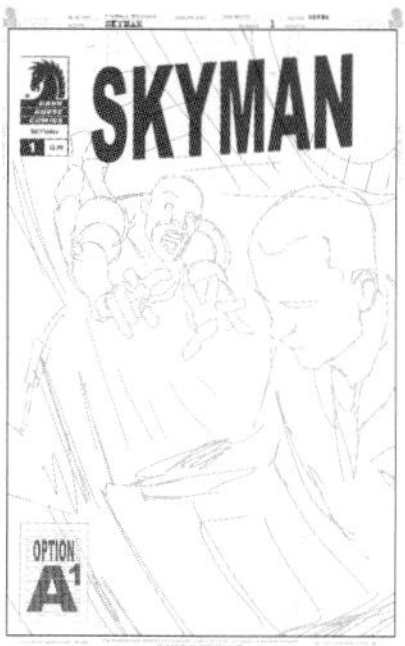
SKYMAN
OPTION
A1

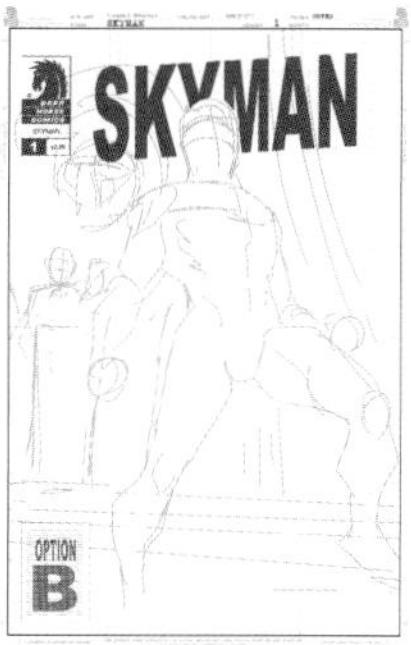
SKYMAN
OPTION
B

Initially a sketch concept for the issue #1 cover, Skyman's almost ill-fated introduction to President Obama became a variant cover for the first issue.

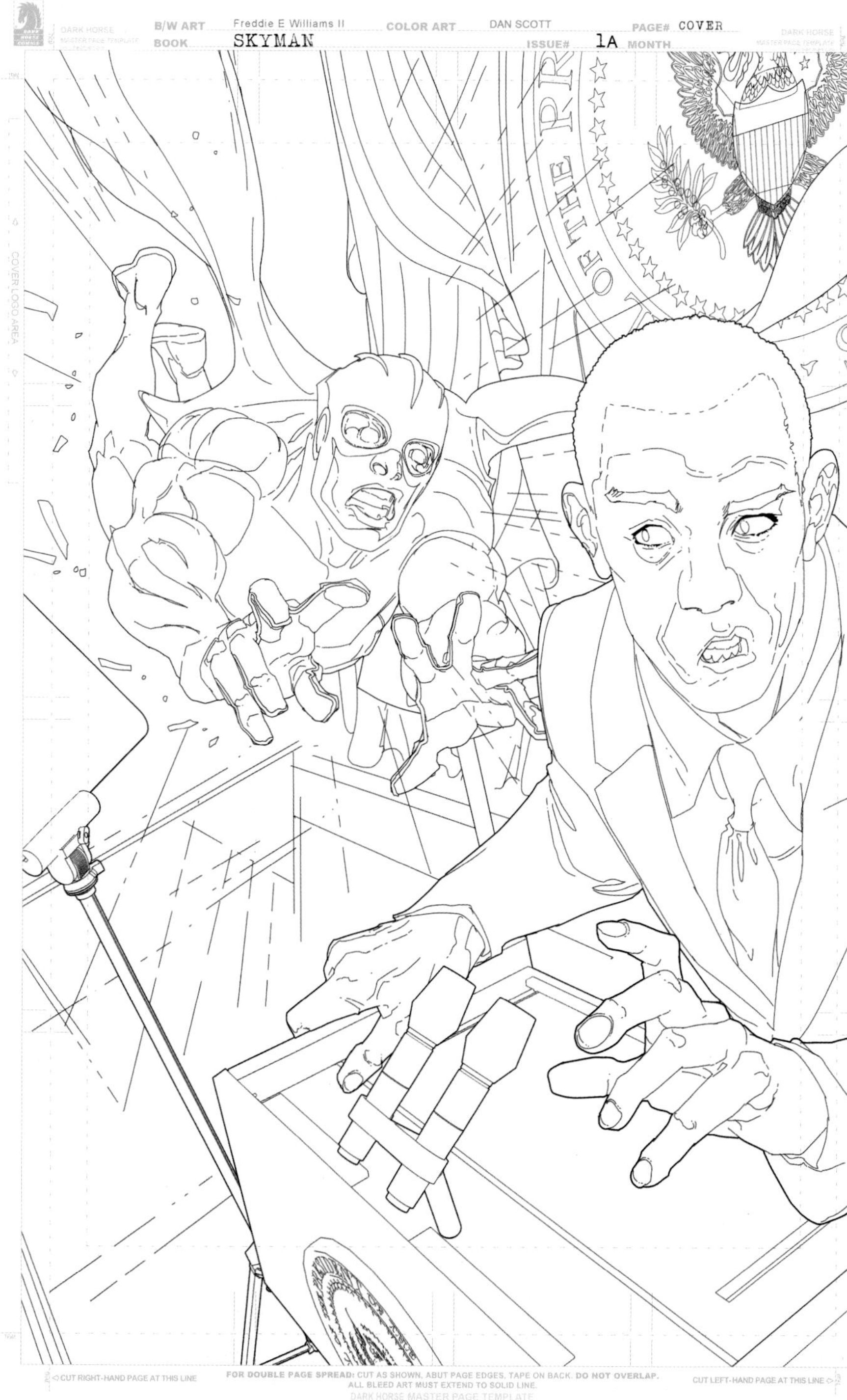
DARK HORSE MASTER PAGE TEMPLATE
B/W ART Freddie E Williams II
COLOR ART DAN SCOTT
PAGE# COVER
BOOK SKYMAN
ISSUE# 1A
MONTH
COVER LOGO AREA
COVER LOGO AREA
CUT RIGHT-HAND PAGE AT THIS LINE
FOR DOUBLE PAGE SPREAD: CUT AS SHOWN, ABUT PAGE EDGES, TAPE ON BACK. DO NOT OVERLAP.
ALL BLEED ART MUST EXTEND TO SOLID LINE.
DARK HORSE MASTER PAGE TEMPLATE
CUT LEFT-HAND PAGE AT THIS LINE

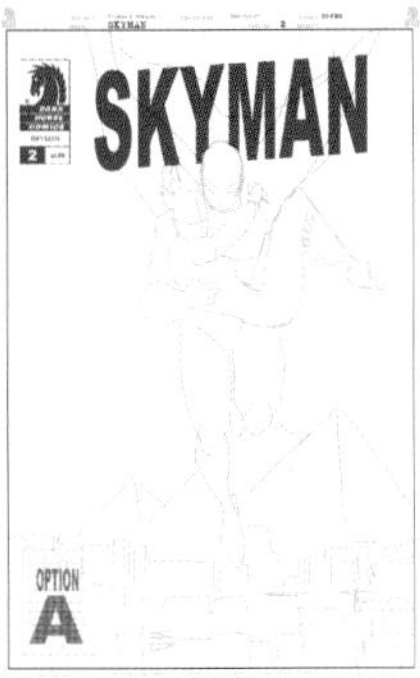
SKYMAN
OPTION
A

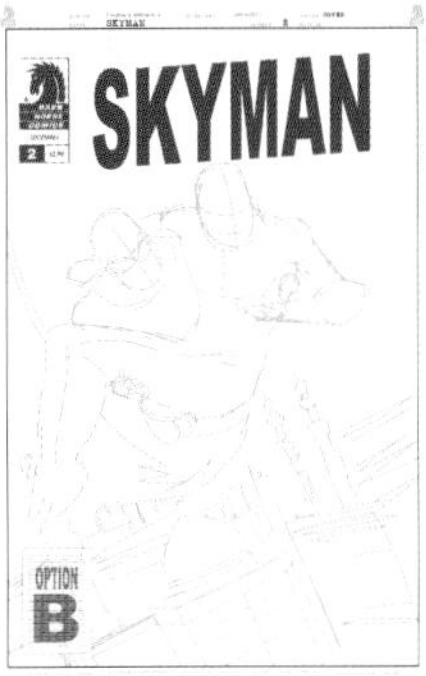
SKYMAN
OPTION
B

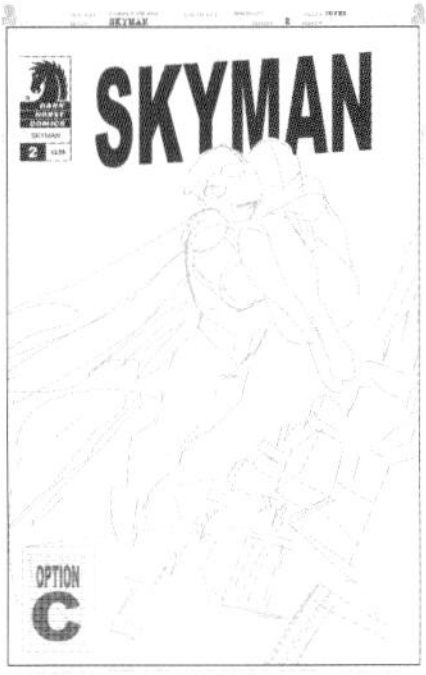
SKYMAN
OPTION
C

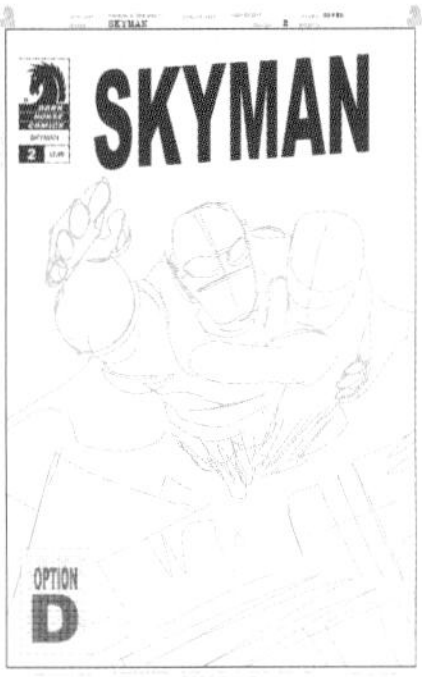
SKYMAN
OPTION
D

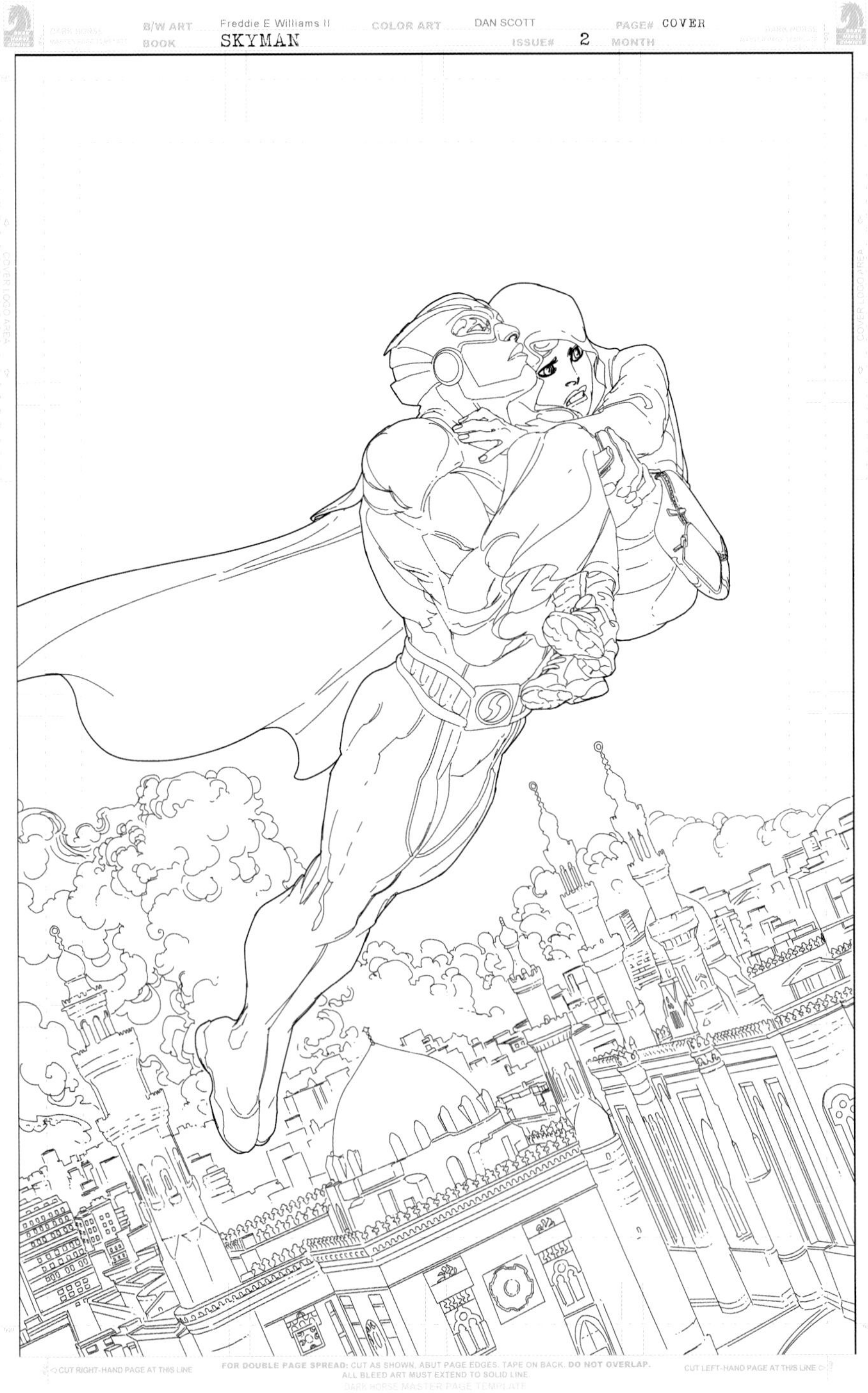
B/W ART Freddie E Williams II
COLOR ART DAN SCOTT
PAGE# COVER
BOOK SKYMAN
ISSUE# 2
MONTH
CUT RIGHT-HAND PAGE AT THIS LINE
FOR DOUBLE PAGE SPREAD: CUT AS SHOWN, ABUT PAGE EDGES. TAPE ON BACK. DO NOT OVERLAP.
ALL BLEED ART MUST EXTEND TO SOLID LINE
CUT LEFT-HAND PAGE AT THIS LINE
DARK HORSE MASTER PAGE TEMPLATE

OPTION
A

OPTION
B

OPTION
C

OPTION
D

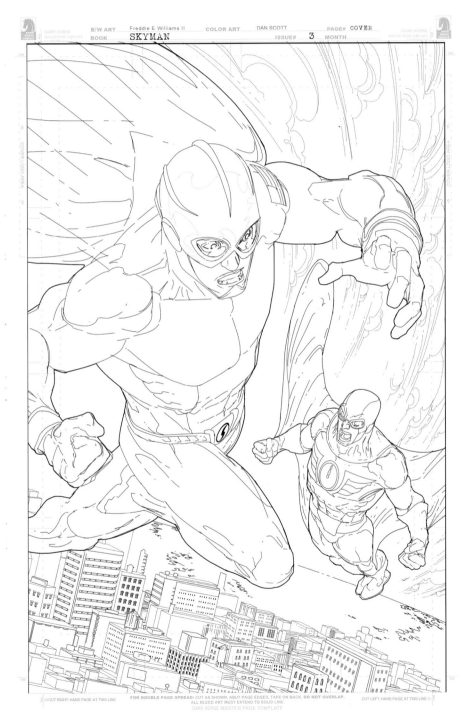

COVER OPTION **A**

COVER OPTION **B**

COVER OPTION **C**

COVER OPTION **D**

B/W ART   Freddie E Williams II      COLOR ART   DAN SCOTT      PAGE# COVER

BOOK   **SKYMAN**                    ISSUE#  **4**    MONTH

CUT RIGHT-HAND PAGE AT THIS LINE      FOR DOUBLE PAGE SPREAD: CUT AS SHOWN, ABUT PAGE EDGES, TAPE ON BACK. **DO NOT OVERLAP.**      CUT LEFT-HAND PAGE AT THIS LINE
ALL BLEED ART MUST EXTEND TO SOLID LINE

# PROJECT BLACK SKY

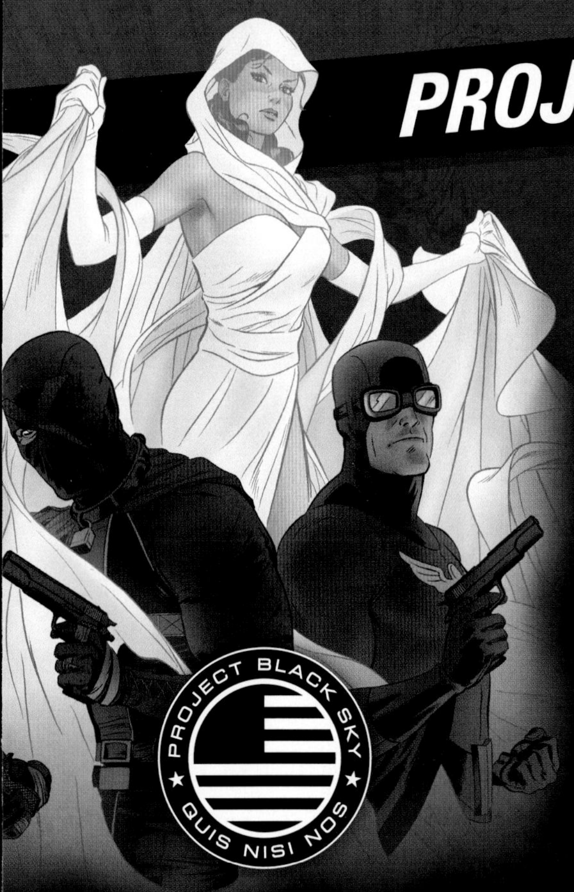
PROJECT BLACK SKY
QUIS NISI NOS

## THE OCCULTIST

*Mike Richardson, Tim Seeley, and Victor Drujiniu*

With a team of hit mages hired by a powerful sorcerer after him, it's trial by fire for the new Occultist, as he learns to handle his powerful magical tome, or suffer at the hands of deadly enemies. From the mind of Dark Horse founder Mike Richardson (*The Secret*, *Cut*, *The Mask*)!

**VOLUME 1**
978-1-59582-745-6 | $16.99

**VOLUME 2: AT DEATH'S DOOR**
978-1-61655-463-7 | $16.99

## CAPTAIN MIDNIGHT

*Joshua Williamson, Fernando Dagnino, Victor Ibáñez, Pere Pérez, and Roger Robinson*

In the forties, he was an American hero, a daredevil fighter pilot, a technological genius . . . a superhero. Since he rifled out of the Bermuda Triangle and into the present day, Captain Midnight has been labeletd a threat to homeland security. Can Captain Midnight survive in the modern world, with the US government on his heels and an old enemy out for revenge?

**VOLUME 1: ON THE RUN**
978-1-61655-229-9 | $14.99

**VOLUME 2: BRAVE OLD WORLD**
978-1-61655-230-5 | $14.99

## X

*Duane Swierczynski and Eric Nguyen*

A masked vigilante dispenses justice without mercy to the criminals of the decaying city of Arcadia. Non-stop, visceral action, with Dark Horse's most brutal and exciting character—X!

**VOLUME 1: BIG BAD**
978-1-61655-241-1 | $14.99

**VOLUME 2: THE DOGS OF WAR**
978-1-61655-327-2 | $14.99

**VOLUME 3: SIEGE**
978-1-61655-458-3 | $14.99

## GHOST

*Kelly Sue DeConnick, Phil Noto, Alex Ross, and Jenny Frison*

Paranormal investigators accidentally summon a ghostly woman. The search for her identity uncovers a deadly alliance between political corruption and demonic science! In the middle stands a woman trapped between two worlds!

**VOLUME 1: IN THE SMOKE AND DIN**
978-1-61655-121-6 | $14.99

**VOLUME 2: THE WHITE CITY BUTCHER**
978-1-61655-420-0 | $14.99

## BRAIN BOY

*Fred Van Lente, Freddie Williams II, and R.B. Silva*

Ambushed while protecting an important statesman, Matt Price Jr., a.k.a. Brain Boy, finds himself wrapped up in political intrigue that could derail a key United Nations conference and sets the psychic spy on a collision course with a man whose mental powers rival his own!

**VOLUME 1: PSY VS. PSY**
978-1-61655-317-3 | $14.99

## SKYMAN

*Joshua Hale Fialkov and Manuel Garcia*

The Skyman Program turns to US Air Force Sgt. Eric Reid: a wounded veteran on the ropes, looking for a new lease on life. *Ultimates* writer Joshua Hale Fialkov pens an all-new superhero series from the pages of *Captain Midnight*!

**VOLUME 1: THE RIGHT STUFF**
978-1-61655-439-2 | $14.99

AVAILABLE AT YOUR LOCAL COMICS SHOP OR BOOKSTORE! • To find a comics shop in your area, call 1-888-266-4226.
For more information or to order direct visit DarkHorse.com or call 1-800-862-0052 Mon.–Fri. 9 AM to 5 PM Pacific Time. Prices and availability subject to change without notice.

# SUPER:POWERED BY CREATORS!

*"These superheroes ain't no boy scouts in spandex. They're a high-octane blend of the damaged, quixotic heroes of pulp and detective fiction and the do-gooders in capes from the Golden and Silver Ages."* —Duane Swierczynski

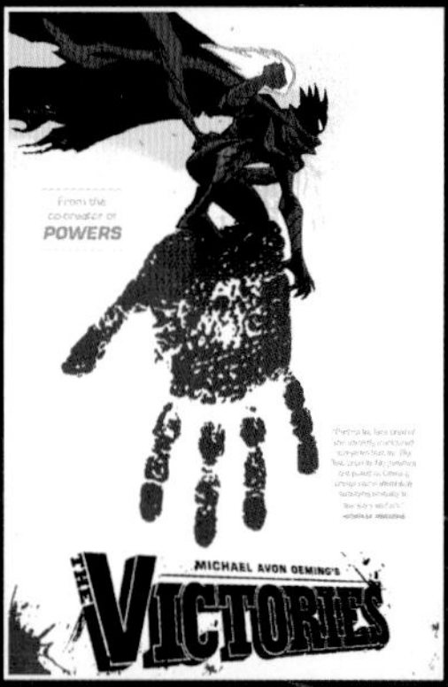
From the co-creator of
POWERS
MICHAEL AVON OEMING'S
THE VICTORIES

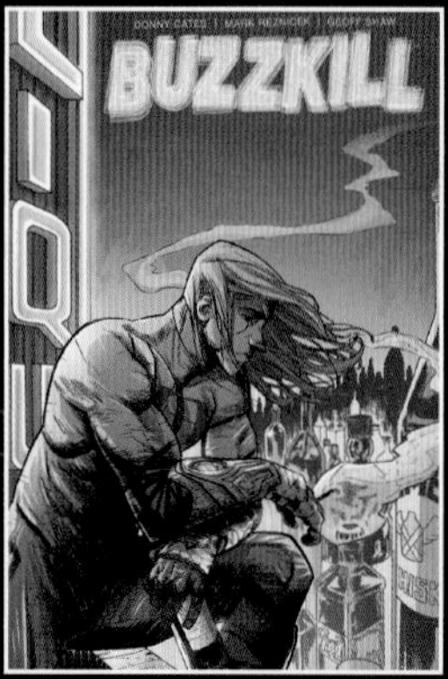
DONNY CATES | MARK REZNICEK | GEOFF SHAW
BUZZKILL

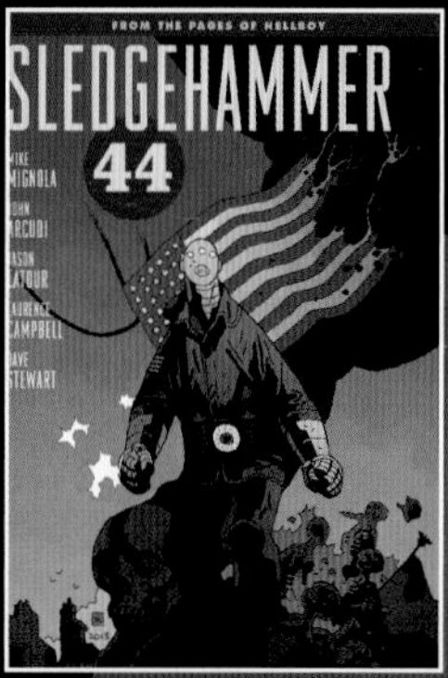
FROM THE PAGES OF HELLBOY
SLEDGEHAMMER
44
MIKE MIGNOLA
JOHN ARCUDI
JASON LATOUR
LAURENCE CAMPBELL
DAVE STEWART

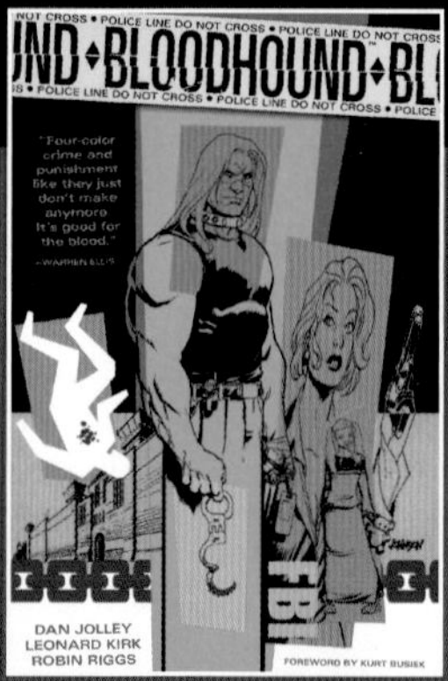
BLOODHOUND
"Four-color crime and punishment like they just don't make anymore. It's good for the blood."
—WARREN ELLIS
DAN JOLLEY
LEONARD KIRK
ROBIN RIGGS
FOREWORD BY KURT BUSIEK

**SLEDGEHAMMER 44**
Mike Mignola, John Arcudi, and Jason Latour
ISBN 978-1-61655-395-1 | $19.99

**DREAM THIEF**
Jai Nitz and Greg Smallwood
ISBN 978-1-61655-283-1 | $17.99

**BUZZKILL**
Mark Reznicek, Donny Cates, and Geoff Shaw
ISBN 978-1-61655-305-0 | $14.99

**THE BLACK BEETLE**
Francesco Francavilla
VOLUME 1: NO WAY OUT
ISBN 978-1-61655-202-2 | $19.99

**THE ANSWER!**
Mike Norton and Dennis Hopeless
ISBN 978-1-61655-197-1 | $12.99

**BLOODHOUND**
Dan Jolley, Leonard Kirk, and Robin Riggs
VOLUME 1: BRASS KNUCKLE PSYCHOLOGY
ISBN 978-1-61655-125-4 | $19.99
VOLUME 2: CROWBAR MEDICINE
ISBN 978-1-61655-352-4 | $19.99

**MICHAEL AVON OEMING'S THE VICTORIES**
Michael Avon Oeming
VOLUME 1: TOUCHED
ISBN 978-1-61655-100-1 | $9.99
VOLUME 2: TRANSHUMAN
ISBN 978-1-61655-214-5 | $17.99
VOLUME 3: POSTHUMAN
ISBN 978-1-61655-445-3 | $17.99

## ORIGINAL VISIONS—THRILLING TALES!

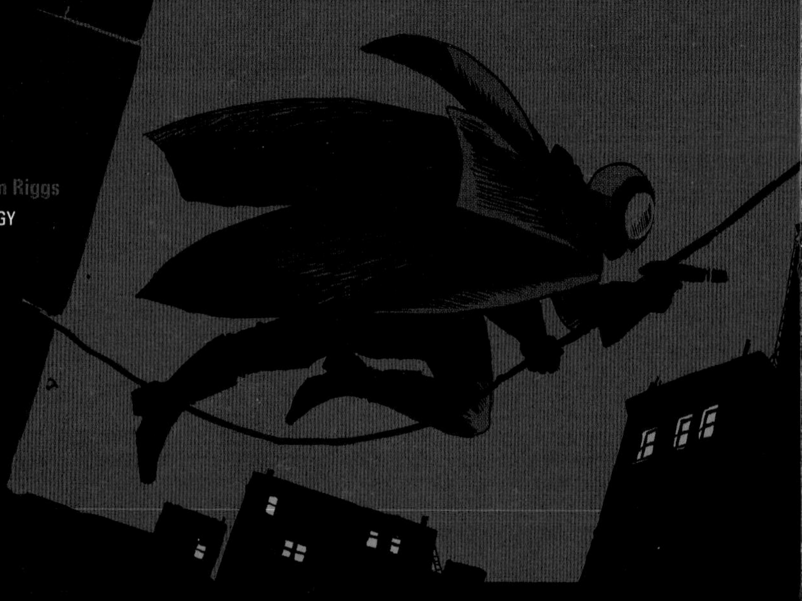

**AVAILABLE AT YOUR LOCAL COMICS SHOP OR BOOKSTORE!** • To find a comics shop in your area, call 1-888-266-4226.
For more information or to order direct visit DarkHorse.com or call 1-800-862-0052 Mon.–Fri. 9 a.m. to 5 p.m. Pacific Time. Prices and availability subject to change without notice.